Persons
in Context

Psychoanalytic Inquiry Book Series

Volume 32

PSYCHOANALYTIC INQUIRY BOOK SERIES

JOSEPH D. LICHTENBERG
Series Editor

Like its counterpart, *Psychoanalytic Inquiry: A Topical Journal for Mental Health Professionals,* the Psychoanalytic Inquiry Book Series presents a diversity of subjects within a diversity of approaches to those subjects. Under the editorship of Joseph Lichtenberg, in collaboration with Melvin Bornstein and the editorial board of *Psychoanalytic Inquiry,* the volumes in this series strike a balance between research, theory, and clinical application. We are honored to have published the works of various innovators in psychoanalysis, such as Frank Lachmann, James Fosshage, Robert Stolorow, Donna Orange, Louis Sander, Leon Wurmser, James Grotstein, Joseph Jones, Doris Brothers, Fredric Busch, and Joseph Lichtenberg, among others.

The series includes books and monographs on mainline psychoanalytic topics, such as sexuality, narcissim, trauma, homosexuality, jealousy, envy, and varied aspects of analytic process and technique. In our efforts to broaden the field of analytic interest, the series has incorporated and embraced innovative discoveries in infant research, self psychology, intersubjectivity, motivational systems, affects as process, responses to cancer, borderline states, contextualism, postmodernism, attachment research and theory, medication, and mentalization. As further investigations in psychoanalysis come to fruition, we seek to present them in readable, easily comprehensive writing.

After 25 years, the core vision of this series remains the investigation, analysis and discussion of developments on the cutting edge of the psychoanalytic field, inspired by a boundless spirit of inquiry.

PSYCHOANALYTIC INQUIRY BOOK SERIES

JOSEPH D. LICHTENBERG
Series Editor

Vol. 13
Self and Motivational Systems:
Toward a Theory of Psychoanalytic
Technique
Joseph D. Lichtenberg, Frank M. Lachmann,
& James L. Fosshage

Vol. 12
Contexts of Being:
The Intersubjective Foundations of
Psychological Life
Robert D. Stolorow & George E. Atwood

Vol. 10
Psychoanalysis and Motivation
Joseph D. Lichtenberg

Vol. 8
Psychoanalytic Treatment:
An Intersubjective Approach
Robert D. Stolorow, Bernard Brandchaft, &
George E. Atwood

Vol. 2
Psychoanalysis and Infant Research
Joseph D. Lichtenberg

Out of Print titles in the PI Series

Vol. 15
Understanding Therapeutic Action:
Psychodynamic Concepts of Cure
Lawrence E. Lifson (ed.)

Vol. 11
Cancer Stories: Creativity and Self-Repair
Esther Dreifuss-Kattan

Vol. 9
Female Homosexuality:
Choice without Volition
Elaine V. Siegel

Vol. 7
The Borderline Patient: Emerging Concepts
in Diagnosis, Psychodynamics, and
Treatment, Vol. 2
James S. Grotstein, Marion F. Solomon,
& Joan A. Lang (eds.)

Vol. 6
The Borderline Patient: Emerging Concepts
in Diagnosis, Psychodynamics, and
Treatment, Vol. 1
James S. Grotstein, Marion F. Solomon,
& Joan A. Lang (eds.)

Vol. 5
Toward a Comprehensive Model
for Schizophrenic Disorders:
Psychoanalytic Essays in Memory of
Ping-Nie Pao
David B. Feinsilver

Vol. 4
Structures of Subjectivity: Explorations in
Psychoanalytic Phenomenology
George E. Atwood & Robert D. Stolorow

Vol. 3
Empathy, Volumes I & II
Joseph D. Lichtenberg, Melvin Bornstein,
& Donald Silver (eds.)

Vol. 1
Reflections on Psychology
Joseph D. Lichtenberg &
Samuel Kaplan (eds.)

Persons in Context

The Challenge of Individuality in Theory and Practice

Edited by
ROGER FRIE and
WILLIAM J. COBURN

Routledge
Taylor & Francis Group
New York   London

Routledge
Taylor & Francis Group
270 Madison Avenue
New York, NY 10016

Routledge
Taylor & Francis Group
27 Church Road
Hove, East Sussex BN3 2FA

© 2011 by Taylor and Francis Group, LLC
Routledge is an imprint of Taylor & Francis Group, an Informa business

Printed in the United States of America on acid-free paper
10 9 8 7 6 5 4 3 2 1

International Standard Book Number: 978-0-415-87143-3 (Hardback) 978-0-415-87144-0 (Paperback)

Library of Congress Cataloging-in-Publication Data

Persons in context : the challenge of individuality in theory and practice / edited by Roger Frie & William J. Coburn.
    p. cm. -- (Psychoanalytic inquiry ; v. 32)
    Includes bibliographical references and index.
    ISBN 978-0-415-87143-3 (hardcover) -- ISBN 978-0-415-87144-0 (pbk.) -- ISBN 978-0-203-86932-1 (e-book)
    1. Individuation (Psychology) 2. Self-analysis (Psychoanalysis) 3. Individuality. 4. Personal construct theory. I. Frie, Roger, 1965- II. Coburn, William J.

BF175.5.I53P47 2010
155.2--dc22
2010006864

**Visit the Taylor & Francis Web site at
http://www.taylorandfrancis.com**

**and the Routledge Web site at
http://www.routledgementalhealth.com**

Contents

PART 3
Developmental contexts   69

PART 4
Reflections on the challenges of individuality   119

Contributors

William J. Coburn, PhD, PsyD, is senior supervising and training analyst and faculty member at the Institute of Contemporary Psychoanalysis, Los Angeles, and at the Northwestern Center for Psychoanalysis, Portland, Oregon. He is editor-in-chief of *International Journal of Psychoanalytic Self Psychology,* is an editorial board member of *Psychoanalytic Inquiry,* and co-editor (with Nancy VanDerHeide) of *Self and Systems: Explorations in Contemporary Self Psychology* (Blackwell, 2009).

Philip Cushman, PhD, is core faculty in the PsyD program at Antioch University in Seattle, Washington. He is the author of *Constructing the Self, Constructing America: A Cultural History of Psychotherapy* (Addison-Wesley, 1995) and of many articles on psychotherapy, psychoanalysis, and the history of psychology and psychotherapy.

James L. Fosshage, PhD, is co-founder, board director, and faculty member of the National Institute for the Psychotherapies of New York City, founding faculty member of the Institute for the Psychoanalytic Study of Subjectivity of New York City, and clinical professor of psychology of the New York University postdoctoral program in psychotherapy and psychoanalysis. He is consulting editor of *Psychoanalytic Inquiry* and editorial board member of the *International Journal of Psychoanalytic Self Psychology* and *Psychoanalytic Dialogues.* He is author of more than 80 publications, including six books; his most recent book, co-authored with Joseph Lichtenberg and Frank Lachmann, is *A Spirit of Inquiry: Communication in Psychoanalysis* (Analytic Press, 2002).

Roger Frie, PhD, PsyD, is associate professor of education at Simon Fraser University, assistant clinical professor of psychiatry at the University of British Columbia, and faculty and supervisor at William Alanson White Institute in New York. He is an editorial board member of *International Journal of Psychoanalytic Self Psychology* and *Psychoanalytic Psychology.* His recently edited books include *Psychology Agency: Theory, Practice, and*

Culture (MIT Press, 2008) and *Beyond Postmodernism: New Dimensions in Clinical Theory and Practice* (Routledge, 2009, with Donna Orange).

Frank M. Lachmann, PhD, is a member of the founding faculty of the Institute for the Psychoanalytic Study of Subjectivity in New York and clinical assistant professor in the New York University postdoctoral program in psychotherapy and psychoanalysis. He is author of *Transforming Aggression: Psychotherapy with the Difficult-to-Treat Patient* (Aronson, 2000), co-author with Joseph Lichtenberg and James Fosshage of *Self and Motivational Systems* (Analytic Press, 1992), *The Clinical Exchange* (Analytic Press, 1996), and *A Spirit of Inquiry: Communication in Psychoanalysis* (Analytic Press, 2002); and co-author with Beatrice Beebe of *Infant Research and Adult Treatment: Co-Constructing Interactions* (Analytic Press, 2002). His most recently published book is *Transforming Narcissism: Reflections on Empathy, Humor, and Expectations* (Analytic Press, 2008).

Jack Martin, EdD, is Burnaby Mountain Endowed Professor of Psychology at Simon Fraser University. His research interests are in philosophy and the history of psychology, especially in the psychology of personhood. His most recent books include *Persons: Understanding Psychological Selfhood and Agency* (Springer, 2009, with Jeff Sugarman and Sarah Hickinbottom), *Psychology and the Question of Agency* (State University New York Press, 2003, with Jeff Sugarman and Janice Thompson), and *The Psychology of Human Possibility and Constraint* (State University New York Press, 1999, with Jeff Sugarman).

Donna Orange, PhD, PsyD, is supervisor and faculty member at the Institute for the Psychoanalytic Study of Subjectivity, and the Institute for Specialization in Self Psychology and Relational Psychoanalysis in Rome. She is author of *Thinking for Clinicians: Philosophical Resources for Contemporary Psychoanalysis and the Humanistic Psychotherapies* (Routledge, 2009) and co-author with Robert Stolorow and George Atwood of *Worlds of Experience: Interweaving Philosophical and Clinical Dimensions in Psychoanalysis* (Basic Books, 2002) and *Working Intersubjectively* (Analytic Press, 1997).

Robert D. Stolorow, PhD, PhD, is clinical professor of psychiatry at the University of California–Los Angeles School of Medicine and training and supervising analyst at the Institute of Contemporary Psychoanalysis in Los Angeles. He is author of *Trauma and Human Existence: Autobiographical, Psychoanalytic, and Philosophical Reflections* (Analytic Press, 2007) and co-author with Donna Orange and George Atwood of *Worlds of Experience:*

Interweaving Philosophical and Clinical Dimensions in Psychoanalysis
(Basic Books, 2002).

Jeff Sugarman, EdD, is professor of education at Simon Fraser University. His
most recent books include *Persons: Understanding Psychological Selfhood
and Agency* (Springer, 2009, with Jack Martin and Sarah Hickinbottom),
Psychology and the Question of Agency (State University New York Press,
2003, with Jack Martin and Janice Thompson), and *The Psychology of
Human Possibility and Constraint* (State University New York Press, 1999,
with Jack Martin). He is a fellow of the American Psychological Association,
past president of the Society for Theoretical and Philosophical Psychology,
and a co-recipient of the George Miller Award for an Outstanding Recent
Article in General Psychology.

Preface and acknowledgments

Individuality is a pervasive and sharply debated theme in contemporary Western culture. Such concepts as autonomy, separateness, and the isolated individual form an integral part of the tradition of individualism. Taken together, these theories have long informed how Western psychologists, psychoanalysts, and psychotherapists think and practice. Yet the recognition that all human activity unfolds within irreducible social, cultural, and biological contexts provides an alternative view of human experience that is not tied to precepts of individualism. Advances in theory, including but not limited to hermeneutics, postmodernism, complexity and systems thought, have helped us to appreciate the extent to which human activity and understanding are always fundamentally contextualized.

From a contextualist perspective, the notion of individuality is a construct produced by particular types of social practices. Individuality is one interpretation of being human, among others; it has no privileged status in telling us about our "true" human nature. We experience ourselves as unique individuals, in some way separate from, yet connected to others, as a result of the social, cultural, and biological contexts that provide us with our framework for understanding human experience.

This book considers the continuing challenge of individuality for psychology, psychoanalysis, and psychotherapy from the perspective of contemporary contextualist theory and practice. We have invited a diverse and distinguished group of psychologists and psychoanalysts, many of whom are also trained academic philosophers, to address the puzzles, challenges, and paradoxes of individuality from the perspective of hermeneutics, systems theory, and contextualism. The initial motivation for this book came from the discussion and debate about the theme of the individual at the International Psychoanalytic Self Psychology Conference in Baltimore, Maryland, in 2008. We invited several presenters from that conference to develop their papers into chapters. An original panel of conference papers, which comprised the beginning of this book, was the inspiration of Joseph Lichtenberg. At the same time, we invited such prominent psychological theorists as Philip Cushman, Jack Martin, and Jeff Sugarman to discuss the contextualized nature of persons and selfhood.

As with any book project, we owe thanks to many people who helped along the way. We are indebted to all of our contributors and especially to Joseph Lichtenberg and Robert Stolorow for suggesting that this book be published. We are grateful to our associate editor at Routledge, Kristopher Spring, who was supportive and enthusiastic about this project from the start. We are also very appreciative of Kristen Leishman's superb editorial assistance and for volunteering her time. Above all, we would like to acknowledge our gratitude for the constant support shown by our families: Roger thanks Emily, Elena, and Andreas; Bill thanks Katalin, Laura, Andy, and William.

Finally, we would like to acknowledge Perseus Publishing for granting us permission to republish a brief selection from *Constructing the Self, Constructing America* (Cushman, 1995), which Dr. Cushman considerably expanded and revised for his contribution to this book.

Roger Frie and William J. Coburn

Introduction: Experience in context

Roger Frie and William J. Coburn

Psychodynamic and humanistic therapies have increasingly dispensed with the notion and values of isolated individuality. The recognition that all human experience emerges within biological, social, and cultural contexts and remains fundamentally embedded in the world has led to the development of new ways of thinking and practicing. A focus on the contexts of human experience is particularly evident in contemporary intersubjective, interpersonal, and relational psychoanalysis and in the existential-humanistic, feminist, gestalt, multicultural, and narrative psychotherapies. For theorists and clinicians who embrace these "post-subjectivist" or "post-individualist" ways of thinking and practicing, the question of individuality can seem confusing, even anachronistic.

Yet, as this book suggests, the challenge of individuality remains a pressing issue for context-sensitive forms of practice. Indeed, therapeutic practice, regardless of orientation, exists within a broader social and cultural milieu that continues to valorize individuality. The belief that the person is fundamentally separate from others and free to make choices that determine life experience is implicit in the tradition of individualism, especially in North America. This way of thinking exerts considerable influence on how we experience ourselves and articulate our relationship to others. As Charles Taylor (1985) points out, "[T]heories serve more than descriptive and explanatory purposes, they also serve to *define* ourselves" (p. 116). By examining the challenge of individuality for contemporary theory and practice, our aim is to foster awareness about the contextualized nature of human experience.

The contributors to this book seek to address the tension between the emergence of contextualism as a dominant mode of theory and practice and the continuing challenge of individuality. As a result of this tension, many clinicians are left to wonder how to understand the notion of "individual" experience either conceptually or clinically. Are there ways to think about the notion of individuality and individual experience without falling back into a one-person model of thinking and practicing? Can the clinician appreciate individuality and maintain a contextualist perspective simultaneously? And in a broader sense, how does a contextualist sensibility respond to the dominant cultural norms and values that emphasize the achievement of individuality?

Using a variety of disciplinary perspectives—psychological, psychoanalytic, philosophical, developmental, biological, and neuroscientific—the contributors develop new insights into the role and place of individuality in the contemporary clinical setting and beyond. In the process, they address a host of important questions about the nature of individual experience. They consider whether individuality is linked to constitutional factors and resides in the realm of genetic predispositions, whether the individual can be defined in terms of the developmental process of self-transformation, or whether individuality is itself a residue of sociocultural norms and values. They address the problem of individuality in terms of a prereflective, embodied self-awareness that is always present in our interactions with other people and the world in which we exist. And they consider what place individuality has in an other-focused perspective on ethics and contemporary practice.

What ultimately makes these essays distinct is the way each contributor seeks to show that individuality, no matter how it is defined, always occurs within the web of social, cultural, and biological contexts. In contrast to radical postmodernists, who seek to undermine the very notion of individuality, the contributors to this volume take a more measured stance in the belief that individuality remains an important topic for consideration (Frie & Orange, 2009). As Martin, Sugarman, and Hickinbottom (2009) suggest,

> It is difficult to dismiss the epiphenomenal and experiential reality in which we understand ourselves as individual agents. Clearly there is little to deny the separateness that is an ostensive condition of human embodiment and the phenomenology of individual subjective experience. However it equally is difficult not to be persuaded by hermeneutic and social constructionist accounts of the last several decades arguing that the self has no pre-given, fixed essence, that it is not constituted naturally, but historically and socioculturally, and thus, that it cannot be understood apart from the interpretations and descriptions given it. (p. 46)

To help the reader appreciate the discussion and debate about individuality in an increasingly post-individualistic age, this introduction has a threefold purpose: (1) to present the broader historical, philosophical, and social contexts that impact the way analysts and therapists understand and conceptualize the problem of individuality; (2) to provide an overview of the understanding of individuality that has developed within psychology, psychoanalysis in general, and contextualist forms of therapy in particular; and (3) to outline the scope and objectives of the book's chapters.

HISTORICAL, PHILOSOPHICAL, AND SOCIOCULTURAL CONTEXTS

Any discussion of individuality must begin by attempting a definition of the term. The notion of individuality has a long and varied history in Western philosophy and can be understand in the broadest sense as the state or quality of being an individual. An individual, in turn, may be defined as a person who is in some way unique, separate from other persons, and possesses his or her own desires, wishes, and needs. The notions of individuality and the individual are an integral part of the tradition of individualism, a philosophical, political, and moral stance that characterizes many Western societies. Our objective is to begin with a brief historical and philosophical discussion of individuality before turning to its role in the evolution of psychology, psychoanalysis, and psychotherapy.

Much of Western philosophy has a long history of valorizing the individual. The "individualist paradigm," to the extent that one can mark out such a broad scope of thinking, is based on the notion that the individual exists in some way separate from and prior to relationship with others. According to this viewpoint, relationships are secondary to the knowing individual who is capable of making choices without reference to others or the world. This perspective finds expression in philosophies as varied as René Descartes and Søren Kierkegaard and has important social and political ramifications.

The individualist paradigm is closely connected to the political tradition of individualism. Modern individualism has its philosophical basis in the work of John Locke (1689/1960), whose political theories became a cornerstone of the American constitution. According to Locke, the individual exists prior to society and forms the primary level of analysis. Individuals come together to form a governable society for the sole purpose of protecting their rights. Society is therefore a product of the individual mind. The Lockean individual is characterized by the ability to rationally choose a course of action that is in his or her best interests. This perspective finds expression in classical liberalism and libertarianism, whose aim is to ensure the freedom of the individuals to determine their own course of action.

The traditional Western understanding of human development and experience is grounded in the politics of individuality. The emphasis on individual self-fulfillment, for example, is a central tenet of individualism. Similarly, the division between so-called private and public experience reflects a belief in the sanctity of the individual mind. As Bellah, Madsen,

Sullivan, Swidler, and Tipton (1985) observe in their study of American attitudes toward individualism:

> Viewing one's primary task as "finding oneself" in autonomous self-reliance, separating oneself not only from one's parents but also from those larger communities and traditions that constitute one's past, leads to the notion that it is in oneself, perhaps in relation to a few intimate others, that fulfillment is to be found. Individualism of this sort often takes a negative view of public life. The impersonal forces of the economic and political worlds are what the individual needs protection against. In this perspective, even occupation, which has been so central to the identity of Americans in the past, becomes instrumental—not a good in itself, but only a means to the attainment of a rich and satisfying private life. (p. 163)

As a set of values and ideals, individualism rests on the not-so-hidden pillars of patriarchy, power, and prejudice. Indeed, the individualist paradigm is strongly gendered because it is grounded in the values of a patriarchal society that privileges thinking, separation, and autonomy over affectivity and relationships. Within individualist-oriented societies, power has traditionally resided in the hands of White men, leaving women and ethnically diverse groups disempowered. From a broadly feminist perspective, individuality, rationality, and the mind are considered masculine values and are elevated above relationships, emotions, and the body, which are considered feminine and generally devalued. Although some progress has been achieved toward bridging the gender gap and securing equal rights among ethnic groups, it is equally the case that the values of individualism remain firmly entrenched and form a challenge to communitarian values.

Indeed, individualism in various forms continues to be dominant in many Western societies, and especially in the United States. At the same time, however, critiques of individuality and reactions to individualism are as widespread as they are varied. Over the preceding decades, the principles and values associated with individuality and individualism have been challenged from multiple disciplinary perspectives. In contrast to the individualist paradigm, critics view the social and cultural as being ontologically prior to the individual. Societies, on this view, are not just a collection of disparate presocial beings, an approach that Charles Taylor (1985) aptly coins "atomism." Rather, society exists as a result of communal practices, beliefs, and associations, and individuals emerge out of them as expressions of these shared identities.

Critical perspectives on individuality and individualism range from "emergentist theories" (Martin, Sugarman, & Hickinbottom, 2009) that see the person as emerging out of biological, developmental, social, and cultural contexts to "postmodern dismissals" of the human subject as fractured, illusory, and momentary. The diversity of critical viewpoints that exist outside of psychology, psychoanalysis, and psychotherapy can be confusing for practitioners who are not trained in these areas. Yet there are many key theories and thinkers that have direct relevance for how clinicians think and practice today.

Contemporary political and moral philosophers have been particularly important in the development of new models of understanding individual experience that avoid the perils of individualism. In contrast to the political model of liberalism, communitarian philosophers (Sandel, 1998; Taylor, 1989) argue for a "communitarian model" of society that recognizes our inherent interdependence. Communitarians question the abstract and intellectualized conception of the individual self in liberalism and argue that the emphasis on individual liberties devalues the importance of attachments, community, and tradition. Social theorists likewise question the notion that individual subjectivity can ever be considered separately from society. They introduce a range of theories—from communicative action (Habermas, 1987) and structuration (Giddens, 1984) to liquid modernity (Bauman, 2000)—to account for the intersubjective, active, and fluid nature of human experience. For anthropologists (Geertz, 1973), meanwhile, individual human nature is always a product of our culture, whereas postcolonial theorists (Bhabha, 1994) question the individualist, colonizing, and imperialist values implicit in Western culture. For feminist theorists, the gendered splits that distort and deform our conceptions of human development (Gilligan, 1993), social interaction (Benjamin, 1988), and scientific study (Keller, 1985) need to be replaced with an ability to see the other as an equal subject in her own right. For postmodern and poststructuralist theorists, the very notion of individual subjectivity is a fiction that overlooks our fundamental embeddedness in systems of language (Derrida, 1977), power (Foucault, 1978), and politics (Lyotard, 1984), of which we remain largely unaware and cannot control. And from the perspective of neuroscience, individual consciousness is increasingly seen as grounded not in isolated cognitive processes but in the body and emotion, "through a feeling of what happens" (Damasio, 1999).*

The contributors to this volume view the "interpretive perspective" that has emerged from hermeneutic (Gadamer, 1996; Taylor, 1989) and existential-phenomenological philosophy (Heidegger, 1995; Merleau-Ponty, 1962) as particularly relevant. For these philosophers, human experience is always and already contextualized and embodied, thus fundamentally undermining the notion of the isolated, disembodied mind.

---

* Neuroscientists argue for the ideas of "connectionism" and "distributed parallel processing" across a network of individual brains—ideas that have led us to the consideration that the particularities of consciousness and their "representations" are distributed across a larger, human network of which each of us is but a constituent (Cilliers, 1998).

The individual, on this view, is a self-interpreting being who can never be separated from his or her contexts of experience. The interpretive perspective (Martin, Sugarman, & Thompson, 2003) acknowledges the biological, social, and cultural basis of all experience, while recognizing that the individual person may experience himself or herself as separate and unique in the presence of other persons. On this basis, then, the contributors seek to account for the nature of lived experience and the contexts in which it unfolds, without reifying the individual self.

PSYCHOLOGY, PSYCHOANALYSIS, AND PSYCHOTHERAPY

The role of individuality in psychology, psychoanalysis, and psychotherapy has a similarly varied history. Within academic psychology, individualism has long held sway to the extent that the individual self has often been considered the main form of reality. Psychological life was historically understood from "the inside out," and human development existed on a singular trajectory toward the achievement of separation, individuation, and autonomy (Mahler, Pine, & Bergman, 1975), norms that reflect the broader values of individualism. Failure to achieve these developmental goals was tagged negatively with terms such as *developmental arrest* or *regression*. For many psychotherapists working within a medical model, meanwhile, treatment objectives focused on changing the behavior and cognition of individual clients with little consideration of the social contexts in which symptoms are manifested and given meaning. As a result, the role of the treatment relationship, or indeed, the culture and values of the society in which both the therapy and client exist, did not factor into the therapeutic process.

The singular focus on the isolated, individual mind in psychology has not been without its critics. Within the history of psychology, three theorists may be identified as being particularly relevant to the perspective developed in this book: Wilhelm Dilthey (1833–1911), Lev Vygotsky (1896–1934), and George Herbert Mead (1863–1931). Dilthey developed his ideas in reaction to the new experimental method in psychology. For Dilthey, psychological phenomena are always constituted by human interpretive practices. In other words, humans are able to perceive and comprehend things, including themselves, only against an ever-present, mostly unarticulated background of their experience. The study of the individual mind in isolation from its contexts thus overlooks the totality of life experience—that is, the lived reality of persons that precedes any distinctions between the mind and body or the self and world. This hermeneutic approach "does not strive for decontextualized facts, but emphasizes meanings as experienced by individuals whose activities are rooted in given sociohistorical settings" (Messer, Sass, & Woolfolk, 1988, pp. xiii–xiv).

The resurgence of interest in Dilthey's hermeneutics is similarly evident in the growing influence of Vygotsky's and Mead's ideas. According to Vygotsky, psychology's emphasis on the isolated individual mind fails to account for the sociocultural nature of human development. He argues that culture and social interaction play primary roles in the development of cognition. As Vygotsky (1978) states:

> Every function in the child's cultural development appears twice: first, on the social level, and later, on the individual level; first, between people (interpsychological) and then inside the child (intrapsychological). This applies equally to voluntary attention, to logical memory, and to the formation of concepts. All of the higher functions originate as actual relationships between individuals. (p. 57)

Vygotsky maintains that mental functions develop through interaction with caregivers as well as through particular cultural groups. A similar perspective is evident in Mead's work. He argues that social development is grounded in a process of symbolic interaction with others. In Mead's (1962) words, "[i]t is the social process of influencing others in a social act and then taking the attitude of the others aroused by the stimulus, and then reacting in turn to his response, which constitutes a self" (p. 171).

Mead's ideas are instrumental to the interpersonal approach of Harry Stack Sullivan and the early interpersonal school. Drawing on Mead's concepts of mind, self, and society, Sullivan views the self as relationally generated and maintained. In an article titled "The Illusion of Personal Individuality," Sullivan (1950) maintains that the content of consciousness is socially derived and gives rise to an illusory sense of self: "No such thing as the durable, unique, individual personality is ever clearly justified. For all I know, every human being has as many personalities as he has interpersonal relations" (p. 221). Sullivan recommends that clinicians give up their attempt to define a unique individual self and try instead to grasp what is going on at any particular time in the interpersonal field. Sullivan's outright rejection of individuality represents an extreme position within the tradition of psychoanalysis, yet most psychoanalysts and psychotherapists today would agree with this basic premise, namely, that human development is always social in nature and that therapy itself is always a relational endeavor.

Indeed, for most practicing psychoanalysts and psychotherapists, the individualist paradigm is highly problematic. It is at odds with the majority of contextualist and systems ideas promulgated today by influential thinkers in psychology, psychoanalysis, infant research, attachment theory, and neuroscience. Many of these perspectives support the contention that individuality and the individual person emerge from within intersubjective, relational matrices and continue to develop in the social contexts of their attachment-based environments.

Despite these recent changes, however, the individualist paradigm is entrenched in the history of psychoanalysis and psychotherapy. In fact, it harmonized quite well with early, rational visions of the individual; with independent psyches ruled by internal, instinctual forces; and with the late 19th-century natural science model that influenced Sigmund Freud and many of his followers. Many of the principles of individualism are likewise inherent in classical psychoanalysis: objectivity, anonymity, interpretation, separation/individuation, patriarchal authority, personal responsibility, and personal independence (as well as, conversely, the pathologizing of dependency). The heartfelt respect many traditional analysts and therapists had for individualism and the individuality of the patient (Freud, 1923, 1933) could easily devolve into distancing, pathologizing, and even blaming the patient when the pendulum of such personal individuality and subjectivity appeared to swing too far afield from the reasonable, the plausible, and the "reality based." Individuality was valued when it was within acceptable limits of the norm, when it was not *too* individual. The irony, or course, is that the values of individualism ultimately ended in conformism, in which each person (and each therapy) sought the same set of valued objectives (Bellah et al., 1985). Furthermore, many analysts were loath to think that they might have to engage relationally or personally with the patient. The individualist paradigm ran counter to the notion that analysts would need to be truly integral as actual persons—not simply as objective, observing analysts—to their patients' emotional lives to effect change (Friedman, 1978).

Since its inception, traditional psychoanalytic theory and practice have been informed by and organized around the notion of individual minds. Psychological problems were thought to reside in the individual's isolated mind or psyche. Freud and many of his followers exemplified and promulgated the Cartesian perspective on "internal" worlds rather than focus on everyday lived experience. Early psychoanalysts pictured the individual person as separate, and at times even estranged, from his or her sociocultural-interpersonal milieu, depending on the degree of "psychopathology." In Freud's model, the mind was left to the whims of biological drives and the vicissitudes of the internal, psychic structures responsible for managing those drives. In the process, other persons took on a purely secondary function.

Whereas, for Freud, instinctual life and its internal management were the psychic engine in the development of the person, D. W. Winnicott (1960) exponentially advanced our focus and appreciation for the uniqueness of the individual. He privileged the primacy of the individual's "spontaneous gesture" and—under good enough circumstances—the environmental (maternal) responsiveness to what emerges as the "true self." Even Winnicott's "false self" was aimed at hiding and protecting the "true self," remaining ever vigilant for relational opportunities in which the true self might see the light of day, grow, and flourish. Winnicott's version of a "contextualized" self was nevertheless more an acknowledgment of the necessity for relational interaction in early life than a lifelong, contextualized, and system-informed sense of self and self-direction.

Similarly, if there was any doubt that individuality and the individual self had become the primary currency of psychoanalytic jargon and interest, Kohut (1971, 1977, 1984) cemented these notions by developing his "psychology of the self." His contribution and initial emphasis (1971, 1977, 1984) regarding the centrality of empathy, or vicarious introspection, in investigating the psychological world of the person laid the groundwork for his subsequent preoccupation with the vicissitudes of the self, including "the self's" ongoing, life-long need for selfobject responsiveness.

Heinz Kohut is often referred to as a transitional force in the movement from a one-person model to a more contextualist sensibility through his emphasis on the inevitability of selfobject reliance. Kohut's "self" is dependent on the surround for its narcissistic sustenance. Yet his psychology of the self continued to propagate the notion of individuality in his presumption of a developing self (and corresponding internal structure) that had its own developmental program and thus remains a striking example of the individualist paradigm. As reliant as this theory of the self may be on the impact of the surround, it should not therefore be conflated with a hermeneutic-contextualist perspective on human development.

Whereas psychoanalysis, in particular, has struggled with how to connect human experience to the surround because of its deep-seated belief in the intrapsychic model of the mind, other therapeutic approaches recognized the ecological model of experience much earlier. For Gestalt therapists, in particular, the self cannot be separated from the field in which it exists (Wheeler, 2000). Similarly, the existential-humanistic therapeutic tradition, responding to the precepts of classical psychoanalysis, turned to Heidegger's (1996) notion of existence as "being-in-the-world," which valued the inextricable connection of self and world. And for the early interpersonal psychoanalysts, starting with Harry Stack Sullivan and Erich Fromm, the self was seen as fundamentally social in nature.

When examined chronologically, psychoanalytic history thus reflects a gradual transformation of attitudes about the individual, the notion of the self, and personal subjectivity. The evolution of psychoanalytic theory and practice takes many forms, from object relations and self psychology through interpersonal, relational, and intersubjective systems theory. Whereas the differences are legion, many psychoanalysts today recognize that individuality and personal subjectivity are reciprocally articulated through interactions with the other and that psychoanalytic practice is itself a fundamentally social exercise. Similarly, the individual person and culture are now understood as mutually informing of one another. Indeed, the idea that individuality is somehow transcendent of culture is an "illusion that is sustained and enabled by culture itself" (Stonebridge, 1998, p. 2). The individual person emerges within historical and sociocultural contexts and through her actions impacts and transforms these contexts: "history flows through people ... [and] constitutes our psyches" just as our psyches have informed our history (Kohut, 2003, p. 226).

Whereas the one-person model eventually gave way to a two-person perspective, the embrace of a more fully intersubjective, contextual viewpoint is relatively recent. From within a contemporary, intersubjective systems and relational perspective, the subjectivities of both patient and analyst are always present and interactive within the context of the analytic relationship as well as within the larger sociocultural surround. Indeed, it is the interactional and enacting capabilities of a living, relational system— whether understood as on the level of procedural/implicit functioning or as within the realm of the conscious/declarative/explicit (Fosshage, 2005)— that provides the framework for determining our therapeutic aims and our therapeutic actions.

These changes in theory and practice give rise to a number of important questions. In light of the focus on the dynamic systems, complexity, and contextualist sensibilities (Coburn, 2002; Galatzer-Levy, 1978; Seligman, 2005; Stolorow, 1997; Thelen & Smith, 1994), what has happened to the individual in psychoanalysis and psychotherapy? How do psychoanalysts and psychotherapists think about individuality? Is there a place for the individual in a contextualist approach to theory and practice? And does an ineradicable contextualist and systems sensibility mesh with an acknowledgement of and appreciation for the uniqueness of the individual and her sense of individuality?

One avenue of resolving the tension between the presumption of the existence of an individual person, on one hand, and the increasing focus on the multiple, sociocultural contexts of human experience, on the other hand, is to distinguish and articulate clearly whether we are speaking *phenomenologically* or *explanatorily*. From the perspective of lived, phenomenological experience, as individual persons we may feel at times quite separate, even estranged, from our social contexts. Whether in theory or practice, psychologists, psychoanalysts, and psychotherapists demonstrate a proclivity toward elevating lived, experience to the level of truth and reality, thus reifying experience and conferring upon it concrete, objective existence. Our propensity to organize unfamiliar stimuli into meaningful patterns of experience is a substantial contributor to this reifying activity, along the lines of: If I feel like an individual entity, I must be one. A sense of separateness, however, does not imply that one *is* fundamentally separate.

Clearly, to navigate the tension between the individual and her surroundings, we can no longer think of ourselves as first existing as individuals and only thereafter entering into contact with others and the world around us.

We are always and already relational beings who exist in worlds that are not of our making (Heidegger, 1996). It is through the process of development and expression over time that we articulate our individuality, in concert with being informed and shaped by our surroundings. Such articulation is made possible by the ever-present background of biological, social, and cultural contexts out of which we emerge and within which we continue to exist. The person and his attendant experiences of individuality, including the values of individualism, are emergent products and properties of the larger bio-sociocultural-historical milieu (or system) of which each of us is a part. And in the process of acting in the world, each of us contributes to the very systems or contexts that give rise to our sense of individuality.

CHAPTER OUTLINE

The challenge of individuality for psychology, psychoanalysis, and psychotherapy thus continues to be a pertinent and pervasive theme. The contributors to this volume, each in his or her own unique way, seek to address and explore the problem of individuality from the perspective of a post-Cartesian, hermeneutic, and contextualist sensibility. As a group, they consider how a contextualist perspective informs, advances, or radically alters our understanding of individuality, along with the presumptions inherent in Western culture's continuing emphasis on individualism. Indeed, a guiding objective of this volume is to elaborate and make explicit the implicit beliefs and values that affect and advance our theory construction and clinical practice. Such attitudes are pivotal in the moment-by-moment, clinical decision-making process that shapes much of what emerges in clinical treatment and what, ultimately, is thought to be useful and mutative.

To facilitate the organization of the book, we have divided the volume into four sections: (1) social, cultural, and political contexts; (2) philosophical contexts; (3) developmental contexts; and (4) reflections on the challenges of individuality. Whereas most contributors address aspects of each of these dimensions, certain themes nevertheless dominate in what contributors discuss. Readers will also note that some chapters are chiefly theoretical in scope, while others are more clinically oriented. Similarly, some chapters address the work of psychologists, and others are concerned primarily with the work of psychoanalysts or philosophers. While psychology, psychoanalysis, and philosophy are often viewed as distinct, we believe that this is an unfortunate and, at times, even artificial distinction. It is our hope that readers will see how much psychologists, psychoanalysts, and philosophers have to learn from one another.

In Chapter 1, Roger Frie addresses the sociocultural contexts that shape theory and practice in psychology and psychoanalysis. He suggests that whereas contemporary theory has increasingly embraced a post-subjectivist outlook, the notion of individuality remains firmly entrenched in North American culture. Social, political, and developmental ideals, grounded in the tradition of individualism, continue to celebrate human autonomy and separation and affect the way human experience is conceptualized and understood. Because clinical practice takes place within the sociopolitical norms and values of the dominant culture, it can appear as though post-Cartesian theory, on one hand, and clinical practice and research, on the other hand, exist on entirely different registers. Frie examines the tension between these different registers and introduces a hermeneutic alternative to the traditional, dualistic conceptions of mind and culture: a conception of the situated person for a post-individualist age.

In Chapter 2, Philip Cushman suggests that the intellectual movement known as the Interpretive Turn has done much to expose the limitations of the Cartesian split (mind–body, nature–nurture, psychological–social), self-contained individualism, and the one-person psychology. Especially noteworthy is how those modern-era ideas have influenced various forms of psychotherapy, including psychoanalysis. Both major branches of the Interpretive Turn—postmodernism and hermeneutics—have been drawn upon to reshape psychotherapy theory over the past 40 years. Cushman argues that this is especially true for relational psychoanalysis, which has relied heavily on postmodern and hermeneutic concepts such as the con-textual, intersubjective nature of human beings. However, he questions whether in its enthusiasm for opposing modern-era ideas such as self-con-tained individualism and the deep, subjective self, postmodern forms of psychoanalysis have lost sight of important human qualities such as human agency and choice. Cushman applies Gadamerian hermeneutics to psycho-therapy so that clinical practices can continue opposing Cartesianism with-out losing sight of important, valuable concepts.

In Chapter 3, Donna Orange examines the responses of recent continental philosophers to the Cartesian tradition of subjectivity. Her chapter attends to the possible meanings of individuality in psychoanalysis and in philosophy, with interwoven references to development and to clinical work. It draws on the dialogic philosophies of Martin Buber and Hans-Georg Gadamer and the ethics of Emmanuel Lévinas to challenge the objectification of self-hood and individuality in psychoanalysis and psychotherapy. In the process, Orange examines central aspects of Buber's, Gadamer's, and Lévinas's phi-losophies as they relate to the problematic of individuality. She suggests that some recent understandings of individuality and of individualized selfhood tend to shift the clinical and ethical focus to the welcomed other.

In Chapter 4, Robert Stolorow explores the relational contexts in which our sense of individualized selfhood takes form. Central to these relational contexts is an attuned relationality, which he defines as the other's attun-ement to and understanding of one's distinctive affectivity. This attuned relationality facilitates and sustains our sense of mineness that is constitutive of experiential life. In developing his thesis, Stolorow draws on concepts from philosophical phenomenology and Heidegger's existential analytic. In the process, he seeks to relationalize Heidegger's conception of authentic selfhood by emphasizing the necessity of integrating the emotional experiences accompanying ownership not only of one's own finitude but also the finitude of all those to whom one is deeply connected.

In Chapter 5, Jeff Sugarman and Jack Martin maintain that psychological inquiry and practice have traditionally sought to explain human psychology through an interior, mentalistic focus or through environmental restriction and simplification. By contrast, they consider persons acting in worldly contexts as the appropriate focus for psychological theorizing and inquiry and for expanding our understanding of individuality—what it means to be individual. Sugarman and Martin outline a conceptual framework for interpreting persons and draw on developmental perspectives grounded in the works of Vygotsky and Mead. They view persons as contextually constituted, embodied, rational, and moral agents. Sugarman and Martin provide an ontological account of persons as unique entities constituted developmentally and emergent within contexts of coordinated activity and interactivity. They conclude that disciplinary psychology should be reoriented to address the psychology of a contextualized personhood.

In Chapter 6, James Fosshage addresses the challenge of individuality in light of the burgeoning contextualist and systems perspectives in contemporary psychoanalysis. Sensitive to this paradigm shift, he argues that these new perspectives do not sufficiently recognize the constitutional factors at play in accounting for the emergence of individuality and uniqueness. Fosshage posits that a deeper consideration of our self-regulatory capacities, temperamental dispositions, strength of motives, and physical and cognitive capacities better facilitates a vital recognition and appreciation of the individual's uniqueness. He argues that motivations and intentions have strong clinical value and that these concepts need to be refined and updated in accordance with recent findings in neuroscience, cognitive science, infant research, dream research, and systems theory. Fosshage tackles this perspective with an emphasis on what he refers to as developmental motivation and developmental direction.

In Chapter 7, Frank Lachmann delineates the emergence of individuality from four perspectives: cellular, organismic, self-psychological, and clinical. Lachmann contends that the current emphasis on contexts and attachments has enriched our understanding of human experience. But it also poses challenges for thinking about and elaborating the nature of individuality. Using an interdisciplinary approach that draws on contemporary self psychology and neuroscience, Lachmann focuses on the evolution and emergence of unique individuality. He maintains that the basic structure at the cellular and organismic levels already contains elements of human uniqueness. Individuality, in turn, emerges from the social contexts in which we live. These contexts provide an ever-present background, much like the oxygen in the air. Yet, on the level of lived experience, we also exist as self-sustaining islands to which we retreat for longer or shorter stretches. Lachmann concludes that this tension is a fundamental characteristic of human experience.

In the concluding chapter, William Coburn considers the previous seven chapters and the ways each contributor subverts and contemporizes the more traditional notions and assumptions emanating from individualism. He highlights and discusses what, for each of the authors, decontextualized persons, stripped of their sociocultural-historical milieu, would have looked like. Coburn then examines a variety of perspectives aimed at envisioning persons whose context-dependent and context-sensitive lives have been restored and whose emotional worlds emanate from an array of interpenetrating complex systems. He asserts that the work of each contributor implies a variety of clinical attitudes that are responsible for therapeutic action in psychoanalysis and psychotherapy and examines these attitudes through the lens of psychoanalytic complexity theory. Coburn concludes by reaffirming the fundamental necessity for distinguishing between two essential dimensions of discourse: the phenomenological and the explanatory. Not doing so, he argues, has been the primary means by which the notion of the person has been decontextualized, reduced, and stereotyped within individualism.

REFERENCES

Bauman, Z. (2000). *Liquid modernity*. Cambridge, UK: Polity.

Bellah, R., Madsen, R., Sullivan, W., Swidler, A., & Tipton, S. (1985). *Habits of the heart: Individualism and commitment in American life*. Berkeley: University of California Press.

Benjamin, J. (1988). *The bonds of love*. London: Virago.

Bhabha, H. (1994). *The location of culture*. London: Routledge.

Cilliers, P. (1998). *Complexity and postmodernism: Understanding complex systems*. London: Routledge.

Coburn, W. J. (2002). A world of systems: The role of systemic patterns of experience in the therapeutic process. *Psychoanalytic Inquiry, 22*, 655–677.

Cushman, P. (1995). *Constructing the self, constructing America: A cultural history of psychotherapy*. Reading, MA: Addison-Wesley.

Damasio, A. (1999). *The feeling of what happens: Body and emotion in the making of consciousness*. New York: Harcourt Press.

Derrida, J. (1978). *Writing and difference*. Chicago: University of Chicago Press.

Fosshage, J. L. (2005). The explicit and implicit domains in psychoanalytic change. *Psychoanalytic Inquiry, 25*, 516–539.

Foucault, M. (1977). *Language, counter-memory, practice: Selected essays.* Ithaca, NY: Cornell University Press.

Freud, S. (1923). *The ego and the id.* In J. Strachey (Ed. & Trans.), *The standard edition of the complete psychological works of Sigmund Freud* (Vol. 19, pp. 3–66). London: Hogarth Press.

Freud, S. (1933). New introductory lectures on psycho-analysis. In J. Strachey (Ed. & Trans.), *The standard edition of the complete psychological works of Sigmund Freud* (Vol. 22, pp. 3–182). London: Hogarth Press.

Frie, R., & Orange, D. (Eds.) (2009). *Beyond postmodernism: New dimensions in clinical theory and practice.* London: Routledge.

Friedman, L. (1978). Trends in the psychoanalytic theory of treatment. *Psychoanalytic Quarterly, 47,* 524-567.

Gadamer, H.-G. (1995). *Truth and method* (J. Weinsheimer & D. G. Marshall, Trans.). New York: Continuum. (Original work published 1960)

Galatzer-Levy, R. (1978). Qualitative change from quantitative change: Mathematical catastrophe theory in relation to psychoanalysis. *Journal of the Ameican Psychoanalytic Association, 26,* 921–935.

Geertz, C. (1973). *The interpretation of cultures.* New York: Basic Books.

Giddens, A. (1984). *The constitution of society.* Berkeley: University of California Press.

Gilligan, C. (1993). *In a different voice* (2nd ed.). Cambridge, MA: Harvard University Press.

Habermas, J. (1987). *Theory of communicative action, vol. 2* (T. McCarthy, Trans.). Boston: Beacon Press.

Heidegger, M. (1996). *Being and time* (J. Stambaugh, Trans.). Albany: SUNY Press. (Original work published 1927)

Keller, E. F. (1985). *Reflections on gender and science.* New Haven, CT: Yale University Press.

Kohut, H. (1971). *The analysis of the self.* New York: International Universities Press.

Kohut, H. (1977). *The restoration of the self.* New York: International Universities Press.

Kohut, H. (1984). *How does analysis cure?* Chicago: University of Chicago Press.

Locke, J. (1960). *Two treatises on government.* Cambridge, UK: Cambridge University Press. (Original work published 1689)

Lyotard, J.-F. (1984). *The postmodern condition.* Manchester, UK: Manchester University Press.

Mahler, M., Pine, R., & Bergman, A. (1975). *The psychological birth of the human infant: Symbiosis and individuation.* New York: Basic Books.

Martin, J., Sugarman, J., & Hickinbottom, S. (2009). *Persons: Understanding psychological selfhood and agency.* New York: Springer.

Mead, G. H. (1962). *Mind, self and society.* Chicago: University of Chicago Press.

Merleau-Ponty, M. (1962). *The primacy of perception.* Evanston, IL: Northwestern University Press.

Messer, S. B., Sass, L. A., & Woolfolk, R. L. (Eds.) (1988). *Hermeneutics and psychological theory: Interpretive perspectives on personality, psychotherapy, and psychopathology.* New Brunswick, NJ: Rutgers University Press.

Richardson, F. C., Fowers, B. J., & Guigon, C. B. (1999). *Re-envisioning psychology: Moral dimensions of theory and practice.* San Francisco: Jossey-Bass Publishers.

Sandel, M. (1998). *Liberalism and the limits of justice* (2nd ed.). Cambridge, UK: Cambridge University Press.

Seligman, S. (2005). Dynamic systems theories as a metaframework for psychoanalysis. *Psychoanalytic Dialogues, 15*, 285–319.

Stern, D. (1985). *The interpersonal world of the infant.* New York: Basic Books.

Stolorow, R. D. (1997). Dynamic, dyadic, intersubjective systems: An evolving paradigm for psychoanalysis. *Psychoanalytic Psychology, 14*, 337–364.

Stonebridge, L. (1998). *The destructive element: British psychoanalysis and modernism.* New York: Routledge.

Sullivan, H. S. (1950). The illusion of personal individuality. In *The fusion of psychiatry and social science* (pp. 198–226). New York: Norton.

Taylor, C. (1985). *Philosophy and the human sciences: Philosophical papers 2.* Cambridge, UK: Cambridge University Press.

Taylor, C. (1989). *Sources of the self: The making of the modern identity.* Cambridge, UK: Cambridge University Press.

Thelen, E., & Smith, L. B. (1994). *A dynamic systems approach to the development of cognition and action.* Cambridge, MA: MIT Press.

Vygotsky, L. S. (1978). *Mind in society.* Cambridge, MA: Harvard University Press.

Wheeler, G. (2000). *Beyond individualism: Toward a new understanding of self, relationship and experience.* Hillsdale, NJ: Analytic Press.

Winnicott, D. W. (1960). The theory of the parent-infant relationship. *International Journal of Psychoanalysis, 41*, 585–595.

Part I

Social, cultural, and political contexts

Chapter 1

Culture and context

From individualism to situated experience

Roger Frie

> Long before we understand ourselves through the process of self-examination, we understand ourselves in a self-evident way in the family, society and state in which we live. The focus of subjectivity is a distorting mirror.
>
> – Hans-Georg Gadamer (1989, p. 276)

INTRODUCTION

Psychologists, psychoanalysts, and psychotherapists traditionally play down the role of historical, social, and cultural forces in human experience. Yet culture in its many forms is always present in the clinical setting and is the context within which all experience unfolds. Each of us is born into and emerges within cultural contexts of shared beliefs, values, rules, and practices. Our cultural contexts determine the language we use to describe ourselves and affect how we exist in the world. The Western emphasis on individuality, autonomy, and separateness is no exception. The belief that each person is unique, that the individual forms the focus of investigation, and that development occurs through a process of separation from others, reflects the dominant cultural values and history of North American society.

The North American preoccupation with the individual self is well documented. Cultural myths of individual self-fulfillment and self-awareness abound and are captured in the image of the "American Dream." The impact of these myths on Western psychology, psychoanalysis, and psychotherapy cannot be underestimated. As numerous critics have shown (Cushman, 1990, 1994; Fancher, 1994, 1995; Martin, Sugarman, & Thompson, 2003; Richardson, Fowers, & Guigon, 1999; Taylor, 1989), the history of psychology and psychoanalysis reads like an ode to the self-determining individual. I will build on the work of these critics and suggest not only that our identity as human beings is shaped by social, cultural, and historical forces but also that individualism—the belief that we are, at the deepest level, self-contained, autonomous individuals—cannot capture the nature of our being as humans.*

Because the transmission of culture is largely tacit, occurring outside of our everyday awareness, the dominant perspective on individuality is firmly entrenched and not easily challenged or changed. Although there has been a strong reaction to the ideology of individualism implicit in many forms of psychoanalysis and psychotherapy, the notion of the self-determining individual remains prevalent in popular culture. The values of autonomy, instrumental reason, and the valorization of the individual continue to impact society as a whole and the practice of therapy in particular. Indeed, many of the goals of therapy are derived from the belief systems and cultural assumptions associated with individualism. These views are implicit in traditional theories of development and often form the basis of the personal narratives that emerge in the therapeutic dialogue, with important consequences.

In this chapter I will suggest that the notion that people are independent and self-determining entities impedes our understanding of the sociocultural contexts of human experience. A theory and practice of psychotherapy that is preoccupied with the inner self and with individual self-fulfillment overlooks our embeddedness in a community of shared values. In the process, human experience becomes strangely disengaged from the social and cultural milieu. When the social world is devalued, social problems also lose their relation to political action (Cushman, 1990). Most importantly, when cultural contexts are overlooked, we are unable to perceive the way self-understanding, gender, race, and ethnicity are all culturally defined and limited.

I will focus on our belonging and indebtedness to the wider sociocultural and historical contexts in which we find ourselves. I will suggest that individuality is a construct produced by particular types of social practices; it is one interpretation of being human among others, with no privileged status in telling us about our "true" nature. My aim is to examine how the notion of individuality forms an intractable part of Western, and particularly American culture, and fundamentally influences the way the clinical situation unfolds. Despite the growing reaction against individualism in contemporary theory and practice, its values, norms, and objectives persist. I believe a crucial step in overcoming this pervasiveness lies in achieving a fuller understanding of the extent to which individualism is ingrained in our thinking about human experience.

I will begin by tracing the historical trajectory of individuality and individualism, which is rooted in the philosophies of René Descartes and John Locke and finds expression in Sigmund Freud's project of psychoanalysis. I

---

* As Charles Taylor (1995) states, "We are of the world through a 'we' before we are through an 'I'" so that "we always find ourselves as a we-consciousness before we can be an I-consciousness" (p. 40).

then consider the determining role of the so-called independent self in psychological theories of human development and cultural experience. I conclude by considering a hermeneutic alternative that is grounded in the works of Martin Heidegger, Hans-Georg Gadamer, and Ludwig Binswanger. This contextualist sensibility undercuts the artificial distinction between self and world by emphasizing the irreducible contexts of understanding that form the basis for human development and experience. Most importantly, a hermeneutic perspective allows us to reconfigure the notion of individuality in terms of a situated (or contextualized) personal experience.

THE DISENGAGED INDIVIDUAL: DESCARTES AND LOCKE

The notion of the autonomous, self-determining individual, which is so deeply embedded in North American culture, is hardly new. It has a long history in western philosophy and forms the basis for models of self-understanding and action, from economic theory to law and politics. The self-determining individual is based on the gendered notion of instrumental, self-responsible reason. The ability to wield reason is grounded in the disengaged mind, which exists separately from bodily drives, the interference of others, and the role of social and political institutions. The iconic image of the Marlboro Man, known throughout the world from the marketing campaign of the cigarette maker Philip Morris provides an apt metaphor. The Marlboro Man is a modern representation of the disengaged individual mind. Here we have the rugged, independent man on horseback, free to determine a course of action, and able to tame the wilds of nature and beasts at will.

The notion of the isolated, thinking mind is most strongly indebted to the philosophy of Descartes. With his famous dictum, "I think, therefore I am," Descartes championed the ability to reason and ushered in the age of the Enlightenment. Following Descartes, the individual mind became the locus of reason and knowledge for the modern tradition of philosophy and psychology (Burston & Frie, 2006). Descartes insists that the knowledge we have of our own minds is not connected in any essential way to the world around us. The external world, other minds, and even the existence of our own bodies are open to question. Our minds are the only thing we can be certain of. In *Discourse on Method* (1637/1949), Descartes writes:

> I attentively examined what I was, and as I observed that I could suppose I had no body, and that there was no world or any place in which I might be...while, on the other hand, if I had only ceased to think, although all the other objects which I had ever imagined had been in reality existent, I would have no reason to think that I existed; I thence

concluded that I was a thinking substance whose whole essence consists in thinking. (p. 27)

The separation of reason from the passions finds its epitome in the work of Descartes. In Descartes model of the mind, reason and passion are adversaries, antagonistic forces that influence behavior by different means. According to Descartes, reason is an active, ordering principle and associated with human agency and choice. By contrast, the passions have a driven involuntary character that effectively places them outside our control and usually puts them at variance with the promptings of reason, an idea that stems from Plato and is later endorsed by Freud. In the Cartesian tradition, therefore, the ability to reason is an "internal property" of the thinking mind that is radically disengaged from the very contexts—biological, social, and cultural—that make it possible to begin with.

Descartes thus presents us with an utterly detached engagement with a world that has itself been cast into doubt. As Charles Taylor suggests, Descartes cogito is an endorsement of "instrumental control" without regard for the outcome. This kind of "dimensionless point of conscious activity" is what Taylor (1989, 1995) calls the "punctual self." According to Taylor (1995), the punctual self is "ideally disengaged, that is…free and rational to the extent that he has fully distinguished himself from the natural and social worlds, so that his identity is no longer to be defined in terms of what lies outside him in these worlds" (p. 7). Or as Wilhelm Dilthey (1976) suggests, in his well-known late 19th-century critique of the thinking subject: "No real blood flows in the veins of the knowing subject…only the diluted juice of reason, a mere process of thought" (p. 162). The knowing subject is an abstraction with little relevance to actual worldly experience. The objectified, individualized subject is thoroughly disengaged from the practical, embodied experience in which any separation of self and world is a false distinction.

While Cartesian philosophy heralds the notion of a disengaged, thinking subject and forms the basis for much subsequent western thought about the mind, the disengagement of the individual from social contexts is fully developed in Locke's political philosophy. Locke's ideas about individuality are particularly relevant to understanding the contemporary culture of individuality because they form the basis for central aspects of the American constitution.* Thomas Jefferson's distillation of Locke's philosophy of

---

* Locke was avidly read by Americans revolutionaries and his ideas played an important part in the formation of American revolutionary thought. As Leo Rauch (1981) states, "It is a sad and ironic fact that the doctrine of the individual's 'natural' rights had already been attacked by Hume and Rousseau before the American founders made use of the idea. Although it may linger on today as the official democratic ideology, it nevertheless shows itself to be a strangely outmoded doctrine—already moribund when it was given such vital use by men who ignored the attacks on it or failed to see it as a relic of the revolutionary thinking of a hundred years before" (p. 72).

"natural rights" is evident in the Declaration of Independence: "We hold these truths to be self-evident, that all men are created equal, that they are endowed by their Creator with certain unalienable Rights that among these are Life, Liberty and the pursuit of Happiness." Indeed, Locke provides a rational picture of the purpose of government: to protect individual rights and to serve individual needs. According to Locke, the individual has a natural right to life, liberty and property that precedes any type of social organization. Individuals come together to form a social contract in order to protect these rights and to limit state power. The role of government is to safeguard an individual's rights, and the individual, in turn, is justified in rebelling if a ruler does not fulfill this obligation.

Locke's ideas have been instrumental to the development of the so-called ideology of individualism. While the American Declaration of Independence proclaimed equality for all its citizens, only those individuals who were defined as white, propertied men were permitted to vote in the new American democracy. In his well-known critique, C. B. Macpherson (1969) introduces the term "possessive individualism" to describe Locke's theory of the formation of a society comprising individuals who act on the basis of market relations. According to Macpherson, Locke sees the acquisition and protection of property as a "rational" exercise. On this view, anyone who fails to acquire property is lacking in rationality. It is this underlying distinction between the propertied and laboring classes that leads Macpherson to describe Locke as an apologist of capitalism. The democratic government envisaged by Locke is set up with the express purpose of protecting the rights of propertied classes. They alone possess the full capacity to be rational actors, and are disengaged from the realities of actual labor and the laboring classes.

The individualist perspective represented in Locke's theory of government finds expression in liberalism and libertarianism. Proponents of these positions broadly hold that the state should protect the liberty of individuals to act as they wish, as long they do not infringe on the liberties of others. They promote the exercise of one's goals and desires, while opposing any external interference upon one's choices. The liberal and libertarian perspective is usually contrasted with the communitarian view of politics and society (Sandel, 1982; Taylor, 1989) which emphasizes communal and societal needs over individual goals. Communitarian thinkers take issue with the abstract concept of an individual self and argue that the emphasis on individual liberties devalues the importance of attachments, community, and tradition.

Locke's political philosophy yields a picture of the sovereign individual who is not bound by nature to any authority. Here we have the emergence of the self-determining individual who is able to remake him or herself through disciplined action, and by force if necessary. Henceforward, the notion of the individual is identified with a specific set of ideas and traditions: the notion of the unified subject; the triumph of reason over nature; the imperial expansion of Western ideas of self-interest and autonomy to the exclusion of non-Western notions of community and selflessness; the celebration of scientific rationalism at the expense of the perils of modern technology; and the homogeneity of such values as universality and equality, which fail to account for differences in gender, race, culture, power and social class.

FREUD AND THE HERALDING OF
THE INDIVIDUAL MIND

The philosophies of Descartes and Locke thus present us with a disengaged individual, whose sole ontological locus, the thinking mind, is deeply ingrained in modern Western culture. The reification of the mind likewise finds expression in the work of Freud and, as I will discuss, also permeates much modern psychology. As a representative of the Enlightenment thinking, Freud believes that the power of reason can be used to strengthen the conscious mind. Like his predecessors, he suggests that the mind is prey to the passions, thus highlighting the inevitability of distortion in our thinking. The purpose of psychoanalysis, according to Freud (1923), is to expand the ego and tame the id, a process captured in his famous dictum, "Where id was, there shall ego become." As such, psychoanalysis is squarely grounded in the Cartesian belief in rational self-mastery.

According to Freud, the rational mind is both dependent on but also exists in opposition to the drives. The need for the thinking mind to achieve mastery over the body has its basis in the history of Western philosophy. Plato is the first in a long line of thinkers who herald the emergence of reason over the passions. Being master of oneself, according to Plato, depends upon the ability to distinguish thought from desire. In contrast to the passions, which may possess us, reason enables us to see and understand. For Plato, the "good man" is one who is able to use thought to become "master of himself." In Freud's project, mind and body are likewise continually at odds with one another. The only way out of this quandary is through the often difficult and painful process of learning self-understanding and self-mastery. However, the very nature of this task perpetuates the Cartesian division between mind and body, cognition and affect (Frie, 1997).

According to Freud (1919), psychoanalytic treatment seeks to strengthen the ego, with the ultimate aim of unifying the ego. As he states:

> In actual fact, indeed, the neurotic patient presents us with a torn mind, divided by resistances. As we analyze it and remove the resistances, it grows together; the greater unity which we call his ego fits into itself all

the instinctual impulses which before had been split off and held apart from it. (p. 161)

Self-mastery is possible only by healing splits and restoring and enlarging the unity of the ego. The enlargement of the ego takes place through the facilitation of the ego's communication with, and integration of, the instinctual forces that it previously defended itself against.

For ego psychology, the expansion of the ego amounts to the pursuit of autonomy and emancipation through the growth of self-knowledge. It is precisely the emphasis on the ego's enlargement that resonates with the tradition of disengagement in the works of Descartes and Locke. Indeed, according to Taylor (1989), Locke's theory forms

> [t]he basis of the mature Freudian conception of the ego, which belongs to the "structural" model. This ego is in essence a pure steering mechanism, devoid of instinctual force of its own (though it must draw power from the id to function). Its job is to manoeuver through the all-but-unnavigable obstacle course set by id, super-ego, and external reality. Its powers are incomparably less than Locke's punctual self, but like its ancestor it is fundamentally a disengaged agent of instrumental reason (p. 174).

Here, then, we have a philosophy of objectification in which the ego is decontextualized, despite its fundamental dependence upon the body, others, and the world in which it exists.*

Although Freud's ideas undergo numerous reformulations, his naturalistic reductionism results in the objectification and isolation of the mind. This disengagement has a strong interpersonal dimension. For Freud, other persons primarily take the role of objects for the gratification of instinctual desires. Interpersonal relations have their origin in the discovery that other people can aid in the reduction of tensions. This mechanistic view similarly influences Freud's understanding of interpersonal love. The diverse forms of human loving, according to Freud, can all be traced back to the drives, whose function is to provide instinctual satisfaction.

Freud's reductionism is also evidenced in the traditional analytic setting, which is based on the twin pillars of objectivity and neutrality. In Freud's view, the analyst is an objective scientist who is able to observe and identify

---

* "There has been a long-standing debate in psychoanalysis over the role of cognitive insight versus affective attachment in the process of therapeutic change. The terms of this debate are directly descended from Descartes' philosophical dualism, which sectioned human experience into cognitive and affective domains. Such artificial fracturing of human subjectivity is no longer tenable in a post-Cartesian philosophical world. Cognition and affect, thinking and feeling, interpreting and relating—these are separable only in pathology" (Stolorow, 2000, p. 683).

the constituents of the mental processes working within the patient. A crucial aspect of this process rests on the analyst's ability to bracket out distorting prejudices. The analyst thereby maintains a neutral stance that allows for objective, "scientific" observation.

The interpersonal ramifications of this approach are captured by Richardson et al. (1999), who suggest that the notion of the individual as a detached knower masks a profound aspiration for separation, if not an actual fear of dependence on others. Indeed, for the traditional analytic patient who works toward achieving self-mastery and autonomy, any dependence on others, including the analyst, can compromise the process of psychological maturation. The failure to separate from others, whether from the parent or the analyst, when combined with a slide back into dependency, is referred to in negative terms as "regression." The process of analysis is itself spurred on by a transference regression, which allows the analyst to perceive the patient's transference needs and desires.

INDIVIDUALITY IN DEVELOPMENTAL AND CULTURAL PSYCHOLOGY

From this perspective, psychological life is located in the drive to satisfy personal, instinctual needs and desires, often to the exclusion of other people's needs or desires. As Taylor (1989) suggests, this "common picture of the self, as (at least potentially and ideally) drawing its purposes, goals, and life-plans out of itself, seeking 'relationships' only insofar as they are 'fulfilling,' is largely based on ignoring our embedding in webs of interlocution" (p. 39). This form of independent individualism is also heavily gendered and finds expression in traditional theories of human development and cultural engagement.

For traditional theorists of development, human growth is premised on such value-laden notions as separation and autonomy. In the main, these theories suggest that the child must learn to separate away from a static representation of his or her mother to achieve an autonomous identity. This process happens in a linear developmental trajectory that reflects the norms of the individually oriented society in which it takes place. The notion of identity formation as an individual developmental achievement was popularized in the works of Erik Erikson in the 1960s. His ego psychological stance is closely associated with the work of Margaret Mahler and her colleagues. In their classic text, *The Psychological Birth of the Human Infant: Symbiosis and Individuation*, Mahler, Pine, and Bergman (1975) build on Freud's theory of a symbiotic union in earliest infancy between mother and child by introducing the role of object relations. They see development as progressing through a series of distinct, linear stages, from normal autism to normal symbiosis and finally to separation-individuation.

By contrast, more recent developmental research focuses on the emergence of social experience. Studies from attachment research (Fonagy, Gergely, Jurist, & Target, 2002), early infant development (Stern, 1985), and mother–infant interaction (Beebe & Lachman, 2002) demonstrate the ongoing social foundations of human experience. Similarly, the work of Vygotsky (1978) has been particularly important in providing a model of human development that demonstrates the ongoing social foundations of human experience. Indeed, the goal of human development, on this view, has less to do with individuation than with creating and sustaining relationships of mutuality that are grounded in practice.

The importance of mutuality and the ability to relate also form the basis of the work of some developmental feminists (Benjamin, 1988; Gilligan, 1993). They take issue with gendered values of individualism and rationalism inherent in the Western conception of the autonomous, bounded self. Benjamin and Gilligan suggest that it is precisely the ability to relate to and care for others that defines the nature of much human experience. As Gilligan (1986) remarks:

> When others are described as objects for self-reflection or as the means to self-discovery and self-recognition, the language of relationships is drained of attachment, intimacy, and engagement. The self, although placed in the context of relationships, is defined in terms of separation. (p. 249)

Gilligan's (1993) analysis of the masculine assumptions of Lawrence Kohlberg's moral psychology highlights the exclusion of an "ethic of care" in psychology. Gilligan questions the reasoning behind Kohlberg's view of autonomy as the goal of moral and psychological development. Gilligan suggests that the morality of a caring orientation arises through the child's ability to develop a connected sense of self. In contrast to Kohlberg, she sees interpersonal responsiveness and caring as fully developed and moral (Frie, in press).

Since Gilligan (1993) first introduced her ideas, theories of gender and development have become considerably more complex, mirroring the way identities are experienced as multiple and fluid. Yet, despite these developments, the ability to separate from one's family and to develop one's independence and autonomy continues to be seen as a sign of psychological maturity by popular Western culture. In particular, the American tradition of "leaving home" is viewed as a crucial step in the achievement of adulthood.

Self-reliance, or what Bellah, Madsen, Sullivan, Swindler, and Tipton (1985) refer to as "ontological individualism," forms the basis of our popular psychological understanding and is seen as the hallmark of psychological maturation. As Hazel Markus (2008) points out:

> Americans explain their own actions and those of others as expressions of individual preferences and choices. Americans know that they should resist influence by others and have the courage of their own convictions. Animated by the independent model, they think they can and they do. They take charge, are in control, and realize their dreams. When things go right, individuals get credit; if not, they get the blame. ... Attention to and concern for others is cast as intentional and voluntary; it is not necessary or obligatory. (p. 656)

Markus uses the notion of the "independent" model of the self to refer to this particular cultural perspective. According to the independent model, "attention to and concern for others is cast as intentional and voluntary; it is not necessary or obligatory" (p. 656).

In cross-cultural psychology, the concepts of independence and interdependence are used to capture the different worldviews of Western and non-Western cultures. A landmark study by cultural psychologists Richard Shweder and Edmund Bourne (1984) summarizes a large amount of cross-cultural literature. Their study creates a psychological typology of different selves: a Western concept of self that is autonomous, abstract, and independent; and a non-Western notion of self that is context dependent, socially defined, and interdependent. This idea has been enlarged by Markus and Kitayama (1991), who characterize two ways of conceptualizing the relationship between self and the social world: (1) an independent way of being, in which agency is organized and made meaningful by one's own internal repertoire of thoughts, feelings, and actions; and (2) an interdependent way of being, in which agency is more relational or conjoint and is contingent on and organized by the thoughts, feelings, and actions of others in a relationship (Markus, 2008).

Cross-cultural psychologists view independence and autonomy as the central attribute of individualism, while interdependence is viewed as the central attribute of collectivism. According to this view, the individualistic self is prevalent in Western European and North American cultures, whereas many Asian and African cultures hold the view that the self is strongly connected to the family, group, and community. For Markus and Kitayama (1991), the implication of this distinction for a theory of the self is significant. "The autonomous, interdependent person" is given to "expressing one's unique configuration of needs, rights and capacities" (p. 8). By contrast, in the "interdependent construal of self," other people "become an integral part of the setting, situation, or the context to which the self is connected, fitted and assimilated" (p. 10). This distinction also reiterates Descartes' dualism, in that the independent self is correlated with "inner" experience, which means roughly "private," while the interdependent self is correlated with "outer" experience, meaning public and including relationships with others.

Whereas individualism and collectivism are traditionally seen as separate and opposed, more recent studies by cultural psychologists enlarge this one-sided depiction of self by accounting for the fact that self-experience can vary widely within cultures and groups. Indeed, recent research (cf. Oyserman, Coon, & Kemmelmeier, 2002; Markus & Kitayama, 2003a, 2003b) suggests that there is considerable diversity in definitions of self-experience within and across cultures. The emphasis on broad cultural categories and concepts not only objectifies humans but also underestimates the idiosyncratic meanings, needs, and desires of personal experience. This is an important point since the process of meaning creation is both cultural and personal in nature.

While the constructs of collectivism and individualism may reflect some global differences among societies, they are more relevant to understanding how persons perceive collective and individual values within their own development. The point is that personal experience always unfolds within specific cultural contexts. As a result, the actions people choose and how they experience their decisions will vary depending on the prevalent structure, ideas, and practices of their cultural contexts.

The importance of cultural contexts in our understanding of human action and the concepts we use to explain it simply cannot be underestimated. As Jerome Bruner (1990) argues:

> To treat the world as an indifferent flow of information to be processed by individuals each on his or her own terms is to lose sight of how individuals are formed and how they function. ... Given that psychology is so immersed in culture, it must be organized around those meaning-making and mean-using processes that connect to culture. This does not commit us to more subjectivity in psychology; it is just the reverse. By virtue of participation in culture, meaning is rendered public and shared. Our culturally adapted way of life depends upon shared meanings and shared concepts and depends as well upon shared modes of discourse for negotiating differences in meaning and interpretation. (pp. 12–13)

Culture provides the person with a system of common symbolic patterns through which to create meanings and organize experience (Frie, 2008). In this view, culture is not a broad, monolithic entity but is continually evolving and contested, made up of different perspectives and narratives that both challenge and support dominant modes of thinking and acting. Whether we think about the meaning as socially constructed, personally created, or biologically based (or some combination of the three), the point is that meaning is possible only within a world of shared, cultural understandings. We can never step outside of our cultural contexts; human beings are expressions of their cultures. As Clifford Geertz (1973) famously states, "There is no such thing as human nature independent of culture" (p. 49). Accounting for culture in this way counters the traditional focus on individuality and interiority and has much in common with the hermeneutic perspective.

THE SITUATED NATURE OF PERSONAL EXPERIENCE: A HERMENEUTIC ALTERNATIVE

In the final section, I wish to outline one way individuality, or what I refer to as *situated personal experience,* can be conceptualized from a hermeneutic perspective. The difficulty is that talk of the individual and individuality usually carries with it the implicit values of individualism. Without accounting for the fundamental contextualism of human experience, we inevitably fall back into the false assumptions of individualism that are grounded in the philosophy of the isolated, bounded, and detached self. These assumptions, as I have suggested, are evidenced in the history of psychotherapy.

Historically, psychoanalysis and psychotherapy have functioned in a monocultural manner and have been largely limited to a specific segment of the population that includes middle- and upper-middle-class, largely White Euro-Americans (Cushman, 1994; Richardson et al., 1999; Markus, 2008). The values of self-fulfillment, autonomy, and individualism enshrined in this segment of the population have much to do with how the goals and objectives of clinical work have been defined over time. The problem, as Cushman points out, is that a culture of psychoanalysis and psychotherapy that promotes "a preoccupation with the inner self" may do little to restore a sense of wider purpose within a community of shared values.

The participants of any therapeutic relationship never exist as an isolated unit. Indeed, therapist and patient alike are always situated in a specific time and place, and their self-understanding is itself a product of their culture and their relationship to one another. When applied to clinical setting, this perspective suggests that the therapist's situated subjectivity and clinical perspective will inevitably influence what he or she knows about his or her patient. The notion of objectivity and the detached thinking mind is thereby placed in question.

To be sure, this response to the individualist values of an independent, autonomous self implicit in traditional psychological theory and practice is becoming more widespread. At the same time, however, the individualist perspective in psychology is not easily overcome. Indeed, because it is so entrenched, it lingers on in the evolving paradigms of psychoanalysis. The progression from a so-called one-person to two-person model of psychoanalysis has been an important step in recognizing the way therapist and patient are inherently interactive and mutually impact one another. Yet the focus on the interpersonal nature of the clinical setting still does not sufficiently take into account the sociocultural contexts in which this interaction unfolds. For example, when focusing chiefly on the conscious and unconscious dynamics of the interaction between the therapist and patient, the cultural impact of the implicit values of interiorization and rationality is easily overlooked. The notions of a "third" or "thirdness" provide an additional perspective on how experience is shared by the participants of therapy and thus can add a crucial further dimension to clinical work. Yet if such distinctions are reified, there remains the possibility that meaning is disengaged from the very social contexts through which it is mediated.

The hermeneutic perspective suggests that all human experience exists within contexts or frameworks of understanding. These frameworks precede all distinctions and make self-interpretation and interaction in the world possible. By contrast, disengaged meaning and knowledge are ultimately an abstraction, which, according to Richardson, Guigon, and Fowers (1999) is "the result of a sort of breakdown in our ordinary being-in-the-world, which gives us no insight into the true nature of reality as we actually encounter it" (p. 207). The point is that meanings do not exist only in our minds, or in separate registers and dimensions. We are not simply monads in a world of objects. Rather, we exist in and through a world of shared understandings. From a hermeneutic perspective, therefore, we are all participants in a shared, situated existence.

A hermeneutic ontology, with its emphasis on understanding and dialogue, seeks to describe and interpret this basic dimension of human life, a practical understanding, which precedes any explanation or conceptualization. The hermeneutic tradition owes much to the ideas of Heidegger (1996) and Gadamer (1995). In his early philosophy, for example, Heidegger seeks to overcome naturalism and determinism in his ontological account of existence. Heidegger rejects the Cartesian view of the subject, arguing that existence manifests itself as "being in the world." The person is not simply *of* a particular sociocultural context. Not only does this context form the background for activity; the embeddedness of the person in sociocultural contexts is so profound as to also render any absolute distinction of action from context nonsensical. We are "always and already in the world" in such a way that there is no possibility of separating the self and world. From this perspective, we can never exist outside of our world of experience. We find ourselves "thrown" into a world we neither create nor control.

Being thrown into the world implies that we exist in specific frameworks of understanding that shape how we experience and interpret ourselves and the world around us. This is also what Gadamer (1995) refers to as our "horizon of understanding." It is from the perspective of our horizon of understanding that we identify things, pose questions, interpret, and know what kinds of answers make sense to us. Our horizon of understanding enables us to communicate and interact and both limits and makes possible what we can make sense of. It is up to each of us to take up the possibilities of self-understanding into which we are thrown and shape them into lives that are our own.

As such, the hermeneutic tradition suggests that there is no psychological experience that is not constituted by the sociocultural and interpretive contexts in which we find ourselves. Our experience is always contingent on contexts that constitute our personhood by way of interpretations and practices. It is not the case that the person is merely "influenced" by socio-cultural factors and contexts. It is not enough to view selfhood and culture as interacting variables (Martin, 2007). Rather, the experience of selfhood is forged within communal contexts and fundamentally embedded.

By emphasizing our embeddedness in cultural contexts I am not suggesting that our actions are entirely determined by sociocultural forces beyond our control. The possibility of making and remaking culture, and of navigating our place within it, is a constantly unfolding process. Culture is being continually transformed as we negotiate common meaning through our social interactions with others (Holland, Lachicotte, Skinner, & Cain, 1998). We are always contributors to the contexts in which we exist and participate, which points to our capacity for agency. In other words, agency and the possibility of change are both made possible and limited (Martin & Sugarman, 1999) by our being in the world.

What makes a hermeneutic perspective so valuable, in my view, is that it provides a means to account both for our situated psychological existence and for the role of the personal agent. As psychological agents we invest activities and practices with practical and personal significance in ways that can modify the sociocultural conventions within which we exist and act. As Martin et al. (2003) suggest, "Once emergent within societies and cultures, psychological beings not only continue to be affected by socio-cultural practices, but also are affected by their own interpretations and conceptions of, and reactions to, such practices" (p. 43).

The potential for personal agency is shaped throughout life as our experiences are learned and transformed in myriad social and cultural contexts. Our agency does not occur in a vacuum but is always and already emergent. The ability to make choices that can affect life experience is dependent on an openness to new possibilities of understanding and relating. This comes about through subtle, and sometimes, painful shifts in our horizons of understanding, never through the self-determining actions of an autonomous, isolated actor.

This approach to working therapeutically was first introduced by Binswanger (1947, 1955). Drawing on Heidegger's concept of being in the world, Binswanger sought to understand how patients configure their worlds, a process that is often outside of awareness. He refers to the patient's horizon of understanding as a "world design," precisely the context through which a person lives and understands his or her experience. Binswanger suggests that within the therapeutic dyad the therapist and patient are together able to begin learning about the limits and possibilities of a particular horizon of understanding. Therapeutic change, in this view, is located not in a patient's interior life or structures of mind but in the development of new and different ways of relating to oneself and others in the world. Psychological experience thus exists not "within" the individual mind but in broader sociocultural contexts that always include other people.

Human experience, as such, is always fundamentally contextualized. Human beings can never stand outside their contexts: there is no such thing as a disengaged person. As Taylor (1989) puts it, "a person without a framework altogether would be outside our space of interlocution," and "in the grip of an appalling identity crisis" (p. 30). This does not imply, however, that such notions as the individual and individuality need to be summarily dismissed. I believe that the individual, or what I refer to as "situated personal experience," can be fully understood and appreciated only from the perspective of the context—the horizon of understanding— in which a person exists. As I have suggested, these contexts are inescapable and the ground upon which reflection, interpretation, and action take place.

Above all, we need to understand the way such concepts as the individual and individuality are used in our culture because they carry hidden and not so hidden values and assumptions, which have very real political and ethical implications. We cannot escape the culture of individualism. Yet, at the very least, we can be cognizant of the values of individualism and seek to ameliorate its impact on how we understand ourselves, other people, and the process of human development.

REFERENCES

Beebe, B., & Lachman, F. M. (2002). *Infant research and adult treatment: Co-constructing interactions.* Hillsdale, NJ: Analytic Press.

Bellah, R., Madsen, R., Sullivan, W., Swindler, A., & Tipton, S. (1985). *Habits of the heart: Individualism and commitment in American life.* Berkeley: University of California Press.

Benjamin, J. (1988). *The bonds of love.* London: Virago.

Bhatia, S. (2007). *American karma: Race, culture, and identity in the Indian diaspora.* New York: New York University Press.

Binswanger, L. (1947). Über die Daseinsanalytische Forschungsrichtung in der Psychiatrie. In *Augewählte Vorträge und Aufsätze, bd. I.* Bern: Franke.

Binswanger, L. (1955). Die Bedeutung der Daseinsanalytik Martin Heideggers für das Selbstverständnis der Psychiatrie. In *Augewählte Vorträge und Aufsätze, bd. II.* Bern: Franke.

Bruner, J. (1990). *Acts of meaning.* Cambridge, MA: Harvard University Press.

Burston, D., & Frie, R. (2006). *Psychotherapy as a human science.* Pittsburgh, PA: Duquesne University Press.

Chodorow, N. (1999). *The power of feelings: Personal meaning in psychoanalysis, gender and culture.* New Haven, CT: Yale University Press.

Cushman, P. (1990). Why the self is empty. *American Psychologist, 45,* 599–611.

Cushman, P. (1995). *Constructing the self, constructing America: A cultural history of psychotherapy*. Reading, MA: Addison-Wesley.

Descartes, R. (1949). *A discourse on method*. New York: Dutton. (Originally published in 1637.)

Fancher, R. (1995). *Cultures of healing: Correcting the image of American mental health*. New York: Freeman.

Fonagy, P., Gergely, G., Jurist, E., & Target, M. (2002). *Affect regulation, mentalization and the development of the self*. New York: Other Press.

Freud, S. (1917). A difficulty in the path of psychoanalysis. In J. Strachey (Ed. & Trans.), *The standard edition of the complete psychological works of Sigmund Freud* (Vol. 17). London: Hogarth Press.

Freud, S. (1919). Lines of advance in psycho-analytic therapy. In J. Strachey (Ed. & Trans.), *The standard edition of the complete psychological works of Sigmund Freud* (Vol. 17). London: Hogarth Press.

Freud, S. (1923). The ego and the id. In J. Strachey (Ed. & Trans.), *The standard edition of the complete psychological works of Sigmund Freud* (Vol. 19, pp. 3–66). London: Hogarth Press.

Freud, S. (1933). New introductory lectures on psycho-analysis. In J. Strachey (Ed. & Trans.), *The standard edition of the complete psychological works of Sigmund Freud* (Vol. 22, pp. 3–182). London: Hogarth Press.

Frie, R. (1997). *Subjectivity and intersubjectivity in modern philosophy and psychoanalysis*. Lanham, MD: Rowman and Littlefield.

Frie, R. (2008). Navigating cultural contexts: Agency and bicultural identity. In *Psychological agency: Theory, practice, and culture* (pp. 223–240). Cambridge, MA: MIT Press.

Frie, R. (in press). Compassion and dialogue: Understanding the other in context. *International Journal of Psychoanalytic Self Psychology*.

Gadamer, H. G. (1975). *Truth and method*. New York: Crossroad.

Gadamer, H. G. (1995). *Truth and method*. (J. Weinsheiner & D. C. Marshall, Trans.) New York: Continuum.

Geertz, C. (1973). *The interpretation of cultures*. New York: Basic Books.

Gilligan, C. (1986). Remapping the moral domain: New images of the self in relationship. In T. Heller, M. Sosna, and D. Wellbery (Eds.). *Reconstructing individualism: Autonomy, individuality, and the self in Western thought*. Stanford, CA: Stanford University Press.

Gilligan, C. (1993). *In a different voice* (2nd ed.). Cambridge, MA: Harvard University Press.

Heidegger, M. (1996). *Being and time* (J. Stambaugh, Trans.). Albany: SUNY Press.

Holland, D., Lachicotte, W., Skinner, D., & Cain, C. (1998). *Identity and agency in cultural worlds*. Cambridge, MA: Harvard University Press.

Locke, J. (1960). *Two treatises on government*. Cambridge, UK: Cambridge University Press.

Macpherson, C. B. (1969). *The political theory of possessive individualism*. Oxford: Clarendon.

Mahler, M., Pine, R., & Bergman, A. (1975). *The psychological birth of the human infant: Symbiosis and individuation*. New York: Basic Books.

Markus, H. R. (2008). Pride, prejudice, and ambivalence: Toward a unified theory of race and ethnicity. *American Psychologist*, 651–670.

Markus, H. R., & Kitayama, S. (1991). Culture and the self: Implications for selves and theories of selves. *Psychological Review, 98*, 224–253.

Markus, H. R., & Kitayama, S. (2003a). Culture, self and the reality of the social. *Psychological Inquiry, 14*, 277–283.

Markus, H. R., & Kitayama, S. (2003b). Models of agency: Sociocultural diversity in the construction of action. In V. Murphy-Berman & J. J. Berman (Eds.), *Cross-cultural differences in perspectives on the self* (pp. 1–57). Lincoln: University of Nebraska Press.

Martin, J. (2007). The selves of educational psychology: Conceptions, contexts, and critical considerations. *Educational Psychologist 42*, 79–89.

Martin, J., & Sugarman, J. (1999). *The psychology of human possibility and constraint*. Albany, NY: SUNY Press.

Martin, J., Sugarman, J., & Thompson, J. (2003). *Psychology and the question of agency*. Albany: State University of New York Press.

Miller, J. G. (2002). Bringing culture to basic psychological theory: Beyond individualism and collectivism. *Psychological Bulletin, 128*, 97–109.

Miller, J. G. (2003). Culture and agency: Implications for psychological theories of motivation and social development. In V. Murphy-Berman & J. J. Berman (Eds.), *Cross-cultural differences in perspectives on the self* (pp. 59–99). Lincoln: University of Nebraska Press.

Oyserman, D., Coon, H. M., & Kemmelmeier, M. (2002). Rethinking individualism and collectivism: Evaluation of theoretical assumptions and meta-analyses. *Psychological Bulletin, 128*, 3–72.

Plato. (1998). *Republic*. Oxford: Oxford University Press.

Rauch, L. (1981). *The political animal*. Amherst: University of Massachusetts Press.

Richardson, F. C., Fowers, B. J., & Guigon, C. B. (1999). *Re-envisioning psychology: Moral dimensions of theory and practice*. San Francisco: Jossey-Bass Publishers.

Sandel, M. (1982). *Liberalism and the limits of justice*. Cambridge, MA: Cambridge University Press.

Shweder, R. A., & Bourne, E. J. (1984). Does the concept of person vary cross-culturally? In R. A. Shweder & R. A. LeVine (Eds.), *Culture theory: Essays on mind, self, and emotion* (pp. 158–199). Cambridge, UK: Cambridge University Press.

Stern, D. (1985). *The interpersonal world of the infant*. New York: Basic Books.

Taylor, C. (1989). *Sources of the self: The making of modern identity*. Cambridge, MA: Harvard University Press.

Taylor, C. (1995). *Philosophical arguments*. Cambridge, MA: Harvard University Press.

Vygotsky, L. S. (1978). *Mind in society*. Cambridge, MA: Harvard University Press.

Wheeler, G. (2000). *Beyond individualism: Toward a new understanding of self, relationship, and experience*. Hillsdale, NJ: Analytic Press.

Chapter 2

So who's asking? Politics, hermeneutics, and individuality

Philip Cushman

Sometime late in the 19th century, an excited, naïve young yeshiva student went to the Hasidic rebbe to ask for permission to travel to Berlin and study at the university there. The rebbe was extremely concerned for the young student and at first refused to let him go. Finally, however, he relented, with one *caveat*: that the young man was to return after one year and they would talk about his experiences. The youngster rejoiced, and his departure was soon arranged.

Instead, after only six months, the young student returned and requested a meeting with the rebbe. Tragically, he was a shadow of his former self, painfully thin with hollow, haunted eyes.

"Rebbe, the professors at the university say that it is not possible to tell what is real from what is illusion. They say that there is no way to tell if truth exists, or if God exists, or even if you or I exist. I don't know what to think—these questions terrify me. Is there really no such a thing as truth, rebbe? Does God exist? Do you exist? Do even I exist? Help me, rebbe! Do I exist?"

"Ah," the old rebbe nodded. "So, who's asking?"

Indeed. Who *is* asking?

This story reminds us that every story is a story about someone; about their sorrows, confusions, joys, and pleasures. A person is more than a narrative on legs or an embodied languaging. The face of the other, Emmanuel Lévinas maintained, calls forth recognition and commitment from us. There is much in the face of the other, worlds, really, if only we notice.

But what are the connections between the face and the voice? The postmodern idea that "language speaks us" is an effective—and poetic—way of pointing to the social, contextual mysteries of human being. Yet there are problems with reducing relationality, agency, and personhood in such a manner, especially in a social world that has constituted us as unique, singular, individuals. This Hasidic story does more than simply illustrate how intellectual movements can become victims of their own jargon and trapped by the allure of the latest philosophical trend. It also highlights questions about the important philosophical and psychoanalytic issues this book sets out to address.

The ideology of self-contained individualism has been both a remarkable social invention and a source of severe trouble and wrong-headed thinking. Is there a way of recasting modern-era understandings of human being in such a way as to draw from the best of Western traditions about freedom, emotion, agency, creativity, and choice and still be aware of (and avoid) the philosophical problems, political suffering, and confusion that self-contained individualism has caused? Can we develop understandings about and an appreciation for personal and political change without falling into the modern-era traps of an acontextual, static, willful, disengaged, Cartesian view of the isolated self? And can we develop psychotherapy practices that appreciate the constitutive nature of language and culture and at the same time attend to the ways psychological processes—such as avoidance, projection, displacement, selective inattention, dissociation, and self-deception—affect how social life is interpreted, embodied, used, and especially modified in everyday relational life?

MODERNITY AND ITS CRITICS

This chapter is informed by the belief that a philosophically sophisticated hermeneutics shows us a way we can articulate an understanding of the self that is both more fully social and psychological. But this is not an easy task, given the history of the last 400 years. The modern era in Western society (starting approximately in 1600 CE) is thought to be framed by interlocking historical forces such as individualism, capitalism, urbanization, and secularism. Indeed, this era was marked by factors such as the undermining of historical traditions; the valorization of self-interested economic motivation and objectivist science; the removal of the peasantry into squalid and dangerous early-modern-era towns and their transformation into a dispossessed urban working class; and, by the 19th century, the increasing power of the bourgeoisie in uneasy alliance with the aristocracy. These historical conditions developed in concert with philosophical trends such as Cartesian dualism, David Hume's radical empiricism, Immanuel Kant's structuralism, *laissez faire* capitalism, the development of the concept of a psychological laboratory, psychiatric diagnostic categories, and scientistic theories about the intrapsychic human mind.

In some ways the modern era has been characterized by revolts, first against medieval beliefs and institutions and then against the very Enlightenment-style ideas that brought the era into being. The Protestant Reformation challenged the all-powerful control of the medieval church, and ideas about equality were used to overthrow the monarchy in the New World and France and to challenge both slavery and the political inequality of women. However, antinomian movements (e.g., Adler, 1972) such as spiritualism, romanticism, and mesmerism reflected understandings of the human spirit that opposed Enlightenment rationalism. And by the beginning of the 20th century intellectual movements identified with Karl Marx (socialism), Friedrich Nietzsche (postmodernism), Wilhelm Dilthey (historical hermeneutics), Mary Wollstonecraft and Margaret Fuller (feminism), and to some extent Sigmund Freud directly challenged the philosophical underpinnings of the modern era.

Then, following the early 20th-century work of Edmund Husserl (phenomenology) and his student Martin Heidegger (ontological hermeneutics), the Interpretive Turn (e.g., Hiley, Bohman, & Schusterman, 1991) in the form of its two major branches—hermeneutics and postmodernism—emerged and became an increasingly powerful force in Europe and then the United States. These intellectual traditions contributed to the 20th-century critique of the Cartesianism, empiricism, scientism, White supremacy, misogyny, and consumer capitalism of the modern era.

Traces of these historical influences, especially the ideas of the Interpretive Turn, can be seen in some psychotherapy theories of the second half of the 20th century. Hermeneutics, in particular, necessitates an appreciation of an understanding of the self that is multiple, entangled with the social, and an active interpreter of the cultural terrain. This is especially true of the current North American psychological interpretation of the philosophical hermeneutics of Heidegger (1996) and his student Hans-Georg Gadamer (1995).*

Hermeneuticists challenge modern-era distinctions such as the split between the monadic individual and the social realm (i.e., the distinction between the sealed-off, intrapsychic mind and the sociopolitical world in which it resides). Importantly, they also challenge forms of postmodern theorizing that verge on a historical determinism and imply that culture imprisons passive subjects. Hermeneuticists believe that arguing against the ideology of self-contained individualism does not necessitate an inability or unwillingness to recognize the existence and salience of psychological processes or an understanding of human being that is agentic and actively interpretive.

Hermeneuticists argue that individual humans have been constituted by, and therefore embody, the dominant moral and political ideology of their time and place (i.e., what cultural anthropologists call the self). This is true even if the ideology that constitutes them denies the contextual nature of human existence or reduces the influence of the social to one of many separate and isolated factors that determine the personality traits that make up

---

* See, e.g., Cushman, 1995, 2005a, 2005b; Faulconer and Williams, 1985; Frie, 2009; Orange, 2009, 2010; Richardson, Fowers, & Guignon, 1999; Sass, 1988; Slife and Williams, 2005; Stern, 1997, 2010; Stolorow, Atwood, & Orange, 2002; Taylor, 1988, 1989.

each unique individual. Cultural understandings of the self, of course, just like any set of ideas, can be good ideas or wrong-headed ideas.

In the modern era, putatively discrete Cartesian categories (e.g., nature and nurture, mind and body, subject and object, individual and society, moral and political, political and psychological) became the foundation of modern-era Western theorizing. To develop a scientific warrant for its practices, academic psychology claimed its *raison d'etre* was to determine which side of the split (e.g., "nature or nurture") the particular "behaviors" under study were caused by. But hermeneutic understandings of the inevitable entanglements of these Cartesian categories disrupt or make irrelevant the pressure to determine whether a particular behavior was caused by social or biochemical influences, by intrapsychic or interpersonal processes. Hermeneutic varieties of the Interpretive Turn should move us to realize that those Cartesian distinctions are not the only way to understand human being and determine psychology's mission. If therapists take Cartesian distinctions for granted, refuse to place them into question, and are unable to contrast and compare them to the distinctions and moral understandings active in other communities, the political arrangements these distinctions reproduce will be further reinforced by the psychotherapy practices those therapists use, even political arrangements that might well be abhorrent to the practitioner. If the way we understand the Interpretive Turn doesn't move us to question those Cartesian distinctions in serious ways, we are not properly understanding and applying it.

Context-sensitive psychotherapies have been deeply influenced by the cultural changes and intellectual movements of the late 20th century, especially the Interpretive Turn. Among these approaches, relational psychoanalysis often consciously draws from the Interpretive Turn for explaining and justifying its clinical practices. However, some theorizing couched in the language of the Interpretive Turn reflects an understanding of psychotherapy that emphasizes the social at the expense of the psychological. Or at least that is the criticism that has been leveled by a more mainstream psychoanalysis against first interpersonal psychoanalysis and more recently the relational variety.

In turn, some relationalists defend their practices against this criticism by emphasizing their dedication to taken-for-granted internal, intrapsychic aspects of mind and claim that they can use both intrapsychic and interpersonal theory, depending on the context of the clinical moment. Unfortunately, however, this strategy is problematic; by using it relationalists reaffirm the very Cartesianism that at other moments they have opposed.

The way out of this dilemma is not to claim the use of both intrapsychic and interpersonal, one-person and two-person, models—that way lies philosophical incoherence. The way out is to fully embrace a hermeneutics that challenges the Cartesian split in a direct, unapologetic manner (e.g., Cushman, 2005a, 2005b, 2009; Stern, 1997, 2010; Stolorow et al., 2002).

In a hermeneutic vision, an understanding of the Interpretive Turn does not mean the end of a nuanced, intellectually sophisticated, "deep" psychoanalysis. It means a critical understanding that recognizes both the pervasive constitutive nature of the social realm and also the vital role played by psychological processes in the life of the individual, who is an active, agentic, intersubjective—sometimes self-deceptive—interpreter.

POLITICS AND THE SELF

One aspect of developing a philosophically sound hermeneutics for psychotherapy is to explore the meanings of and interrelationships between the political and the self. Myriad psychotherapy books have been written about the self. In one way or another each of these books has been about politics, because the self is all about politics. Usually we use the term *politics* to refer to many events and activities within our late 20th- early 21st-century world: there is the politics of the American electoral process; the politics of race, gender, and class; the politics within the field of psychotherapy, the community, the family, the workplace, the romantic couple, and so on. In general politics refers to the arrangements and exercise of power. But what frames each struggle, the bedrock of all political struggles, is the ongoing moral negotiation over what it means to be human, over what hermeneuticists call the self.

The self is configured in ways that both reflect and influence the very foundations of social life and everyday living. Without the cultural guidance set by a particular set of moral understandings about what it means to be human, political conflict would be impossible because social life itself would be impossible. The shape of the self in a particular era indicates which goals individuals are supposed to strive toward and how individuals are to comport themselves while striving; it indicates what is possible, what is worthwhile, who is worthwhile, and which institutions determine worthwhileness. In other words, the self emerges out of a moral dialogue that sets the stage for all other political struggles. Once the self is set, the rest of the struggles begin to appear in the clearing: they become visible.

Hermeneutics calls on us to question and examine the distinctions of the modern age, those central to the moral understandings, power relations, and professional territories of the last 500 years. These include the boundaries between discrete academic departments in the social sciences and humanities, the intellectual differences between intrapsychic and interpsychic, mind and body, self and other, rational and irrational, subjectivity and objectivity, history and narrative, scientific discovery and poetic metaphor, the one truth and· a multitude of falsehoods. As a result, hermeneutic, interpretive views encourage us to notice how entangled those split categories are, to embrace those entanglements, to enjoy them.

Entanglements are thought to be unavoidable, pervasive, inevitable, omnipresent. We are also called upon to recognize them and comment on them. In this way we can develop interpretations about our world and the political functions of various artifacts, such as the self and its healing technologies, that prosper in our time. Discourse about the self is never removed from the political realm. For instance, psychologists might work in what is called a "laboratory" and refer to their work as science, but one of the things they are unintentionally doing is using the approved practices of their era to carry on a disguised moral discourse to justify a particular view about what is the proper way of being.

The point is that it is impossible to step outside the entanglements of the social world and see one pure, uncontaminated truth. The language we use, the issues that we deem worthy of examination, the happenings we identify as problems and solutions, the information we consider data, the procedures we believe to be scientifically proper—all are embedded in a specific cultural terrain. Although psychologists might claim to have "discovered" a scientific truth about being human, those results, as Smedslund (1985) suggests, are inevitably "necessary and true," a product of the cultural frame that had already been set long ago.

If we believe that the psychological laboratory can and is producing an objective, unimpeachable truth about a universal human nature, and if we believe that laboratory results prove that the late 20th-century Western self is the one, universal way of human being, then how do we evaluate cultures that do not configure the self in the way we do? Do we think they are misguided, primitive, disabled? If we think them less than us—less civilized, accomplished, moral, learned—will we then believe ourselves justified in trying to dominate them and make them more like us? Will imperialism, racism, cultural chauvinism, or noblesse oblige be considered justified once the one scientific truth about, say, infant development or locus of control is thought to be the property of one profession? If psychology can prove that separation-individuation is the universal process of psychological maturation, then how do we evaluate communities that do not envision a world in which the individual separates from family and clan, communities that instead value the well-being of the group over that of the individual? If psychology can prove that autonomy and personal agency are the cornerstones of the universal self, then how will this affect our ideas about unemployment benefits, welfare, social security, and national health care? If psychology can prove that the highest form of morality is an expression of unattached monads who have no moral commitments to one another beyond their own subjective sense of good and bad, then what are we saying about group solidarity, discipline in the ranks of striking workers, or personal sacrifice for the common good? If psychologists can prove that each individual possesses a unique self the potential of which is present at conception or soon after and that the self is a natural entity that grows organically with the proper nourishment, will that putative scientific truth be used to justify banning abortion?

One can see the centrality of the configuration of the self in these political debates. If psychology is one of the guilds most responsible for determining what is thought to be the truth about the self, then psychology wields a certain amount of power. This is especially true in our current era, in which the moral authority of many religious and philosophical institutions has been undermined. By unknowingly propping up the hegemony of individualism through laboratory findings, psychology is hindering our ability to realize how political structures impact the individual and the degree to which these structures are responsible for the suffering of the victims and the crimes of the perpetrators. These opinions will determine our response to future political crises. Should we interpret a petty burglary solely as a manifestation of the criminal's psychopathology or also as the result of economic desperation? Should we interpret the increased popularity of African American, Asian, and Latino youth gangs as a genetic defect that causes young people of color to be unable to develop a "mature" psychological autonomy or as a reflection of the consequences of centuries of racial discrimination, economic exploitation, community devastation? Should we interpret family violence solely as a product of the isolated, psychologically "dysfunctional" family system of the perpetrator or also the absence of meaningful moral traditions, communal support, gratifying work, and extended family aid and advice?

THE DISAPPEARANCE OF THE CITIZEN AND A TWO-PERSON PSYCHOLOGY

Currently, the outer limits that most psychotherapy theories can conceive of as the social realm are the isolated parent–child or patient–therapist dyad, or at most the nuclear family. This vision of the social is an aspect of what is referred to as "two-person" psychology. In many ways it is a welcome improvement over older, more extreme forms of self-contained individualism, so-called one-person psychologies. But, ultimately, some forms of two-person psychologies, such as object relations theory and self psychology, fall short of what is needed. If, under the influence of individualism, this shortsightedness continues, it will be difficult for us as a nation to address problems that appear as a result of larger political and cultural arrangements. If we psychologize and medicalize human action by attempting to rid it of any significant political cause, we condemn ourselves to denying the effects of the macro structures of our society. Therefore, we will leave those structures intact while we blame the only positions in our cultural clearing that show up as responsible, culpable entities: the individual, the dyad, sometimes the family. If we cannot entertain the realistic possibility that political structures can be the cause of personal, psychological distress, then we cannot notice their impact, study them, face their consequences, mobilize to make structural changes, and have few ideas about what changes should be made. We will become politically incompetent. Perhaps we already are.

Ultimately, the hermeneutic critique is important because of the ways late 20th-century populations are controlled by the state: less by military repression and more by the state's ability to set and exploit the cultural frame of reference. The most significant battles of our era are not joined at the barricades but occur in the corporate boardroom. They are battles fought through the manipulation of words, symbols, and electronic images, by the power to describe "the other," to define gender, and to determine the particulars of consumer desire. Today political lines are drawn in protracted white-collar battles over the content of the nightly news, judicial decisions regarding the meanings of sanity and culpability, "expert" opinion regarding the causes of crime and homelessness, the personality of the latest soft drink mascot or celebrity spokesperson, the ideological positions of radio talk show hosts, the direction of a new beer advertising campaign, the shape of this year's fashion trends, or the definition of *terrorist*.

The process by which "the other" is constructed, defined, and used is the face of war in our time. The constructed content of the self and the determination of what is split off, disavowed, and then relocated into the unconscious and onto "the other" goes a long way toward legitimizing political decisions regarding the identity of the enemy, the content of major political issues, the distinctions between male and female and White and Black, the understandings of right and wrong. The addict, the homeless, African American, Asian American, criminal, female, Jew, Muslim, or Latino can carry what is despised and disavowed; these distinctions, and the intellectual discourse that follows them, then justify previous injustices and present or future governmental policies.

We have difficulty solving our political problems today in part because we do not experience ourselves as political beings. Our cultural clearing is configured in such a way as to exclude the social connectedness of the commons, a phrase used to connote a process whereby citizens exercise their political obligations to their community and experience a sense of common purpose and group solidarity. Mostly in our current terrain we understand ourselves as discrete, isolated individuals who have few loyalties and identities beyond our individual selves and families and few available activities beyond acquiring and consuming. It is difficult to develop communal commitments because it is difficult to think of ourselves as citizens—as active, involved, caring political beings. In our world—a world in which the individual is pictured as separate and apart from, actually opposed to, a dangerous, potentially controlling state and rigid, authoritarian traditions—*freedom* is usually defined as the absence of social influences and political allegiances.

Although psychologists do not intend to do so, our practices reflect the current terrain by producing theories that glorify individuation, proclaim separation as the ultimate goal of child development, view psychological boundaries as essential to proper adjustment, and consider their absence or permeability a major cause of pathology. In the early 21st-century clearing, caring could well show up as "codependence" and a sense of political responsibility as an "obsessive-compulsive" trait.

TOWARD A POLITICALLY SUBVERSIVE HERMENEUTICS: A THREE-PERSON PSYCHOLOGY

The concept of a two-person psychology was articulated and elaborated by radical interpersonalists such as Edgar Levenson and Merton Gill. It was meant by them to emphasize the importance of a nonhierarchical, non-mechanistic, interpersonal, and intersubjective process between patient and therapist. However, as a result of various shifts and misconceptions in the history of psychotherapy during the post-World War II era, the concept of a two-person psychology has often been identified more with a historical, politically accommodating theory than with its more radical originators. Levenson's and Gill's innovative, nonmainstream perspectives were reflections of a courageous, free-thinking posture that is more critical and philosophically sound, in fact closer to the three-person approach Neil Altman (1995) and I (Cushman, 1995) introduced than what the discipline has come to accept as the mainstream two-person approach. Object relations theory and self psychology—usually considered two-person approaches—have had difficulty developing a historical perspective on their practices; this violates the central tenet of the three-person, hermeneutic approach. Perhaps this is why Gill (1983, 1994) and his colleague Irwin Hoffman (1983, 1998) turned increasingly to a "social constructivist" vision and why Levenson (1991) referred to his work as "an *at least* two-person psychology" [emphasis added].

Philosophical hermeneutics helps us learn more about the exercise of power within a political landscape and how power shows up in a particular shape as a result of the moral understandings that frame that landscape. However, hermeneutics does not rely on a deterministic view of cultural influence, nor does it conceive of the individual as passive and powerless in relation to cultural prescriptions and the status quo. Instead, hermeneutics encourages us to become aware of and emphasize the ongoing psychological processes that we unknowingly use as a means of maintaining compliance with a particular cultural terrain. These unconscious processes are indispensable to the individual as he or she attempts to fit into and be considered an approved of member of a particular society.

The hermeneutic stance is important because it is an attempt to formulate a psychology that does not conform to our dominant consumerist frame. Many post-World War II psychotherapy theorists have unintentionally developed theories that are consumerist in nature (see Cushman, 1990, 1995). For instance, object relations theory and self psychology reflect views of human being that are dependent on the metaphor of consuming: infant development is conceptualized as growth through the process of taking in (consuming) and finally internalizing (metabolizing) parental supplies. Of course, clinicians aren't aware of, and most would not want to be complicit in, the reproduction of a consumerist status quo. But because we are not trained to historically situate our theories and to interpret the political functions of our theories, psychotherapists do not usually notice our subtle contributions to the continuing reproduction of our current way of life.

By describing the self as being "built" by the ingestion of supplies, psychopathology as the consequence of ingesting bad supplies or the consequence of the absence of supplies, and psychotherapy as an activity that provides good supplies, object relations theory and self psychology seem to be unknowingly enacting a covert strategy not unlike that used by 19th-century mesmerism. Mesmerism (see Cushman, 1995) provided a covert, compensatory response to a political problem—the loss of community—by describing an invisible spiritual substance that connected the patient with all humankind and with the cosmos and by providing a healing technology that featured an ongoing group experience. However, although American mesmerism provided a compensatory response to a political problem, it did so covertly; it did not help patients recognize the political nature of their distress and challenge the political arrangements that caused it.

Could the current emphasis on providing supplies to neglected, deprived selves in psychotherapy be a covert, compensatory response to a political problem? By blaming parents (especially mothers) for the development of poorly built or "dysfunctional" selves, could we be drawing attention away from the larger culprit, a sociopolitical system in which the concept of the properly built self is so riddled with contradiction that it is impossible to achieve? Could the culprit be a sociopolitical system that is structured in such a way as to deprive the majority of the population of emotional guidance and a sense of security and then to convince people that what they need is to be found in empty calories, new electronic gadgets, and glitzy clothes? By conceiving of the self as a structure that can be properly built by good parents and by conceiving of psychotherapy as the activity in which proper supplies are offered or a proper environment for the true self provided, are we unknowingly offering an indirect solution to an unacknowledged political problem best attacked directly? And by doing so are we preventing our patients from understanding the political nature of their distress and challenging the political structures that cause it?

Mesmerism provided a compensatory connective "glue" to a world that was falling apart while at the same time remaining silent about the political causes of the wreckage. Are object relations theory and self psychology providing a small measure of compensatory emotional sustenance and safety while at the same time not adequately relating emotional ills to their political sources? Are some current psychotherapists making the same mistakes mesmerists did?

Philosophical hermeneuticists draw our attention to the historical and cultural and thus to the moral implications and political functions of various discourses and practices. An awareness of these implications could move psychotherapy toward adopting a more comprehensive hermeneutic perspective, a "three-person psychology."

The third player I referred to is the ever present, interpenetrating social realm. By "three-ness" I intended to convey that the individual, the therapist, and the historical-cultural context are inextricably intertwined, that moral understandings are a foundational aspect of a culture, and that our discipline needs to be concerned with how various psychotherapy theories affect political structures and activities. By emphasizing the "givenness" of the cultural terrain and the powerful psychological processes that, outside of awareness, reproduce features of that terrain, philosophical hermeneutics demystifies psychopathology and grants a certain respect and efficacy or agency to persons that is sometimes lost in other theories within the Interpretive Turn. With a three-person psychology might also come an increase in hope and a willingness to continue to fight for the very thing that most of us have despaired of: institutional change.

A three-person psychology encourages us to think of psychotherapy as a set of social practices shaped by its historical-cultural habitat and unable to be bracketed away from moral discourse. It reminds us that humans exist only in a culture and that cultures simultaneously make possible some opportunities and limit others. It presumes that every era and every culture develops images of the correct way to be human, that each era's self has its idiosyncratic vulnerabilities, which must then be healed by those designated as healers. Because humans must accommodate to their settings, each society develops practices that lessen suffering or remove it from view and return persons to their place in society. The question is not whether healers work hand in glove with a specific terrain, and thus with a particular set of moral understandings and political arrangements. This is a given. The important questions pertain to how they make use of their knowledge of the terrain in their work: can they develop the insight to see the connections between the political arrangements within their society and the emotional suffering those arrangements cause, can they develop strategies to address that connection, can they find the courage to dedicate themselves to changing the terrain, and can they generate enough power to shift it?

In other words, hermeneutics implies that there are various types of healers. One type scrutinizes and owns up to the political consequences of therapy, and another avoids that task and contends that therapy is apolitical. The hermeneutic view is a measured but hopeful one: if as therapists we determine that our work has been unknowingly colluding with political forces that we oppose, then we can shift our practices so that our work does not support that with which we disagree and perhaps even add to the development of social relations or political arrangements of which we approve. If we abstain from this overt, active role, then we become accomplices in social arrangements that run the risk of producing some of the very ills we are responsible for healing.

A WAY OUT OF THE DILEMMA

But how can we find ways of practicing that do not reproduce the Cartesian split and the social world that it has generated yet also avoid losing sight of intersubjectivity, agency, and choice? During the mid 1980s I was struggling with these issues and trying to find a way to practice psychotherapy that would not violate my political and hermeneutic commitments. After awhile, I noticed I was beginning to use the same metaphor with my patients that I use in historical research: the metaphor of the cultural clearing. In retrospect I suppose I could say I started doing this because I wanted to limit my use of the metaphors, language, theories, and therapeutic interventions that have been so much in tune with the current sociopolitical terrain. I wanted my language to stop being taken over by the language of the masterful, bounded self. I wanted to stop reinforcing in an unquestioned, unqualified way what Michel Foucault called the isolated individual with the "richly furnished interior," because I had come to realize that one of the essential ingredients of that interior was the absence of a vibrant connection with the social world of communal and shared meaning. Currently, our richly furnished interiors are mostly furnished with things; our connection with others rarely shows up in our clearing, and if others do show up "inside" us, as some forms of therapy suggest, usually they are thought of as "objects," things to be used instrumentally. Our connection to consumer items often seems to be one of the only connections available to us, and our experience of the self has been attenuated to the point that our interiors often seem to have become simply a giant vacuum, what I called the empty self (see Cushman, 1990).

I wanted to conduct therapy in ways that reflected a more hermeneutic, relational, intersubjective way of being. On the other hand, I didn't want to start sounding so weird that no one would understand me. I didn't want to start sounding like I was from Mars (or, more accurately, postmodern France). I wanted to resist negative aspects of the status quo, but I also knew I couldn't, and wouldn't want, to do away with the emotional, agentic, intersubjective individual either. So I wondered what I could do to live in this very Western, modern, individualistic world and work within it with more integrity. It was soon after this that I began, tentatively, to use the horizonal metaphor in therapy.

Over time I began to draw on an interpretation of Gadamer's (1995; pp. 300–307) horizonal metaphor that I could live with in my work. It goes like this: At birth, each of us is thrown into a particular world. Growing up is the process of living through social practices and by doing so learning the background procedures, shared understandings, rules, and meanings of that very particular world, from the larger world of history and culture to the very particular, local world of families, friends, and communities that exists within and as a result of the larger cultural world. That world is communicated to us through myriad social practices and interactions that make up the little moments of everyday life.

We must come to be a part of that background so fully, so completely, that we embody it—it is sedimented in our bodies. It comes to constitute us. We need to do that so that we can reproduce it instantaneously upon waking each morning, upon meeting and interacting with others, upon performing any of the innumerable but indispensable tasks we are called upon to perform each day. The world that we must reproduce shifts slightly according to the particular requirements of various situations, and especially with regard to particular persons within particular situations. Others, of course, are doing the same thing, and as a consequence of our shared social practices, we continuously coconstruct a viable, understandable, predictable world. In other words, we are called upon to reproduce a particular world each morning and recall and act according to specific procedural rules and moral understandings, depending on the individuals we encounter and the context in which we encounter them. Outside of our awareness we sense which particular areas of the clearing we must emphasize or focus on at any given moment.

We also—and here is the most difficult part—reproduce this world without being able to admit it or even be aware of it. There is something in the very nature of being human that makes it extremely difficult to realize our role in reproducing that social world or differentiating what we can be from what our horizon allows us to be. We reproduce the social world in such a way that we can consider it, experience it, as reality itself—the one, true, concrete truth. To do otherwise would be to open up the existential abyss for us, to force us to confront our own lacks, absences, and emptiness, to challenge the taken-for-granted moral understandings, power relations, economic privileges, and status hierarchy of our era, and to acknowledge the relational rules, alliances, and secrets of our family of origin. For various reasons, for most of us an awareness of the constructed nature of the world of our everyday lives appears to be too difficult to acknowledge and too frightening to live with.

As a result, we have no conscious control over our part in the structuring of the world as we immediately know it and live it. This is good in that we can be involved in many complex tasks without having to clutter our consciousness with questions pertaining either to performing detailed tasks or the overall frame (Heidegger [1995] called this "everydayness"). We can also go about our everyday lives without confronting the lack of at-homeness that follows from an awareness of what Berger and Luckman (1966) call the social construction of reality. But our lack of consciousness in reproducing that world is also bad in that we experience the constructed world as an immutable, unchallengeable given: Usually we can't imagine an alternative configuration or the possibility of changing our current configuration. Unfortunately, some aspects of the world that we have learned so well and shaped our behavior to accommodate to—aspects of the world that we are perhaps most at home with—do not necessarily make for a good world.

This world first emerged in our childhood and may not be very compatible with the world that others live in; it may not fit well with the present-day relational world that we, as adults, live in; and it may not be the kind of world we would want to live in. But it is the world we cuddle up with when it is cold outside and things go bump in the night. It is the world we induce others to play a role in, and we do that in skillful and unconscious ways. It may be a distant or mean "parent" we sidle up to, but we are drawn to that relational space, that position in the terrain, just the same. It may be an irrational or distasteful moral frame that we feel a strong, embodied allegiance to, but it may be the only one available or the only one we dare embrace at that given moment, the only one that would keep our old emotional attachments in place. It is precisely this conspiring, this unknowing, embodied collusion that psychotherapy is designed to reveal and question. There is a subtle and complex dialectic at work in human life: the world we are thrown into constitutes us, and then we must continually reproduce it. It limits us by its givenness, and then we, in turn, recreate it. Where does the givenness end and our semiconscious collusion begin?

Hermeneutically, the therapeutic task might be conceived of in this way: we work to confront our thrownness, discover experientially and cognitively how we cooperate in reproducing the world the way we do, more fully face the consequences of that construction, begin imagining alternative configurations and allowing them to emerge, and then develop ways of letting a different world come to light.

This slightly shifted psychological terrain, hermeneuticists take pains to emphasize, does not appear out of nowhere. It is not simply the product of one's singular, isolated imagination or even the product of two singular imaginations, the mistake some two-person or postmodern psychotherapy theories make. Humans, hermeneuticists argue, are constituted through historical traditions that are "inescapably moral" traditions. Each of our lives is a point of intersecting traditions. We are in a continuing encounter with different moral traditions simply by virtue of our everyday relational lives as well as our intellectual activities. When we encounter a different perspective through interaction with someone, we are presented with the opportunity to reexamine our embodied understandings and perhaps to shift, slightly, our perspective and therefore the moral understandings that frame our world. This is what some have called an encounter with difference (e.g., Cushman, 2005a), and if we are willing and adequately self-reflective, it can lead to what Gadamer (1995, pp. 367–369, 383–389) calls dialogue or "genuine conversation." The resulting process can lead to an embodied, often not conscious, reevaluation and change. This is what saves hermeneutics from the kind of cultural and historical determinism that plague forms of postmodernism that conceive of culture and political arrangements as forms of imprisonment from which there is no escape.

I do not mean that this process is solely or even predominately rational, calculating, cognitive, or conscious—I have written that it is more like a dance than a worksheet or decision tree. Also, we must realize that this process is most difficult—the concept of the clearing implies not only the potential for perspectival change but also the very real limitations of givenness. Above all, let us not fool ourselves: the process of human change is not really understandable; it is a profound mystery. But perhaps there is also a place for thinking and feeling and evaluating, for choosing as well as feeling, a place for hope as well as resignation.

A POP-UP WORLD

Many years ago I was listening to a patient, a troubled mid-30s male professional who was one of the most tortured patients I ever worked with. He was in a particularly excruciating experience that day, one that he sometimes slipped into: he was certain that no one would want to know how he really felt, everyone would hate him and reject him for what he thought, and no one would allow him what he needed. And it occurred to me that day that he was describing a world to me, the world that he lived in when he was in this particular state of mind. Suddenly, I saw that world, spread out before him on all sides, peopled with certain characters and voices from his past, from a time when the horizon of his family life was originally formed. I thought of those pop-up books made for children: when we open them, a whole little world of mountains, cities, individuals, and homes instantly pops up and comes to life before us.

Before I could think much about it, before I knew what would happen next, I told him it seemed to me as though a world had suddenly appeared before us, a world that encompassed him on all sides. In this world, the people of his young life live and interact, all according to the rules that he had described to me or enacted with me. These rules create certain positions in the clearing in which certain people must live, and these positions determine destinies. I described some of these rules as I had come to understand them, especially those that pertained to how he felt that day.

"Well," he said, "that's life. That's all there is." He paused, cocked his head, and looked puzzled. "What do you mean—there's some other world?" He paused and then put his head back and laughed, a relaxed, pleasant kind of laugh I had rarely heard from him. For a moment, he had glimpsed an alternative perspective, or the possibility of one, and the experience momentarily released him from the tortuous imprisonment he experienced in that old terrain.

But there is much that prevented him from experiencing a different world. We tried to understand how that old world got evoked and recreated in his everyday life and in the therapy hour. Occasionally, he could get a sense of what he did, what I did, and what we did together, to summon that world. When he could do that he would get very frightened, very angry, and for a moment almost hopeful. He hated that hopeful, alive feeling. It caused him unbearable kinds of trouble. Once, after he was remarking about how drawn he was to the old world and how guilty he felt if even for a moment he escaped it, I said to him, "You know, I wonder if this is what Freud meant when he talked about Oedipus?" He looked sad and then quietly joked, "You mean I want to go to bed with my old world?" "I mean," I replied, "that I think you want to lie down with it each night." He looked up at me, eyes filled with longing: "It is so warm on a cold night."

His response demonstrated one of the reasons why humans are driven to reproduce the old terrain, even though it is so destructive to us: my patient did to himself and to others what was done to him, in part to evoke the terrain that contained the relationships with those he loved and needed so desperately and the moral frame that created, explained, and justified their particular pattern of relating. We unknowingly reproduce old ways of living and loving and being loved by sending a multitude of signals and cues to others and by selectively attending and not attending to the signals and cues of others regarding what are permissible and preferred behaviors, feelings, and interactions. Through such semiconscious communications, the horizon of understanding gets positioned so that only the old terrain has room to show up. By using the horizonal metaphor, for instance, we can describe what are sometimes called self-defeating behaviors or repetition compulsions without as much recourse to the interiorizing, hyperindividualistic language—and the passive, historical determinism—that unknowingly contributes to the reproduction of the relational and political status quo.

In ways difficult to notice we induce others, even (or especially) loved ones, to be players in that terrain. And, as many relationalists have pointed out in recent years, it is the living out of those pop-up rules and relations that inevitably get enacted in the therapy hour. When that happens, if the therapeutic dyad can face the truth of that moment, the opportunity for a slight shift in perspective, a slight change in where we stand, becomes a possibility (e.g., Stern, 2010).

THROWNNESS AND COMPLICITY

By emphasizing the relationship between thrownness, the individual's unconscious complicity in maintaining the cultural and relational *status quo*, and one's personal emotional suffering, the hermeneutic perspective can aid in undoing the mechanistic, passive, helpless view of human being that tends to be unknowingly reflected and reproduced in several current psychotherapy theories. If clinicians conceptualize adult pathology as a mechanistic process that is determined solely by what prominent figures in an individual's life did or did not do to the individual, patients will never come to understand what they unknowingly do to remember and reproduce the old cultural, moral, and relational terrain of their youth. And then they will not be able to develop understandings about how they currently collude with or even arrange situations that reproduce the same old dissatisfactions and pain or that risk further trauma, and thus they will not be able to protect themselves against the indifference or maliciousness of others—indeed, they will welcome it. The issue becomes more important when we consider that most therapy theories do not usually help patients think of themselves as active moral agents, who live in an intersubjective world constructed by political arrangements and moral understandings about those arrangements. Instead they picture a world in which the pathogenic agent—whether a toxic parent, a traumatic incident, or an addictive drug—is all powerful and they are helplessness in relation to it.

If as therapists we can develop an increased understanding of how social worlds are constructed and reconstructed, perhaps we will be able to notice our unintentional contributions to the status quo, be less naive and seducible about claims of truth and scientific authority, be better able to enter into effective collective efforts with community members and colleagues, and finally be freer to address the structural arrangements of our time. Everyday social interaction calls upon us to develop a multitude of interpretations about the immediate social context, and philosophical hermeneutics challenges us to become more effective at noticing those daily interpretations: those we are aware of and those that we are not aware of; those that help us open our awareness to new possibilities and those that close off possibilities; those that help us be open to those who are different from us, who embody different moral understandings and be able to question our own, cherished, understandings in relation to them; those that help us see the forbidden and those that shut off or help us disown and avoid the forbidden; those that reproduce an old, destructive terrain and those that help us develop a world in which new possibilities have the opportunity to emerge.

Relational psychoanalysis has been deeply influenced by the Interpretive Turn. We might speculate that alternative understandings of human being—of the self—must already be coming to light in our cultural clearing for us to be troubled by the dilemmas pertaining to individualism and intersubjectivity and struggling with the issues they cause. Perhaps this means, in the mysterious way of human creativity, that some of the answers to our questions are already present, already in the process of being lived out by us, and what we are doing when writing about our questions is trying to find the words to explain an embodied cultural shift that in some inchoate ways has already been taking shape. If that is true, then could one of the political functions of relational psychoanalysis be the articulation of a new way of being, a (very) quiet revolution in the cultural and moral understandings about what it means to be properly human? Could relational psychoanalysis be a harbinger of a potentially new political force?

However, despite the growing interest in relational psychoanalysis, the continuing influences of managed care, scientism, technicism, and instrumentalism are continually and forcefully influencing psychotherapy. They influence therapists to develop practices that preclude a critical, historical, political vision of human being coexisting with a nuanced understanding of dark, complex psychological processes. They influence therapists to believe they can—and should—be able to operationalize and measure the mystery of human creativity and change through disengaged, positivist practices and thereby eventually prove the efficacy of their practices (see Hoffman, 2009, for a critique of this approach). These next few years will be a time marked by many important decisions in the field of health care. It could be an important turning point in the history of psychotherapy—an opportunity to transcend the limitations, distortions, and demands of Cartesianism and to apply therapy practices to a concept of the person as a relational, active, interpretive agent who is simultaneously both a sociopolitical and an intersubjective being. But if these technicist trends continue, then an important opportunity will be lost. And in our current world, dominated as it is by psychological compartmentalizations and political stratifications of many kinds, that would be a tragedy of significant proportions. Let us hope for and work toward a philosophically sound hermeneutic, relational psychotherapy that contributes to other, better ways of being human. Let us remember that each data point in a managed care calculus or epidemiological study symbolizes an individual person whose suffering calls out to us. Let us, in the spirit of the old Hasidic rabbi, remember who is asking.

REFERENCES

Adler, N. (1972). *The underground stream: New life styles and the antinomian personality*. New York: Harper & Row.

Altman, N. (1995). *The analyst in the inner city: Race, class, and culture through a psychoanalytic lens*. Hillsdale, NJ: Analytic Press.

Berger, P., & Luckman T. (1966). *The social construction of reality*. Garden City, NY: Doubleday.

Cushman, P. (1990). Why the self is empty: Toward a historically situated psychology. *American Psychologist, 45*, 599–611.

Cushman, P. (1995). *Constructing the self, constructing America: A cultural history of psychotherapy*. Reading, MA: Addison Wesley.

Cushman, P. (2005a). Between arrogance and a dead-end: Psychoanalysis and the Heidegger-Foucault dilemma. *Contemporary Psychoanalysis, 41*, 399–417.

Cushman, P. (2005b). Clinical applications: A response to Layton. *Contemporary Psychoanalysis, 41*, 431–445.

Faulconer, J., & Williams, R. (1985). Temporality in human action: An alternative to positivism and historicism. *American Psychologist, 40*, 1179–1188.

Frie, R. (2009). Reconfiguring psychological agency: Postmodernism, recursivity, and the politics of change. In R. Frie & D. Orange (Eds.), *Beyond postmodernism: New dimensions in clinical theory and practice* (pp. 162–182). London: Routledge.

Gadamer, H.-G. (1995). *Truth and method* (J. Weinsheimer & D. G. Marshall, Trans.). New York: Continuum. (Original published in 1960)

Gill, M. M. (1983). The distinction between the interpersonal paradigm and the degree of the therapist's involvement. *Contemporary Psychoanalysis, 19*, 200–237.

Gill, M. M. (1994). *Psychoanalysis in transition: A personal view*. Hillsdale, NJ: Analytic Press.

Hiley, D. R., Bohman, J. F., & Schusterman, R. (Eds.) (1991). *The interpretive turn: Philosophy, science, culture*. Ithaca, NY: Cornell University Press.

Heidegger, M. (1996). *Being and time* (J. Stambaugh, Trans.). Albany: State University of New York Press. (Original published in 1927)

Hoffman, I. Z. (1983). The patient as the interpreter of the analyst's experience. *Contemporary Psychoanalysis, 19*, 389–422.

Hoffman, I. Z. (1998). *Ritual and spontaneity in the psychoanalytic process: A dialectical-constructivist view*. Hillsdale, NJ: The Analytic Press.

Hoffman, I. Z. (2009). Doublethinking our way to "scientific" legitimacy: The desiccation human experience. *Journal of the American Psychoanalytic Association, 57*, 1043–1069.

Levenson, E. A. (1991). Character, personality, and the politics of change. In *The purloined self: Interpersonal perspectives in psychoanalysis* (pp. 239–253). New York: Contemporary Psychoanalysis Books.

Orange, D. (2009). Toward the art of living dialogue: Between constructivism and hermeneutics in psychoanalytic thinking. In R. Frie & D. Orange (Eds.), *Beyond postmodernism: New dimensions in clinical theory and practice* (pp. 117–142). London: Routledge.

Orange, D. (2010). *Thinking for clinicians: Philosophical resources for contemporary psychoanalysis and the humanistic psychotherapies*. New York: Routledge.

Richardson, R. C., Fowers, B. J., & Guignon, C. B. (1999). *Re-envisioning psychology: Moral dimensions of theory and practice*. San Francisco, CA: Jossey-Bass.

Sass, L. (1988). Humanism, hermeneutics, and the concept of the human subject. In S. Messer, L. Sass, & R. Woolfolk (Eds.), *Hermeneutics and psychological theory: Interpretive Perspectives on personality, psychotherapy, and psychopathology* (pp. 222–271). New Brunswick, NJ: Rutgers University Press.

Slife, B. D., & Williams, R. N. (2005). *What's behind the research: Discovering hidden assumptions in the behavioral sciences*. Thousand Oaks, CA: Sage.

Smedslund, J. (1985). Necessarily true cultural psychologies. In K. J. Gergen & K. Davis (Eds.), *The social construction of the person*. New York: Springer-Verlag.

Stern, D. B. (1997). *Unformulated experience: From dissociation to imagination in psychoanalysis*. Hillsdale, NJ: Analytic Press.

Stern, D. B. (2010). *Partners in thought: Working with unformulated experience, dissociation, and enactment*. New York: Routledge.

Stolorow, R., Atwood, G., & Orange, D. (2002). *Worlds of experience: Interweaving philosophical and clinical dimensions in psychoanalysis*. New York: Basic Books.

Taylor, C. (1988). The moral topography of the self. In S. Messer, L. Sass, & R. Woolfolk (Eds.), *Hermeneutics and psychological theory: Interpretive perspectives on personality, psychotherapy, and psychopathology*. New Brunswick, NJ: Rutgers University Press. 298–320.

Taylor, C. (1989). *Sources of the self: The making of the modern identity*. Cambridge, MA: Harvard University Press.

Part 2

Philosophical contexts

Chapter 3

Beyond individualism

Philosophical contributions of Buber, Gadamer, and Lévinas

Donna Orange

> I am defined as a subjectivity, as a singular person, as an "I," precisely because I am exposed to the other. It is my inescapable and incontrovertible answerability to the other that makes me an individual "I."
>
> – Emmanuel Lévinas

In everyday usage, "individuality" connotes desirable qualities like creativity, self-possession, singularity, unique personality, and style. Whether human or household pet, individuality is what sets one apart from the crowd, what makes one particular. We often contrast individuality with conformity and boredom. In North American cultures in particular, we have learned to admire the rugged individual who can struggle against adversity, whether natural or resulting from poverty or immigrant history. But concepts of the individual and of individuality carry not only these informal connotations but also formal and philosophical meanings that background their uses in psychoanalytic and psychotherapeutic discourse. It is these meanings that I will bring into focus in dialogue with three 20th-century philosophers. Finally, I will suggest that some recent understandings of individuality and of individualized selfhood tend to shift the clinical and ethical focus to the welcomed other.

WHAT IS INDIVIDUALITY?

In formal logic, an individual is a member of a class, set, or collection. Notice that there is yet no reference to psychoanalysis or even to abstractions like self, personality, or subjectivity. Nor is there any explicit reliance on individualism, whether philosophical or political in kind or on cultural ideals of independence and self-sufficiency.

In modern philosophy, from René Descartes through the Enlightenment and the Romantics, the concept of the human became ever more identified with the concept of an individual, inner, subjective, self-enclosed "mind" or "self" distinguished from an outside, objective, extended universe. The mind's relation to this outer universe was to reflect and represent it. Charles Taylor's (1989) masterful *Sources of the Self* shows that this development was not inevitable and is grounded in a specific and fascinating history of ideas throughout the modern period. Despite a few dissenting voices, the unquestioned assumption of the individual "punctual self," desituated and detached from relations with others, served as the basis for modern conceptions of democracy, religion, psychology, and even psychoanalysis. Only in the 20th century with Ludwig Wittgenstein and Martin Heidegger, and those they influenced, did this picture of the human being come into serious question.

Mainstream psychoanalysis has made little explicit use of concepts of individuality. In the Freudian tradition, the closest idea is probably ego, that "agency which [Sigmund] Freud's second theory of the psychical apparatus distinguishes from the id and super-ego" (LaPlanche & Pontalis, 1973). Nothing in this definition, of course, evokes the meanings of uniqueness, particularity, or singularity that we tend informally to associate with individuality. In Kleinian psychoanalysis, I find no concept similar to individuality, though others may be able to supplement my ignorance on this score.

In self psychology, of course, we find the idea of selfhood, which refers, in its least reified (concretized) and thus more phenomenological uses, to a subjective sense of continuity, stability, and personal value, emergent within the relational, or selfobject, environment. Though Heinz Kohut's own talk of core self and nuclear self could sound like Aristotle's acorn just growing into its predestined oak, he also taught a fine awareness of the background of needed "selfobject" support for anyone to grow into a sense of one's own being.

In Winnicott (1965), there is potentially the "true self," referring to the spontaneous gesture not excessively adapted to social expectancies. "The good-enough mother meets the omnipotence of the infant and to some extent makes sense of it. She does this repeatedly [and] a True Self begins to have life. ..." (p. 145). Much like Kohut's (1977) sense of self lost under various forms of narcissism, long considered untreatable, Winnicott's true self seemed invisible in the mass of social compliance that he unfortunately named the "false self."

Only the interpersonal school, forever inspired and challenged by Sullivan's (1950) "The Illusion of Personal Individuality," has paid central attention to the concept of individuality itself—only to reject it. Sullivan read the operationalism of Percy Bridgman to mean that unless one could specify a procedure for "checking" the applicability of a concept, it had no place in science. Thus, Sullivan claimed, since operational definitions require repeatability and the individual, if such there be, could never be repeated, the concept of individuality had no place in the science of psychiatry. Psychiatry could concern itself only with observable and repeatable social interactions, not with the individual or the subjective or the private. Concepts of selfhood like those of Winnicott, Kohut, and everyday discourse, not to mention more careful phenomenological views, did not belong in scientific psychiatry or psychoanalysis.

Intersubjective systems theory as well (Stolorow & Atwood, 1992; Stolorow, Atwood, & Orange, 2002), with its unremitting challenge to the "isolated mind" of modern philosophy and of most psychoanalysis, may seem to have obviated all concepts of individuality. It has challenged both the psychoanalytic concepts of intrapsychic mind and the cultural ideals of existence independent of emotional support and personal connection. But a strong interest remains—central to psychoanalysis as theory and as practice—in personality development (Atwood & Stolorow, 1993; Stolorow, Atwood, & Orange, 2008), in self-delineating intersubjective processes, and in individuality as experienced. This appears most clearly in the discussions of "self-delineating selfobject transferences" and in the work of Brandchaft (2007) on the imprisoning systems of "pathological accommodation."

But what is individuality? How can it still be personal individuality and escape the critiques of the isolated mind? Is the concept of individuality—in the human realm, apart from abstract logic—worth rescuing? While chaos, systems, and complexity theories can surely help us see how someone might self-organize into an unrepeatable individual, they do not help us very much with the concept of individuality itself. Let us therefore look to the work of three 20th-century philosophers for some clues. We will consider the work of Martin Buber, Hans-Georg Gadamer, and Emmanuel Lévinas, each of whom advances a profoundly relational (i.e., nonindividualistic) account of personal individuality that could support our psychoanalytic and psychotherapeutic work.* At the same time, these relational accounts tend to challenge the American cultural ideals of independence and self-sufficiency and may lead to a further shift of emphasis. I will introduce each philosopher biographically (i.e., situate him in personal and historical context). We will see that each one's challenge to the notion of individual and identical selfhood developed nonetheless within life worlds both singular and shared with many others.†

---

* Wittgenstein was another possibility. His critique of private language, however, belongs more to the overcoming of isolated-mind psychology and philosophy, while my intent here is to suggest some positive contents for a psychoanalytic and philosophical concept of individuality, which in turn may obviate the concept.

† For more extensive treatment of each of these thinkers, and of the themes treated here, see Orange (2009).

MARTIN BUBER AND THE ICH-DU

The contribution of Martin Buber (1878–1965), philosopher of dialogue, inclusion, and confirmation, has gone largely unnoticed in the psychoanalytic world. At the same time, his work has been warmly welcomed by the communities of humanistic psychotherapists, especially by Carl Rogers (Agassi, 1999) and by gestalt therapists (Hycner & Jacobs, 1995; Yontef, 1993). How can we explain this difference? First, as we can see in Buber's correspondence (Agassi; Buber, 1999; Glatzer & Mendes-Flohr, 1991), he challenged Freud, finding him too reductionistic and mechanistic, too inclined to reify the unconscious, and too dismissive of religious experience (Agassi). Freud had considered real guilt as if it were merely neurotic, thus precluding actual reconciliation (Buber, 1948). Buber's form of humanism and nondogmatic religion found much greater welcome among more existentially oriented psychiatrists in Europe like Ludwig Binswanger and Hans Trueb (Glatzer & Mendes-Flohr, 1991), psychoanalysts stopped listening.

But who was Buber? Born in Vienna in 1878, into a world of culture both grand and innovative in literature, music, science, philosophy, psychology, art, and architecture, Martin Buber grew up in a world in which Jews were demeaned—the young Freud could not hope for a professorship, for example. In spite of this, significant contributions were being made by the likes of Freud, Wittgenstein, Gustav Mahler, and Arthur Schnitzler (Janik & Toulmin, 1973). It was also a world from which all these geniuses, if they lived into the *Nazizeit*, had to depart. Buber, whose parents separated in 1882, grew up in Poland with his paternal grandparents, with whom he was very close and from whom he learned his love for languages and literature. Later he studied literature, philosophy, and some psychology in Vienna, Leipzig, Berlin, and Zurich. The year 1904 found him in Frankfurt working with Franz Rosenzweig and filling a lectureship in Jewish religious studies and ethics at the university. There he became involved in publishing and remained in the Frankfurt area until 1937 when the family emigrated to Jerusalem, where he taught at Hebrew University. His writings in religious studies and philosophy—*I and Thou* (Buber & Kaufmann, 1970) and *Tales of the Hasidim* (Buber & Marx, 1947)—made him a revered figure consulted by people from around the world (Glatzer & Mendes-Flohr, 1991).

Buber was reticent about his private life but did furnish a series of "autobiographical fragments" for the volume of the Library of Living Philosophers devoted to him (Schilpp & Friedman, 1967). The first of these, written when Buber was only 3, may be the most interesting from the perspective of psychoanalysis and psychotherapy:

> The house in which my grandparents lived had a great rectangular inner courtyard surrounded by a wooden balcony extending to the roof on

which one could walk around the building at each floor. Here I stood once in my fourth year with a girl several years older, the daughter of a neighbor to whose care my grandmother had entrusted me. We both leaned on the railing. I cannot remember that I spoke of my mother to my older comrade. But I hear still how the big girl said to me "No, she will never come back." I know that I remained silent, but also that I cherished no doubt of the truth of the spoken words. It remained fixed in me; from year to year it cleaved ever more to my heart, but after more than ten years I had begun to perceive it as something that concerned not only me, but all men. Later I once made up the word *Vergegnung*—"mismeeting" or "miscounter"—to designate the failure of a real meeting between men.* When after another twenty years I again saw my mother, who had come from a distance to visit me, my wife, and my children, I could not gaze into her still astonishingly beautiful eyes without hearing from somewhere the word *Vergegnung* as a word spoken to me. I suspect that all that I have learned about genuine meeting in the course of my life had its first origin in that hour on the balcony (pp. 3–4).

The centerpiece of Martin Buber's philosophy—he called it his "believing humanism"—is the dialogic encounter or meeting between I and Thou, which differs radically from all I-It relations, in which we regard the other as a thing or as an object to be known, used, or discarded. Unfortunately, translating Buber's Ich-Du as I-Thou creates and perpetuates a false impression, as Walter Kaufmann (Buber, 1970) explained. *Du* is the intimate form of "you," used with lovers, children, and very close friends. The English "Thou," instead, implies that the other is some kind of transcendent deity. For Buber, even addressing a deity, we use the Du.

But what is this intimate dialogic contact, and why does it become so important it for our work? For Buber there are two basic words: I-You and I-It. Both parts differ: "The I of the basic word I-You is different from that in the basic word I-It" (Buber, 1970, p. 53). How we stand in relation to the other changes us. We can stand above or outside as observer, investigator, or artist (Buber, 1962). When, however, we allow the other to speak to us, something very different occurs:

> This person is not my object; I have something to do with him. Perhaps I have something in him to complete; but perhaps I have only something to learn, and it only comes about that I "accept." Maybe I immediately have to answer this person; maybe speech would involve a long, complex transmission, and I must answer somewhere else, some other

---

* Translators usually render Buber's *Mensch* and *Menschen* as *man* and *men* in English, but the German word has a much more inclusive sense, more like *people*.

time, to someone else, in who knows what sort of language, and it comes about that I take the answer into myself. But a word happened to me that demands an answer. (p. 152, translation mine)*

Buber's other, his Du, is not part of me, but speaks into me as I do into him or her. Meeting the other as a Du changes us both by the word that is spoken. (I think, by the way, that such a concept of meeting makes complex mechanistic concepts like projective identification in psychoanalysis less inviting). Concepts of personal individuality tend to drop out of Buber's writing: they become unimportant.

Instead, two relational ideas take center stage: *Bestätigung* (confirmation), and *Umfassung* (inclusion.) Confirmation shares the self-building quality of Kohutian mirroring but goes further:

> Man wishes to be confirmed in his being by man, and wishes to have a presence in the being of the other. The human person needs confirmation because man as man needs it. An animal does not need to be confirmed, for it is what it is unquestionably...secretly and bashfully [man] watches for a Yes which allows him to be and which can come to him only from one human person to another. It is from one man to another that the heavenly bread of self-being is passed. (Buber in Agassi, 1999, p. 16)

Such a confirmation means that the other continues to exist in my being, much as Winnicott (1965) describes for the infant who can be alone because of his or her continued existence in the very being of the mother.

In our clinical work, we sometimes notice confirmation by its failure. A patient whom I had seen only once or twice a month for many years recently entered a devastating suicidal crisis, apparently precipitated by my failure to make my summer vacation plans fully clear to her. When she could not reach me and could not remember knowing where I was or when I would return, she panicked. Many factors, on her side and on mine, more and less conscious, went into this loss of communication. It would make a long, interesting, and complex clinical story. But my Buberian point is that our solid relational tie had confirmed her in being for so many years, and her fear that "something had happened to you" made her feel that her own being could not continue. It would be argued, perhaps, from some theoretical points of view, that I have allowed too much dependence. I share, instead, Buber's "believing humanism," according to which confirmation—making

---

* Gadamer (1975/1991) says something very similar: "The person with understanding does not know and judge as one who stands apart and unaffected; but rather, as one united by a specific bond with the other, he thinks with the other and undergoes the situation with him." (p. 323).

firm together—means holding in being someone who otherwise, so devastated, could not have survived to raise her children.

Inclusion (*Umfassung*), in turn, another relational idea in Buber, has a double meaning in German: both belonging and embrace. Inclusion, in Buber's use, replaces the Romantics' empathy or *Einfülhung*:

> It is the extension of one's own concreteness, the fulfillment of the actual situation of life, the complete presence of the reality in which one participates. Its elements are, first a relation, of no matter what kind, between two persons, second, an event experienced by them in common, in which at least one of them actively participates, and third, the fact that this one person, without forfeiting anything of the felt reality of his activity, at the same time lives through the common event from the standpoint of the other. (Buber & Smith, 2002, p. 115)

Buber's use of the term to describe what human I-You relatedness involves, implies both belonging to the human community together and a warmth of embrace within this commonality. He makes it clear that individuality could be at most a secondary value for him. He often said that relation is first, implying that individuality could be only derivative.

HANS-GEORG GADAMER: PHILOSOPHER OF DIALOGIC UNDERSTANDING

Hans-Georg Gadamer, too, lost his mother young. Born in Marburg in 1900 to a mother who died when he was 4 years old, Gadamer was raised in Breslau (now part of Poland) by his chemistry professor father: "The way I was raised when I was a child I would wish on no one today. No child would be likely to get through it without rebellion" (Grondin, 2003). Two dominating relationships shaped his life and work: his father, who relentlessly ridiculed his interests in the humanities and arts; and his mentor, Martin Heidegger, who considered Gadamer "not gifted enough" to do philosophy. After his 100th birthday, Gadamer would still speak of how disappointing he had been to both these men. Nevertheless, he found his own way through his intensive studies of Greek and especially of Plato, back into philosophy, where he developed his hermeneutics, or study of meaning and interpretation, into a whole philosophy of understanding emergent in dialogue. He survived the Nazi and early communist periods in Leipzig by keeping quiet[*] but also protected and hid Jewish colleagues. Called to a professorial chair in Heidelberg in 1950, he taught there until

---

* Some have seen him as too acquiescent, even cowardly; see Palmer (2002) and Wolin (2002). For Gadamer's own account, see Gadamer, Dutt et al. (2001).

his retirement and lived there until his death in 2002. There too, he wrote his *Truth and Method* (1997), for which he is best known. After having retired, he began to study languages and traveled and taught, especially in the United States and South America. He loved conversation and hated writing, too lonely and individualistic a pursuit for him, haunted as he always was by his sense of Heidegger looking over his shoulder.

Hermeneutics, the study of interpretation and meaning (Hermes was the messenger god in ancient Greece), had before Gadamer been a set of rules for interpreting texts, originally biblical texts. Two major figures intervened. In the Romantic period, Friedrich Schleiermacher (1768–1834) extended the reach of hermeneutics to law and literature and emphasized its difficulty: "misunderstanding occurs as a matter of course," he taught, "and so understanding must be willed and sought at every point"(Schleiermacher & Kimmerle, 1977, p. 110). Understanding (Frank, 1977) involved both linguistic and psychological contexts for Schleiermacher. At the end of the 19th century, Wilhelm Dilthey emphasized the difference among explanation, the task of the natural sciences, and understanding, the hermeneutic role of the human sciences.

In Gadamer's (1975/1991) hands, hermeneutics became the dialogic process of understanding in which what emerges from a conversation is something unique and unexpected:

> We say that we "conduct" a conversation, but the more genuine a conversation is, the less its conduct lies within the will of either partner. Thus a genuine conversation is never the one that we wanted to conduct. Rather, it is generally more correct to say that we fall into conversation, or even that we become involved in it. The way one word follows another, with the conversation taking its own twists and reaching its own conclusion, may well be conducted in some way, but the partners conversing are far less the leaders of it than the led. No one knows in advance what will "come out" of a conversation. Understanding or its failure is like an event that happens to us. (p. 383)

Note that Gadamer (1975/1991) refers to the interlocutors in a dialogue as "partners" or as "we," not as individuals. For him, the concept of individuality represents a reversion to romantic hermeneutics, with its attempts to enter the mind of the author. Understanding, he continues, "is not based on transposing oneself into another person. ... To understand what a person says is ... to come to an understanding about the subject matter, not to get inside another person and relive his experiences" (p. 383). In a genuine dialogue, people attempt to convince each other, but always also with the expectation that the other can teach us something. Under this condition, understanding can emerge in the play of conversation:

> Hermeneutics is die *Kunst der Verständigung*—the art of reaching an understanding—of something or with someone...this "coming to an understanding" of our practical situations and what we must do in them is not monological; rather, it has the character of a conversation. We are dealing with each other. Our human form of life has an "I and thou" character and an "I and we" character, and also a "we and we" character. In our practical affairs we depend on our ability to arrive at an understanding. And reaching an understanding happens in conversation, in a dialogue. (Gadamer, 2001, p. 79)

So for Gadamer, individuality and any kind of emphasis on the individual that prioritizes the "self" over the shared search for understanding is a reversion to the romantic hermeneutics and to the Cartesian view of the self-enclosed mind.

In his later years, Gadamer (1977/2000), concerned that Husserlian intersubjectivity depended on a traditional Cartesian concept of subjectivity, approached this topic through a study of the history of the concept of subjectivity. He concluded that Heidegger had been right to insist that our more primordially shared being in the world made individual subjectivity derivative. It could never be the foundational reality founding epistemology that modern philosophy had presumed it to be, the one certainty. All we had instead was our experience of concerned thrownness. Our individuality, such as it is, is our always already finding ourselves in a situation with others, a situation over which we have little control of how and when it is going to end but anxiously know that it will. What Gadamer adds is a sense of the genuine pleasure that can come from finding oneself in a situation of Aristotelian friendship and dialogic truth seeking with the others likewise thrown (Gadamer, 1999). The Heidegger of destiny, resoluteness, solitary death, and individual authenticity holds little attraction for Gadamer. For him, as for Critchley (Schürmann, Critchley, & Levine, 2008), the more important temporal dimension is the past that conditions the possibility of present and future coming into understanding.

EMMANUEL LÉVINAS AND THE FACE OF THE OTHER

Finally, there is Emmanuel Lévinas, part philosopher, part Talmudic scholar, and part prophet. Born in Lithuania in 1906, Lévinas and his family, who were refugees from the German occupation, moved to Ukraine in 1915 and back to Lithuania in 1920. He studied in Strasbourg and for one year (1928–29) in Freiburg with Husserl and Heidegger. His thesis introduced Edmund Husserl to French philosophers, but he abandoned his book on Heidegger when that philosopher joined the Nazis and tried to impose their program on Freiburg University. In 1939 he became a French citizen and enrolled in the officer corps. In 1940 he was imprisoned in a labor camp for the rest of the war, while his wife and daughter were hidden by nuns. All of his Lithuanian family died.

After the war, he was principally involved with Jewish education in Paris but also continued to write in philosophy. His doctoral thesis, "Totality and Infinity," was published in 1960, and by 1967 he was professor at the University of Paris, along with Paul Ricoeur. Many books and lectures later, he died in 1995. He wrote that his life was "dominated by the presentiment and the memory of the Nazi horror" (Lévinas, 1990, p. 291). Interest in his work has grown immensely since his death, in part because an ethical void was left by postmodernism.

The "big idea" of Emmanuel Lévinas was, in the words of Simon Critchley (2002), "that ethics is first philosophy, where ethics is understood as a relation of infinite responsibility to the other person" (p. 6). To understand this idea, we must remember that Heidegger, for whom ontology, the study of being, was everything and by whom the young Lévinas had been fully convinced, used his philosophy to support the regime that imprisoned and enslaved Lévinas for five years and murdered all his family. Lévinas became convinced that something "otherwise" than being or knowledge must be fundamental. He contrasted what he called "totalizing," or treating others as something to be studied or understood,* with relating to the face of the other. This irreducible "face" always transcends our concepts and ideas: "The way in which other presents himself, exceeding the idea of the other in me, we here name face" (Lévinas, 1969, p. 50). The other (*Autrui*, the human other) presents me with an infinite demand for protection and care. The face says: you shall not kill. The face, in Critchley's words, "is not something I see, but something I speak to" (p. 12).

The relation to the other (*Autrui*) creates what Lévinas (1969) called a "curvature of intersubjective space" (p. 291). To express this curvature Lévinas used words like *height* and *transcendence*:

> The neighbor concerns me before all assumption, all commitment consented to or refused. I am bound to him, him who is, however, the first one on the scene, not signaled, unparalleled; I am bound to him before any liaison contracted. He orders me before being recognized. Here there is a relation of kinship, outside of all biology, "against all logic." It is not because the neighbor would be recognized as belonging to the same genus as me that he concerns me. He is precisely other. The

---

* Clearly "understanding" means something different to Gadamer and to Lévinas. For Lévinas, to understand the other is to reduce the other to a member of a category, to "the Same," to totalize. For Gadamer, understanding means treating the other as a source of truth, my partner in conversation whose word and voice has a quality much like of the face of the other in Lévinas.

community with him begins in my obligation to him. The neighbor is a brother. (p. 87)*

The ethical relation is not between equals but is asymmetrical (compare with Aron, 1996, and Buber (Agassi, 1999)), that is, from "inside that relation, as it takes place, at this very moment, you place an obligation on me that makes you more than me, more than my equal" (Critchley, 2002, p. 14). Because I cannot expect the same responsibility without limits of the other toward whom I bear it, society is needed:

> The other stands in a relationship with the third party [society], for whom I cannot entirely answer, even if I alone answer, before any question, for my neighbor. ... Justice, society, the State and its institutions, exchanges and work are comprehensible on the basis of proximity. This means that nothing is outside of the control of the responsibility of the one for the other. (Lévinas, 1981, pp. 157–159)

Proximity, a key word in Lévinas (1981), means to him both the nearness and distance of our relation to the stranger: "In proximity is heard a command come as though from an immemorial past, which was never present, began in no freedom. This way of the neighbor is face" (p. 88). Thus, my singularity is not a kind of self-identification; instead, it is unutterable, cramped, ill at ease; it is exposure to wounding and outrage, unable to take a distance from itself, radically responsible for the other prior to any contact or choice (Bernasconi, 2002). It is "uniqueness without interiority, me without rest in itself, hostage of all, turned away from itself in each movement of its return to itself" (Lévinas, 1987, p. 150). "My relation to the Other individualizes me."

This means that individuality in Lévinas is no longer subjectivity but accusativity. To the stranger's need I say the biblical *hineni* or *me voici*. The English "here I am" does not translate this well, because it reintroduces the "I," the I of domination and violence. Lévinasian ethics challenges us, much as Buddhism does, to keep ourselves smaller in the world, to let ourselves just respond, traumatized by the suffering stranger.

In fact, the Lévinasian ethic gives meaning to the clinician's own "traumatism":

> ... There is a radical difference between the suffering in the other, where it is unforgivable to me, solicits me and calls me and suffering in me, my own experience of suffering, whose constitutional or congenital uselessness can take on a meaning, the only one of which suffering

---

* Though Lévinas seriously tried to keep his philosophical and "confessional" writings separate, the resonances come through, as here with the biblical sense of covenant.

is capable, in becoming a suffering for the suffering (inexorable though it may be) of someone else. (Lévinas, 1998, p. 94)

My own being, my own suffering take on importance as they enable me to respond to the widow, the orphan, and the stranger, who come to me suffering, naked, and impoverished. Otherwise, he often said, I am dethroned: I am defined as a subjectivity, as a singular person, as an "I," precisely because I am exposed to the other. It is my inescapable and incontrovertible answerability to the other that makes me an individual "I." So that I become a responsible or ethical "I" to the extent that I agree to depose or dethrone myself—to abdicate my position of centrality—in favor of the vulnerable other. (Lévinas, in Cohen, 1986, pp. 26–27)

INDIVIDUALITY: WHAT REMAINS?

Martin Buber's Ich-Du leaves us with the primacy of relation, confirmation, and inclusion. His philosophy of meeting and dialogue poses a profound challenge to the Western tradition's assumptions and values and inspired generations of thinkers who have sensed that something has been profoundly awry with our culture's focus on instrumental and technical rationality, especially in the human sciences. But where does the Buberian alternative lead us? No one has seemed to know.

Next we have the dialogic hermeneutics of Hans-Georg Gadamer. Situated within traditions, we find ourselves in conversation trying to learn from each other and to reach understanding together. We never know in advance where the process will lead us but must surrender ourselves to it anyway, doing our best to seek emergent truth together. But where is the Cartesian self, or any familiar notion of subjectivity—even one needed for a theory intersubjectivity—in Gadamer? Has the person disappeared into the dialogue? Or is a dialogic person now a differently understood person? I think these questions remain really unresolved.

Emmanuel Lévinas leaves us with, perhaps, even more questions. When the face of the suffering other (the widow, the orphan, the stranger) accuses me, traumatized me, and holds me hostage, what has happened to my "self," my "mind," my "agency?" I have become a first responder to the other, "the first one on the scene" (Levinas, 1981, p. 87). To avoid reducing the other an object of knowing, to a category, I have dethroned myself. Is this the only option? Is the *hineni, me voici* enough?

So what have we left of individuality? For Buber and Gadamer, we have a dialogical "I" that little resembles the private individual or self known to us from modern philosophy, personality psychology, diagnostic manuals, or even romantic philosophy and literature. In fact, the question of individuality as something we should seek to develop never shows up in these philosophies of dialogue and understanding. For Lévinas, the individual is not the speaker or knower, but the Other (the stranger/neighbor) to whom one speaks, whose face constitutes an infinite responsibility for me. Any individuality that makes the notion of the self central is unthinkable for him.

What can these challenges to personal individuality mean to the working psychoanalyst or psychotherapist? Especially in this moment when psychoanalysis has begun to consider both people as full participants in the process, with all our own history and struggles and psychological organization in play, all our fears, hopes, sufferings, and temptations to despair, even our radical hope, what can we learn from these thinkers?

It may be that East and West are coming closer at some points, that *anatta* (*an-atman*), the Buddhist ideal of no-self, is becoming speakable in Western languages too. Perhaps these thinkers, who all lived through—as exile, "inner exile," and prisoner—the horrors of the *Nazizeit*, are telling us that concepts of individuality have served us badly. Maybe they invite us to develop a therapeutic culture in which generosity, care, and protection of the other become our central values. In Gadamer's (1993) words, "It is the other who breaks my self-centeredness by giving me something to understand" (p. 9).*

Clinically, this makes it more than reasonable for therapists and analysts to accept being "actors in a supporting role" as opposed to protagonists, a position already familiar to self psychologists and to intersubjective systems clinicians. While we are fully involved in every clinical encounter, we need not insist that the other see how much effort we are making on the other's behalf. Our presence can be nondramatic: we are always already infinitely responsible to and for the other.

How then, a humanistically oriented analyst or therapist might ask, do we get our own relational needs met in our "infinitely demanding" work (Critchley, 2007)? I think there are several answers to this query. In some instances, for a long time, we simply will not. Instead, these needs for friendship and welcome will feel thwarted and rejected by the other whose suffering has transformed itself into complaint or contempt against us. At other moments, our welcome and care for the other will feel met by the suffering other. Sometimes, we must support our work from the outside, in friendships that make our infinite responsibility bearable. We have "promises to keep" and miles to go before we sleep.

---

* "Da ist es der Andere, der meine Ichzentriertheit bricht, in dem er mir etwas zu Verstehen gibt" (my translation).

REFERENCES

Agassi, J. (Ed.) (1999). *Martin Buber on psychology and psychotherapy: Essays, letters, and dialogue.* Syracuse, NY: Syracuse University Press.

Aron, L. (1996). *A meeting of minds: Mutuality in psychoanalysis.* Hillsdale, NJ: Analytic Press.

Atwood, G., & Stolorow, R. (1993). *Faces in a cloud: Intersubjectivity in personality theory.* Northvale, NJ: Jason Aronson.

Bernasconi, R. (2002). To which question is "substitution" the answer? In S. Critchley & R. Bernasconi (Eds.), *The Cambridge companion to Lévinas* (pp. 234–261). Cambridge, UK: Cambridge University Press.

Brandchaft, B. (2007). Systems of pathological accommodation and change in analysis. *Psychoanalytic Psychology, 24,* 667–687.

Buber, M. (1948). *Guilt and guilt feelings.* Paper presented at the International Conference on Medical Psychotherapy, International Congress of Mental Health, London.

Buber, M. (1962). *Das Dialogische Prinzip.* Gerlingen: Verlag Lambert Schneider.

Buber, M. (1970). *I and thou: A new translation with a prologue "I and you" and notes.* New York: Scribner's Sons.

Buber, M. (1988). *The knowledge of man.* Amherst, NY: Humanity Books.

Buber, M. (1999). *Martin Buber on psychology and psychotherapy: Essays, letters, and dialogue.* Syracuse, NY: Syracuse University Press.

Buber, M., & Kaufmann, W. A. (1970). *I and thou.* New York: Scribner.

Buber, M., & Marx, O. (1947). *Tales of the Hasidim.* New York: Schocken Books.

Buber, M., & Smith, R. G. (2002). *Between man and man.* London: Routledge.

Cohen, R. A. (1986). *Face to face with Lévinas.* Albany: State University of New York Press.

Critchley, S. (2002). Introduction. In S. Critchley & R. Bernasconi (Eds.), *The Cambridge companion to Lévinas.* Cambridge, UK: Cambridge University Press.

Critchley, S. (2007). *Infintely demanding: Ethics of commitment, politics of resistance.* London: Verso.

Frank, M. (1977). *Das individuelle Allgemeine: Textstrukturierung und interpretation nach Schleiermacher.* Frankfurt am Main: Suhrkamp.

Gadamer, H.-G. (1975/1991). *Truth and method.* New York: Crossroads.

Gadamer, H.-G. (1977/2000). Subjectivity and intersubjectivity, subject and person. *Continental Philosophy Review, 33,* 275–287.

Gadamer, H.-G. (1999). *Hermeneutics, religion, and ethics.* New Haven, CT: Yale University Press.

Gadamer, H.-G. (2001). *Gadamer in conversation: Reflections and commentary.* New Haven, CT: Yale University Press.

Gadamer, H.-G. (2001). *Gadamer in conversation: Reflection and commentary* (R. E. Palmer, Trans.). New Haven, CT: Yale University Press.

Glatzer, N., & Mendes-Flohr, P. (Eds.) (1991). *The letters of Martin Buber: A life of dialogue.* Syracuse, NY: Syracuse University Press.

Grondin, J. (2003). *Hans-Georg Gadamer: A biography.* New Haven, CT: Yale University Press.

Hycner, R., & Jacobs, L. (1995). *The healing relationship in Gestalt therapy: A dialogic/self-psychological approach*. Highland, NY: Gestalt Journal Press.

Janik, A., & Toulmin, S. E. (1973). *Wittgenstein's Vienna*. New York: Simon and Schuster.

LaPlanche, J. & Pontalis, J. B. (1973). *The language of psycho-analysis*. New York: Norton.

Lévinas, E. (1969). *Totality and infinity: An essay on exteriority*. Pittsburgh, PA: Duquesne University Press.

Lévinas, E. (1981). *Otherwise than being or beyond essence*. The Hague: Marinus Nijhoff.

Lévinas, E. (1987). *Collected philosophical papers*. The Hague: Martinus Nijhoff.

Lévinas, E. (1990). *Difficult freedom: Essays on Judaism*. Baltimore, MD: Johns Hopkins University Press.

Lévinas, E. (1998). *Entre nous: On thinking-of-the-other*. New York: Columbia University Press.

Orange, D. (2009). *Thinking for clinicians: Philosophical resources for contemporary psychoanalysis and the humanistic psychotherapies*. New York: Routledge.

Palmer, R. (2002). A response to Richard Wolin on Gadamer and the Nazis. *International Journal of Philosophical Studies*, 10, 467–82.

Schilpp, P., & Friedman, M. (Eds.) (1967). *The philosophy of Martin Buber*. London: Cambridge University Press.

Schleiermacher, F., & Kimmerle, H. (1977). *Hermeneutics: The handwritten manuscripts*. Missoula, MT: Scholars Press for the American Academy of Religion.

Schürmann, R., Critchley, S., & Levine, S. (Ed.). (2008). *On Heidegger's being and time*. London: Routledge.

Stolorow, R., & Atwood, G. (1992). *Contexts of being: The intersubjective foundations of psychological life*. Hillsdale, NJ: Analytic Press.

Stolorow, R., Atwood, G., & Orange, D. (2002). *Worlds of experience: Interweaving philosophical and clinical dimensions in psychoanalysis*. New York: Basic Books.

Stolorow, R., Atwood, G., & Orange, D. (in press). Heidegger's Nazism and the hypostatization of being. *International Journal of Psychoanalytic Self Psychology*.

Sullivan, H. S. (1950). The illusion of personal individuality. *Journal for the Study of Interpersonal Processes*, 13, 317–332.

Taylor, C. (1989). *Sources of the self: The making of the modern identity*. Cambridge, MA: Harvard University Press.

Winnicott, D. W. (1965). *The maturational processes and the facilitating environment*. New York: International Universities Press.

Wolin, R. (2002). Nazism and the complicities of Hans-Georg Gadamer: Untruth and method. *New Republic*, 36–45.

Yontef, G. (1993). *Awareness, dialogue, and process: Essays on Gestalt therapy*. Highland, NY: Gestalt Journal Press.

Chapter 4

Individuality in context

The relationality of finitude*

Robert D. Stolorow

i am through you so i.

– e. e. cummings

Philia begins with the possibility of survival. Surviving—that is the other name of a mourning whose possibility is never to be awaited.

– Jacques Derrida

A common misconception among critics of relational perspectives in psychoanalysis is the notion that an emphasis on the relational or intersubjective contexts of emotional experience defocuses, or even nullifies, experiences of individualized selfhood. As my collaborators and I (Stolorow, Atwood, & Orange, 2006) have emphasized, such criticisms tend to collapse the distinction between phenomenological description and theoretical explanation. As a phenomenon investigated by the psychoanalytic method, individualized selfhood is grasped always and only as a dimension of personal experiencing. Explanations of this dimension (or of disturbances in it) in terms of its taking form within intersubjective systems do not in any way imply a neglect or annulment of it. Contextualizing is not nullifying.

Husserl (2001), widely regarded as the founder of philosophical phenomenology, claimed that careful phenomenological description of structures of experience is a precondition for adequate theoretical explanations of them. Individualized selfhood is a dimension or structure of experience. For more than 25 years, my collaborators and I[†] have sought both to illuminate this structure (phenomenological description) and to conceptualize the intersubjective systems that facilitate or obstruct its consolidation (theoretical explanation).

---

* This is an expanded and substantially revised version of "Individuality in Context," *International Journal of Psychoanalytic Self Psychology*, 4(4), 2009, pp. 405–413.

† See, for example, Atwood and Stolorow (1984, Ch. 3), Socarides and Stolorow (1984–85), Stolorow, Brandchaft, and Atwood (1987, Ch. 4), and Orange, Atwood, and Stolorow (1997, Ch. 4).

The present chapter is a continuation and deepening of this twofold effort. Drawing on concepts from philosophical phenomenology—the work of Zahavi (2005), in particular—I will first argue that at the core of the experience of individualized selfhood is the sense of "mineness" of one's experiential life. Next I will contend that attuned relationality—the other's attunement to and understanding of one's distinctive affectivity—is a central constituent of the relational contexts that facilitate and sustain the mineness that is constitutive of experiential life. Then I will explore Heidegger's (1962) contention that it is authentically taking ownership of our finitude that individualizes us. Last, I seek to "relationalize" Heidegger's conception of individualized selfhood by emphasizing the necessity of integrating the emotional experiences accompanying ownership of not only one's own finitude but also the finitude of all those to whom one is deeply connected.

THE EXPERIENCE OF INDIVIDUALIZED SELFHOOD

A book by Zahavi (2005), *Subjectivity and Selfhood: Investigating the First-Person Perspective*, provides valuable philosophical tools that can help us in clearing up conceptual muddles about "the self" that pervade contemporary psychoanalytic discourse. He delineates three distinctive conceptions of self found in philosophy.

The Kantian self: The self of Kantian philosophy is not directly experienced; it is the inferred locus of identity in the midst of changing experiences. Our changing experiences all have something in common: they all have the same subject; they are all lived through by one and the same self. The Kantian self remains one and the same through time. This selfsame subject, according to Immanuel Kant, stands apart from our experiences and constitutes their unity and coherence. Although Zahavi does not make this point, the Kantian subject seems also to be the agent of choice and action.

The narrative self: In this conception, the self is assumed to be an interpretive construction, an evolving narrative or story about one's life and personality that reflects one's developmental and relational history and one's values, ideals, aims, and aspirations. One might say that, whereas the Kantian self is the inferred subject or agent of reflection, the narrative self is an object or product of reflection.

Experiential selfhood: From the experiential perspective, selfhood is claimed to possess immediate experiential reality and to be found in the structure of subjectivity itself. Specifically, originary selfhood is identified with what Zahavi calls the first-personal givenness or mineness of all of our experiences. All of my experiences are given to me as mine, as experiences that I am undergoing or living through. According to the experiential conception of selfhood, to which Zahavi gives primacy, the first-personal givenness or mineness of experiential life is claimed to be the source of our most basic or core sense of self.

The self-awareness that is intrinsic to the first-personal givenness of experience is not to be equated or confused with the positing of the self as an entity or object of reflection. Rather, the self-acquaintance that is inherent to the mineness of experience is variously characterized as immediate, prereflective, implicit, unthematized, and nonobjectifying.

Nor is the prereflective self-awareness that constitutes the core sense of selfhood to be equated with the self-enclosed interiority of a Cartesian worldless subject. On the contrary, this basic self-awareness is world immersed—that is, intrinsic to the first-personal givenness of our experiential engagement in the world. As my collaborators and I (Stolorow, Atwood, & Orange, 2002) have claimed, experiences of selfhood and of the world we inhabit are inextricably bound up with one another in a broader contextual unity, such that "any dramatic change in the one necessarily entails corresponding changes in the other" (p. 145).

Zahavi's (2005) position on the interrelations among subjectivity, intersubjectivity, and the forms of selfhood is quite complex. He wishes to replace the Kantian self with experiential selfhood grounded in the mineness of experience but then does not explain how he would account for personal agency. Experiential selfhood is a condition for the possibility of the narrative self. The narrative self is intersubjectively constituted, but mineness (along with otherness) is a condition for the possibility of both the narrative self and intersubjectivity. Zahavi does not consider the formative intersubjective contexts that promote or undermine the experience of mineness itself. That is a task for psychoanalysts, who are less concerned with the *a prioricity* of the sense of mineness than with the variations and modifications of it that occur within lived experience.

THE INTERSUBJECTIVE CONTEXTS OF EXPERIENTIAL SELFHOOD

I contend that, both developmentally and in the therapeutic situation, it is the other's ongoing validating attunement to and understanding of one's distinctive affectivity that strengthen and consolidate the mineness of one's emotional experiences, the foundation stone of one's sense of individualized selfhood. My distinctive affectivity, if it finds a hospitable relational home, is seamlessly and constitutively integrated into whom I experience myself as uniquely being.* In contrast, as Brandchaft (2007) elegantly shows, the mineness of experiential

---

* Elsewhere I have claimed (Stolorow, 2007), "Linguisticality, somatic affectivity, and attuned relationality are constitutive aspects of the integrative process through which the sense of being takes form" (p. 30).

life and the sense of individualized selfhood are undermined when, to maintain a needed tie with a malattuned other, one sacrifices one's own emotional experience and accommodatively adopts what is perceived to be required by the other. Under such circumstances, my emotional experience is no longer felt to be truly mine; it has been coopted, it now belongs to you.

Kohut (1977) made important contributions to our understanding of the context embeddedness of experiential selfhood, but his tendency to reify self-experience muddied the phenomenological waters. Zahavi's (2005) delineation of the three philosophical conceptions of self can help disambiguate conceptual difficulties found in Kohutian self psychology. According to Kohut, the self is a bipolar structure composed of two basic constituents—nuclear ambitions at one pole and guiding ideals at the other—deriving from the person's developmental and relational history. The two poles are said to be joined by a "tension arc," which is seen as the source of motivation for the person's basic pursuits in life. The Kohutian bipolar self would seem to fit well with Zahavi's characterization of the narrative self—an evolving construction or story about who one is, was, and is seeking to become.

But consider the following sentence, whose structure is typical of many that appear in the self psychology literature: "The fragmented self is striving to restore its cohesion." Who is the self that is engaging in such striving? Clearly it cannot be Kohut's bipolar self, since a narrative construction, particularly one that has fallen to pieces, cannot engage in an action such as striving. So it must be a Kantian self, a subject or an agent, who stands apart from the fragmenting self-experience and engages in actions to restore its cohesion. Or perhaps it is just the particular person—Bob Stolorow, for example, not Bob Stolorow's "self"—who performs such actions. And who is the self that is fragmenting? Is it merely the person's story about himself or herself that is falling apart? Or is it something much more profound, such as the person's basic experience of selfhood, the enduring and unifying sense of mineness lying at the core of his or her being? Applying Zahavi's (2005) typology makes it clear that "the self" of Kohutian self psychology confusingly conflates the three philosophical conceptions of self and coalesces them into a reified entity that tells a story, fragments, and restores its own cohesion. This conflation and reification obscure Kohut's central and most valuable contribution—illuminations of the phenomenology of self-experience in varying relational contexts.

Unlike the Kantian and narrative selves, experiential selfhood, at whose heart is the mineness of emotional life, is not an entity or a thing. It is a central dimension of personal experiencing and, as such, is exquisitely context dependent and context sensitive. Transforming such a dimension of emotional experiencing into an ossified thing automatically severs and isolates it from its constitutive relational contexts.

SELFHOOD AND FINITUDE

The emphasis on the mineness of experience as being constitutive of experiential selfhood brings to mind Heidegger's (1962) conception of authenticity, or *Eigentlichkeit*, which literally means ownedness or mineness. Authentic existence for Heidegger is owned, as opposed to disowned or unowned, existence. Does Heidegger's conception of authenticity as entailing ownership of one's existence deepen our understanding of how individualized selfhood is constituted within formative relational contexts? At first glance, Heidegger's idea does not seem to help us, as he appears to regard authentic existing as a singularly nonrelational affair.

For Heidegger (1962), authentic existing is grounded in nonevasively owned being toward death. Torn from the sheltering illusions of conventional everyday interpretedness (*das Man*), one who exists authentically apprehends death, not as a distant event that has not yet occurred or that happens to others (as the "idle talk" of *das Man* would have it) but as a distinctive possibility that is constitutive of his or her very existence, as his or her "ownmost" and "uttermost" possibility, as a possibility that is both certain and indefinite as to its "when" and that therefore always impends as a constant threat. Authentic existing is disclosed in the mood of anxiety, in which one feels "uncanny"—that is, no longer safely at home in an everyday world that now fails to evade being toward death. I have shown (Stolorow, 2007) that Heidegger's characterization of existential anxiety bears a remarkable resemblance to the phenomenology of traumatized states and that emotional trauma plunges one into a form of being toward death.

Heidegger (1962) claims that death as one's ownmost possibility is "nonrelational," in that death lays claim to one as an individual, nullifying one's relations with others.* One's death is unsharable: "No one can take [another's] dying away from him. ... By its very essence, death is in every case mine. ... Mineness ... [is] ontologically constitutive for death" (p. 284). Thus, in Heidegger's view, it is authentic being toward death as our ownmost, nonrelational possibility that individualizes and singularizes us, enabling us to seize ownership of and responsibility for our own existence.

THE RELATIONALITY OF FINITUDE

Heidegger's (1962) claims about the nonrelationality of authentic existing might seem jarring in view of his monumental efforts to recontextualize the

---

* A careful reading reveals that Heidegger (1962) is specifically claiming that it is relating to others in the inauthentic mode governed by *das Man* that is nullified in authentic being toward death. Authentic being toward death, according to Heidegger, frees us from the grip of deindividualizing conventional interpretedness.

Cartesian isolated mind and his insistence that human existing is always a "being in the world" and a "being with one another." I have contended (Stolorow, 2009c), however, that another view of authentic existing, in which it is relationally constituted, is implicit in Heidegger's conception of "solicitude." Authentic or emancipatory solicitude, for Heidegger, is a mode of being with in which we "leap ahead" of the other, welcoming and encouraging his or her individualized selfhood by liberating him or her to exist for the sake of his or her ownmost possibilities of being. But recall that, for Heidegger, being free for one's ownmost possibilities also always means being free for one's uttermost possibility—the possibility of death—and for the existential anxiety that discloses it. So if we are to leap ahead of the other, freeing him or her for his or her ownmost possibilities of being, we must also free him or her for an authentic being toward death and for a readiness for the anxiety that discloses it. Therefore, according to my claims about the contextuality of emotional life, we must be with—that is, attune to—the other's existential anxiety and other painful affect states disclosive of being toward death, thereby providing these feelings with a relational home in which they can be held, so that he or she can seize upon his or her ownmost possibilities in the face of them. And, as I have been contending, such attunement to the other's distinctive emotional experience contributes to the consolidation of his or her core sense of individualized selfhood.

What makes such integrating attunement possible? Vogel (1994) points us toward an answer to this question by illuminating a dimension of the relationality of finitude. Just as finitude is fundamental to our existential constitution, so too is it constitutive of our existence that we meet each other as "brothers and sisters in the same dark night" (p. 97), deeply connected with one another in virtue of our common finitude. I have contended (Stolorow, 2007) that our existential kinship in the same darkness is a condition for the possibility of forming bonds of deep emotional attunement within which the devastating emotional pain inherent to the traumatizing impact of our finitude can be held and integrated.

Critchley (2002) points the way toward a second, and to my mind essential, dimension of the relationality of finitude:

> I would want to oppose [Heidegger's claim about the non-relationality of death] with the thought of the fundamentally relational character of finitude, namely that death is first and foremost experienced as a relation to the death or dying of the other and others, in being-with the dying in a caring way, and in grieving after they are dead...With all the terrible lucidity of grief, one watches the person one loves—parent, partner or child—die and become a lifeless material thing. That is, there is a thing—a corpse—at the heart of the experience of finitude. This is why I mourn. ... Death and finitude are fundamentally relational...constituted in a relation to a lifeless material thing whom I

love and this thing casts a long mournful shadow across the self. (pp. 169–170)

Authentic being toward death entails owning up not only to one's own finitude but also to the finitude of all those with whom we are deeply connected. Hence, I have contended (Stolorow, 2007) that authentic being toward death always includes being toward loss as a central constituent. Just as, existentially, we are "always dying already" (Heidegger, 1962, p. 298), so too are we always already grieving. Death and loss are existentially equiprimordial (Agosta, in press). Existential anxiety anticipates both death and loss.

Recently I encountered unexpected support for my claim about the equiprimordiality of death and loss in some works by Jacques Derrida. In *Politics of Friendship* (Derrida, 1997), for example, he contended that the "law of friendship" dictates that every friendship is structured from its beginning, a priori, by the possibility that one of the two friends will die first and that the surviving friend will be left to mourn. In *Memoirs for Paul de Man* (Derrida, 1989), he similarly claimed that there is "no friendship without this knowledge of finitude" (p. 28). Finitude and the possibility of mourning are constitutive of every friendship. Derrida (2001) makes this existential claim evocatively and movingly in *The Work of Mourning*:

> To have a friend, to look at him, to follow him with your eyes, to admire him in friendship, is to know in a more intense way, already injured, always insistent, and more and more unforgettable, that one of the two of you will inevitably see the other die. One of us, each says to himself, the day will come when one of the two of us will see himself no longer seeing the other. ... That is the ... infinitely small tear, which the mourning of friends passes through and endures even before death. ... (p. 107)
> [This is] the mourning that is prepared and that we expect from the very beginning. ... (p. 146)
> From the first moment, friends become ... virtual survivors. Friends know this, and friendship breathes this knowledge ... right up to the last breath. (p. 171)

Consider, with regard to the relationality of finitude, the emotional impact of collective trauma, such as the terrorist attack of September 11, 2001 (see Stolorow, 2009b). As we watched the twin towers of the World Trade Center collapse right before our eyes and witnessed the instant death of more than 3,000 people, did we experience terror only about our own finitude and the possibility of our own deaths? Or were we terrified as well, or even primarily, for the lives of those we loved—our children, for example?

It might be objected that being toward loss cannot be a form of being toward death because, whereas the uttermost possibility of death is "the possibility of the impossibility of any existence at all" (Heidegger, 1962,

p. 307), loss does not nullify the entirety of one's possibilities for being. Yet, I would counter, in loss as possibility, all possibilities for being in relation to the lost loved one (other than imaginary and symbolic possibilities) are extinguished. Thus, being toward loss is also a being toward the death of a part of oneself—toward a form of existential death, as it were. Traumatic loss shatters one's emotional world (Stolorow, 2007), and, insofar as one dwells in the region of such loss, one feels eradicated. Derrida (2001), once again, captures this claim poignantly and poetically:

> [T]he world [is] suspended by some unique tear...reflecting disappearance itself: the world, the whole world, the world itself, for death takes from us not only some particular life within the world, some moment that belongs to us, but, each time, without limit, someone through whom the world, and first of all our own world, will have opened up. ... (p. 107)
> [A] stretch of [our] living self ... a world that is for us the whole world, the only world ... sinks into an abyss. (p. 115)

My effort to relationalize Heidegger's conception of being toward death is captured in my poem, "Finitude" (Stolorow, 2009a):

> If we're not self-lying,
> we're always already dying.
> If we're not self-deceiving,
> we're always already grieving.
> The answer to the existential quiz?
> "Good-bye" is all there is.

CONCLUSIONS

I have contended that attuned relationality, the other's attunement to and understanding of one's distinctive affectivity, including the horror and anguish that derive from the traumatizing emotional impact of our finitude and the finitude of all those with whom we are deeply connected, is a central constituent of the relational contexts that facilitate and sustain a sense of individualized selfhood and of the often excruciating mineness of our experiential life, indeed, of our very being. In the course of developing this thesis, I have delineated two constitutive dimensions of the relationality of finitude— our kinship in the same darkness and our being toward loss.

Grasping the relationality of finitude holds, as Vogel (1994) alludes, significant ethical implications insofar as it motivates us, or even obligates us, to attune to and provide a relational home for others' existential vulnerability and pain. Imagine a world in which this ethical obligation has been universalized. In such a world, human beings would be much more capable of living in their existential anxiety rather than having to revert to the defensive, destructive, deindividualizing evasions of it that have been so characteristic of human history. A new form of identity would become possible, based on owning rather than covering up our existential vulnerability. A new form of human solidarity would also become possible, rooted not in shared ideological illusion but in shared recognition and understanding of our common human finitude. If we can help one another bear the darkness rather than evade it, perhaps one day we will be able to see the light—as individualized, finite human beings, finitely bonded to one another.

REFERENCES

Agosta, L. (in press). *Empathy in the context of philosophy*. New York: Palgrave Macmillan.

Atwood, G. E., & Stolorow, R. D. (1984). *Structures of subjectivity: Explorations in psychoanalytic phenomenology*. Hillsdale, NJ: Analytic Press.

Brandchaft, B. (2007). Systems of pathological accommodation and change in analysis. *Psychoanalytic Psychology, 24*, 667–687.

Critchley, S. (2002). Enigma variations: An interpretation of Heidegger's *Sein und Zeit. Ratio, 15*, 154–175.

Derrida, J. (1989). *Memoirs for Paul de Man* (C. Lindsay, J. Culler, E. Cadava, & P. Kamuf, Trans.). New York: Columbia University Press.

Derrida, J. (1997). *Politics of friendship* (G. Collins, Trans.). London: Verso.

Derrida, J. (2001). *The work of mourning* (P.-A. Brault & M. Naas, Eds.). Chicago: University of Chicago Press.

Heidegger, M. (1962). *Being and time* (J. Macquarrie & E. Robinson, Trans.). New York: Harper & Row. (Original work published 1927)

Husserl, E. (2001). *The shorter logical investigations* (J. Findlay, Trans. & D. Moran, Ed.), New York: Routledge. (Original work published 1900 & 1913)

Kohut, H. (1977). *The restoration of the self*. Madison, CT: International Universities Press.

Orange, D. M., Atwood, G. E., & Stolorow, R. D. (1997). *Working intersubjectively: Contextualism in psychoanalytic practice*. Hillsdale, NJ: Analytic Press.

Socarides, D. D., & Stolorow, R. D. (1984–85). Affects and selfobjects. In C. Kligerman (Ed.), *The annual of psychoanalysis, vol. 12/13* (pp.105–119). New York: International Universities Press.

Stolorow, R. D. (2007). *Trauma and human existence: Autobiographical, psychoanalytic, and philosophical reflections*. New York: Analytic Press.

Stolorow, R. D. (2009a). Finitude. *Psychoanalytic Perspectives, 7*, 74.

Stolorow, R. D. (2009b). Identity and resurrective ideology in an age of trauma. *Psychoanalytic Psychology, 26*, 206–209.

Stolorow, R. D. (2009c). Trauma and human existence: The mutual enrichment of Heidegger's existential analytic and a psychoanalytic understanding of trauma. In R. Frie & D. M. Orange (Eds.), *Beyond postmodernism: New dimensions in clinical theory and practice* (pp. 143–161). London: Routledge.

Stolorow, R. D., Atwood, G. E., & Orange, D. M. (2002). *Worlds of experience: Interweaving philosophical and clinical dimensions in psychoanalysis.* New York: Basic Books.

Stolorow, R. D., Atwood, G. E., & Orange, D. M. (2006). Contextualizing is not nullifying: Reply to Mills (2005). *Psychoanalytic Psychology, 23,* 184–188.

Stolorow, R. D., Brandchaft, B., & Atwood, G. E. (1987). *Psychoanalytic treatment: An intersubjective approach.* Hillsdale, NJ: Analytic Press.

Vogel, L. (1994). *The fragile "we": Ethical implications of Heidegger's* Being and Time. Evanston, IL: Northwestern University Press.

Zahavi, D. (2005). *Subjectivity and selfhood: Investigating the first-person perspective.* Cambridge, MA: MIT Press.

Part 3

Developmental contexts

Chapter 5

Persons acting in worldly contexts

Jeff Sugarman and Jack Martin

Given the mission of disciplinary psychology to explain human behavior across the variety of social, cultural, and biophysical contexts in which it occurs, it might be expected that the focus of psychological investigation is persons acting in worldly contexts. However, historically and currently, seldom is such the case. Introspective, cognitive, and biological psychologies have taken the focal phenomena of interest to be thoughts, mental forms and functions, or neurophysiological structures and processes. Functional and behavioral approaches to psychology have investigated human behavior, but restrictively so, as responses of research subjects to highly contrived tasks in "stripped down" experimental settings purposefully denuded of practical, cultural, and historical relevance. Psychoanalytic, humanistic, phenomenological, and existentialist traditions frequently have been preoccupied with the inner experiences, desires, and tensions of persons rather than with their activity in the everyday contexts in which their lives are composed. Even evolutionary psychologists, who might be expected to emphasize the worldly activity of persons when theorizing about psychological selection and adaptation, appear instead to favor a combination of narrative speculation and mathematical modeling. As this brief synopsis shows, past and present psychological scientists have looked to explain individual human action and experience primarily through an interior mentalistic focus or environmental restriction and simplification, not in terms of persons acting in everyday worldly contexts.

Despite the ascent of psychology over the last century to the scientific legitimacy it currently enjoys, claims as to the success of its disciplinary mission are less than compelling. Research in social, personality, developmental, industrial-organizational, and psychometric psychology has met with disappointment when persons routinely fail to behave in everyday situations as would be predicted by their self-reports, performance on psychological instruments, or observed responses on experimental tasks. Cognitive scientists continue to be vexed by frame problems and associated difficulties that severely restrict the explanatory value and applicability of their models and simulations in real-world contexts. Clinical, counseling, forensic, school, and other professional psychologists have been reconciled to administering assessments and implementing interventions that boast only limited predictive success, with levels of diagnostic and prognostic accuracy other health-related sciences would find unacceptable. Over the sum of psychological research, there is an absence of findings shown to be robust across the myriad social, cultural, historical, and biophysical contexts.

We do not wish to deny that psychology has contributed to the understanding and betterment of persons' lives. However, in our view, the progress of psychological theorizing, research, and practice has been impeded by inadequate conceptions of psychological subject matter and widespread inattention to the ontology of phenomena of interest. Such conceptual and ontological considerations have monumental implications for psychology. For not only are appropriate conceptions of the phenomena of interest necessary for relevant and consequential psychological theorizing, research, and practice, but, moreover, unless features of human psychology can be shown to be ontologically exceptional (i.e., irreducible to physical, biological, or sociocultural properties) then psychology has no subject matter of its own and can be absorbed by other fields of inquiry judged more fundamental to the nature of their subject matter (e.g., neurophysiology, cultural studies; Sugarman & Martin, 2010). In this chapter, we offer *persons acting in worldly contexts* as the distinctive and appropriate subject matter for psychology and discuss why this conception should serve to orient psychologists in their investigative and theoretical pursuits.

But why have psychologists neglected the study of persons acting in everyday contexts? There is a strongly dualistic assumption implicit in much psychological theory that divides mind from body, action from reflection, selves from each other, and persons from the world in which they act and exist. It also is widely assumed that the objects of psychological inquiry are natural phenomena with fixed universal characteristics that preexist scientific investigation and whose components can be isolated, reductively analyzed and classified, formulated in causal mechanistic laws, made predictable, and eventually brought under instrumental and technical control by psychological scientists. At work here is an implicit endorsement of scientific naturalism along with the belief that "person" is not a proper scientific concept. Scientific naturalism concerns study of the nature of things in the world. But *person*, by definition, denotes those features of human beings that make them more than mere things. Persons are individuals of a particular kind. If persons are beings with reflexive self-understanding, with moral and rational agency, with freedom of choice and action, who can be said to be justly deserving of praise or blame, who can originate genuine purposes, who possess identities, and so forth, then persons cannot be described solely in terms of physical, biological, or other kinds of constituents that exclude features of existence that mark human individuals distinctively as persons and rendering them unique among other kinds of entities. However, it would appear that psychologists have become so entrenched in the traditions of dualism and naturalism and so thoroughly persuaded by the methods of natural science and its reductionistic strategies that they seem to prefer to distrust and dismiss their everyday understanding of themselves as persons acting in the world rather than to regard it as a basis for their discipline.

In this chapter, we consider conceptually, ontologically, and epistemologically *persons acting in worldly contexts* as the appropriate focus for psychological theorizing and inquiry, and for expanding our understanding of individuality—what it means to be individual and to be an individual. In our account, persons are individual in vital ways. The realization of one's unique and particular existence provides for a phenomenal presence of being and infuses experience and action in the world with significance. However, as will become clear, the individuality of persons is not comprehended in some atomistic sense, separated from conditions of history, society, and culture. Rather, as we reveal, such conditions are constitutive of who and what individuals are and can become through their emergence as psychological persons.

We begin by outlining a conceptual framework for interpreting persons. We then introduce briefly two developmental theories that support an emergent ontology of persons. These theories reveal the constitutive role of coordinated activity and interactivity in the developmental emergence of reflexive self-understanding, moral and rational agency, and social and psychological identity—features attributed exclusively to persons in our conceptualization. Subsequently, we examine epistemological consequences of this ontology and, moreover, how psychological description is connected ontologically with the differing forms personhood can take. We conclude that disciplinary psychology should be reoriented to address the kind of psychology of personhood we advocate.

A CONCEPTUAL FRAMEWORK

If psychology is to be directed toward the study and understanding of persons acting in worldly contexts, it is important first to be clear as to what persons are. In the conceptualization we have advanced (see Martin, Sugarman, & Hickinbottom, 2009), persons are embodied, reasoning, and moral agents, with self-consciousness, self-understanding, and social and psychological identity. As we shall discuss, when personhood is comprehended as developmentally emergent within worldly contexts of coordinated activity and interactivity, persons can be identified and interpreted as uniquely constituted ontological entities.

Our conceptualization of persons is based on concepts of embodiment, selfhood, identity, and agency. Embodiment refers to a physical, biological, human body embedded in, and in continuous exchange with, the biophysical and sociocultural world. Self is the first-person experience and understanding that discloses and extends a person's particular being and activity, while, at the same time, providing existential and experiential stability within ongoing processural change. Self is recognizable to itself, even as it develops and changes. Importantly, our conception of the self is one of relational understanding and awareness, not of physical or transcendental substance. Self is not a thing but rather a mode of being. Social identity refers to those social classifications and designations appropriated and adopted by individuals as descriptive of themselves or various groups to which they belong (e.g., White, male, American, spouse, parent, professor, psychologist). Psychological identity is a person's recognition by self and others as a unique individual with a biography (autobiography) and personality.

Agency is of particular significance in our conceptualization of persons acting in worldly contexts. Human agency is the deliberative, reflective activity of a human being in framing, choosing, and executing his or her actions in a way that is not fully determined by factors and conditions other than his or her own understanding, reasoning, and moral consideration (Martin, Sugarman, & Thompson, 2003). As we have argued elsewhere (Martin et al., 2003), because persons (as agents) may and frequently do act for reasons and purposes of their own, personal determination must be considered a source of human action. The further implication is that the actions of persons are thus not reducible to biophysical or sociocultural determinants alone. Once psychologically capable persons have emerged developmentally within their biophysical and sociocultural contexts, their interpretations, understandings, and deliberations are causally influential in any further determination of their being and activity. Agentive psychological capabilities are not only causally implicated, but moreover, once they have emerged, they have distinct ontological status and are irreducible to their biophysical and sociocultural determinants.

Human agent causation, as conceived in the tradition of 18th-century philosopher Thomas Reid, is imputed to the deliberations and actions of persons as rational and moral agents. However, deliberative rational and moral action is only a portion of human worldly activity, much of which is less formally rational and deliberative and which often occurs prereflectively. Further, psychological capacities requisite for deliberative rational and moral action are not present at birth but rather must be acquired developmentally. It is from a developmental perspective that persons capable of moral and rational action can be seen to emerge gradually within human social and cultural contexts in which coordinated activity and interactivity enable and shape agentive psychological development.

It is the developmental emergence of persons as ontologically distinctive entities to which we now turn. More specifically, we discuss two recent developmental theories that draw attention to the worldly activity and interactivity of embodied and situated human agents and that do so in a way that gives priority to relations and coordinations over individual cognitive or neurophysiological processes. We wish to make clear that we do not dispute that persons require particular evolved biological bodies and brains for the kinds of coordinated social activity and interactivity within which psychological development takes place. What we do argue is that psychological development can ensue only when biophysically embodied humans are immersed and participate in uniquely human sociocultural contexts of coordinated action and interaction.

In addition, we emphasize that in our conceptualization, it is persons who act in the world, not parts of persons. As Hacker (2007) admonishes, talk of brains making decisions, brains learning, creative brains, and criminal brains are mereological fallacies—not just mistaken, but meaningless. Brains cannot decide, learn, be creative, or commit crimes. Only persons can be said to do and be these things. Consequently, any psychology of personhood, if it is to be grammatically and theoretically coherent, must attend to the kinds of entities that persons are, how they act as integral human beings in the world, and what follows from their worldly activity and interactivity.

THE DEVELOPMENTAL ONTOLOGY OF PERSONHOOD

In support of a developmental ontology of persons acting in worldly contexts, we present briefly Cultural-Historical Activity Theory (CHAT) as it recently has been extended and advanced by Stetsenko and her colleagues, followed by the neo-Meadian approach elaborated by Martin. These theories are consistent with our conception of persons acting in worldly contexts. They are concerned with persons functioning as integral agents, not with parts of persons, and draw attention to developmental contexts of coordinated activity and interactivity within which psychologically capable persons emerge as ontological entities.

Cultural-historical activity theory and psychological development

The work of Stetsenko and her colleagues (see, e.g., Stetsenko, 2002, 2005, 2008; Stetsenko and Arievitch, 1997, 2004, 2010; Vianna and Stetsenko, 2006) is an extension of Cultural-Historical Activity Theory, which originated in the early 20th century with the investigations of Vygotsky and his colleagues, Leontiev and Luria. Like his contemporary Jean Piaget, Vygotsky believed that humans are part of the natural order and that every living organism exists in dynamic exchange with its environment. It is thus that Vygotsky and Piaget both looked to explain psychological development as a result of the activity and interactivity of individuals as they endeavor to adapt to the contexts they inhabit. However, in following Karl Marx and Fredrick Engels, Vygotsky believed not only that humans adapt to their environments but, moreover, that they also labor collectively to transform them. According to Vygotsky, by transforming their environments, humans transform themselves, acquiring subjectivity, moral and rational agency, and other psychological functions.

Vygotsky asserted that collaborative social practice is a uniquely human kind of material and practical exchange with the world. He also believed that the ontology of psychological development was to be traced to historically situated and sustained, but nonetheless continually evolving, sociocultural practices. In Vygotsky's Marxian inspired analysis, these sociocultural forms of coordinated activity and interactivity, and the varieties of individual psychology they engender, have developed precisely because they are necessary to regulate the collective material production of human life. Vygotsky thus theorized that human phylogenesis is unique among living organisms. It not only follows a trajectory of biological evolution but also a cultural historical evolution of coordinated activity and interactivity that has coalesced into socially and culturally organized material practices. These practices regulate individual and collective life and furnish contexts suitable for the development of psychologically capable persons.

Central to Vygotsky's developmental theory is the cultural mediation of action. While Marx was concerned with the dynamics of the material conditions of human life and collectively produced forms of labor and social regulation, Vygotsky explored how the dynamics of social practice create conditions for the emergence of psychological functions. More specifically, Vygotsky observed the ways social exchange is mediated by cultural tools such as language and other modes of symbolic representation and how such cultural tools are used to shape thought, action, and experience. Vygotsky interpreted words and symbols as the "material" used in the production of psychological capacities. Individuals acquire psychological functions by appropriating meditational means deployed initially in the coordination of social exchange and subsequently using them as tools to regulate their thoughts, actions, and experiences. Humans shape their existence collectively and individually through the use of cultural tools and, by relaying these tools from one generation to the next, perpetuate the historical development of psychological capacities.

Vygotsky revealed that transmission of the means for a distinctively human psychological existence occurs not by genetic inheritance but rather by institutionalized practices of coordinated activity and interactivity. The cultural tools that connect social and psychological being are conveyed and acquired through teaching, learning, and multitude practices of enculturation. What this implies, from the Vygotskian perspective, is that the subject of development is not simply the psychological individual but also social and cultural contexts and, more specifically, meditational means and patterns of coordinated activity and interactivity through which social and individual life are lived.

In contrast to Vygotsky, who became concerned largely with semiotic mediation in the development of psychological functions, Leontiev played down the importance of signs and, instead, gave priority to material forms of practical activity and the ways tools are used to change the structure of activity (Stetsenko, 2005; Stetsenko & Arievitch, 2004, 2010). Dissenting from Vygotsky, Leontiev insisted that the primary vehicles for implementing social forms as psychological functions are not signs but rather are material practices (by which signs are carried and conveyed) that structure the child's concrete actions and relations with others and objects. For Leontiev, practical activity and its objects are the fundamental medium of psychological development.

Leontiev held that psychological processes, as forms of activity, are object related. All activity is directed toward objects and is differentiated by them. At the same time, however, objects are represented only as a result of acting with or toward them. According to Leontiev, activity and objects exist in a mutually constitutive relation. Leontiev also claimed that psychological activity never can be reduced to individual activity and always reflects its origins in collective experience. This is because the cultural tools with which actions and experiences are mediated delineate the features of objects that make them objects of concern or interest for us and, thus, cultural tools contribute to our comprehension of objects—a comprehension that finds its original expression and develops in collective practices. Our actions and experiences are shaped by our interpretations of objects and forms of engagement with them that have arisen in specific collective, historically situated practices.

In the tradition of CHAT initiated by Vygotsky and elaborated by Leontiev and their successors, the basis of psychological development is initiation into historically situated social and cultural practices. This initiation is assumed to occur predominantly through child–adult interactions and the adult's purposeful regulation of the child's activity beginning with its material forms. Through practices of teaching and learning, there is gradual transformation of the child's material forms of activity into corresponding mental forms of activity. Mental activities (e.g., attending, remembering, motivating, symbolizing) emerge developmentally and incrementally within material forms of coordinated activity and interactivity. It is in this way, according to Vygotsky's famous maxim, that higher psychological functions (i.e., mental functions that involve cultural mediation) always appear twice: first interpsychologically, in collaborative action, and then intrapsychologically, internalized by the individual.

While adopting much of the account of psychological development advanced by CHAT, Stetsenko argues that insufficient attention has been paid to the ways subjectivity and agency figure in the transformative processes of social and psychological life. According to Stetsenko, while Leontiev recognized a role for subjectivity, he interpreted it as an outcome and device of material production serving primarily to orient individuals in social interaction. By designating subjectivity and other psychological forms and processes as features of social interaction, Leontiev was attempting to overcome problems associated with metaphysical dualism. Stetsenko alleges, however, that in seeking to specify the properties of objects that precipitated psychological images, Leontiev and other CHAT theorists reified both material objects and their corresponding mental images and, in so doing, inadvertently reconstructed the sort of dualism they had intended to escape.

Stetsenko proposes that to avoid dualism and its attendant problems Leontiev's principle of object-relatedness needs to be reconceptualized such that objects and agents are understood to function integrally but as aspects of ongoing and evolving dynamic processes of activity. According to Stetsenko, objects and their attributes are never severed from their functions in social practice. The significance of objects consists in the ways they are made manifest and employed in social practices, and this significance becomes part of our perception and understanding of objects. This implies that the significance of objects is subject to change as our aims and practices change, and, consequently, so too are our perceptions and understanding of objects.

Importantly, Stetsenko emphasizes a dialectic relation between objects and subjective agency. We work on objects, and, conversely, objects work on us. Our actions with and on objects can alter our conceptions and understandings of ourselves. As we labor to transform an object, reinterpreting its practical significance, we transform our means of engagement with the world, and, because we are constituted through our actions, this can change our understanding of ourselves.

Stetsenko claims that it is our activity with objects and dialectical relation with them that creates the conditions for asserting our agency within the materiality of our practices. It is within the dialectic relation of acting and being acted on that persons, as subjects and agents, are realized and transformed. Stetsenko notes that the transformative dialectical relation between object and subjective agency can be comprehended only within the broader context of social and cultural institutions necessary to sustaining this relation. But, at the same time, she asserts strongly that such institutions can exist only through the coordinated actions and interactions of psychologically capable, embodied agentive subjects. The implication is that it is only by virtue of the activity and interactivity of agentive persons that collective social structures and practices can be transformed. Thus, not only are persons constituted through the objects of social activity, but, moreover, they also create these objects, transform them, and, in so doing, make manifest their agentive personhood in the world. As Stetsenko (2005) summarizes:

> By returning to the world through activity processes in their endless manifold transitions, human subjectivity inevitably changes the world, positing (externalizing) itself in the materiality of human practice in its reified objective forms. The latter forms, that is, the cultural-historical objects, not only come to embody communal social practice as they "reflect" and carry on the history and vicissitudes of their social production...but also appear as coming into being only when being again involved—further transformed and creatively developed—in human practice that is carried out by concrete individuals. That is, the world of cultural-historical experience (reified in tools and objects) and human subjectivity appear as co-evolving and existing through conjoint constant reenactments in, and by the processes of, active transformation of the world. (p. 83)

In Stetsenko's extension of CHAT, psychological development is not bridging a metaphysical divide between external social practice and an interior mental realm. Rather, psychological development can be comprehended as the emergence of a new sphere of action that affords possibilities for transformative social practice and social and individual life. The mental realm is conceived as a realm of action. According to Stetsenko, agency, material social practice, and intersubjectivity "form a three-fold unified dialectical system of mutually co-determining and co-evolving facets of human life" that combine developmentally to "represent processes aimed at actively transforming the world" (2005, p. 81).

Mead's perspectival realism and psychological development

According to Martin (2007a), the work of George Herbert Mead elucidates the metaphysics of psychologically capable personhood as developmentally emergent within contexts of coordinated dynamic interaction. In his interpretation and elaboration of Mead's ideas, Martin (2005, 2006, 2007a, 2007b) focuses on the function of perspectives in structuring social interactions and making them intelligible to participants and in facilitating the developmental transition from prereflective to reflective forms of agentive activity. Psychological development proceeds from the situating of individuals in multiple perspectives and a growing ability to recognize, occupy, and coordinate differing perspectives within established patterns of social interaction. By occupying and exchanging perspectives, individuals gradually become capable of comprehending and regulating their actions with increasing psychological sophistication and complexity. In Martin's view,

Mead's perspectival realism reveals developmental conditions for the emergence of an ontologically unique psychological agency that is socially and culturally constituted but also self-interpreting and self-determining. In so doing, Martin (2007b) submits, Mead's account "resists essentialist and foundationalist formulations by achieving a pragmatic grounding in the contingent, but far from arbitrary, practices and perspectives that constitute our forms of life" (2007b, pp. 437–438).

According to Martin (2007b), the fundamental unit of analysis in Mead's metaphysics is "a relationship between an organism and its world" (p. 443). It is in the relationship between individuals and their biophysical and sociocultural contexts that perspectives are formed as ways of orienting to the world that contain possibilities for individual and collective action. According to Mead, from birth, human individuals are immersed in a social matrix of coordinated perspectives that structure our actions and interactions. However, perspectives serve to orient persons not only toward events, objects, and others but also psychologically toward our own subjectivity. Acquiring the capacity for perspective taking enables us to take perspectives toward ourselves, creating the possibility for reflexive self-consciousness.

All perspectives originate in human sociality, as collective acts organized around social objects (e.g., persons, events, locations, and ideas as well as physical objects). Importantly, however, in Mead's theory, perspectives do not simply function epistemologically. Rather, perspectives have ontological force. Psychological reality is perspectival in that all understanding and experience arises from the relation between persons and the contexts within which they are embedded and act. Perspectives are real. However, they are not static and can be modified or discarded if they are no longer functional. Perspectives arise within contexts of practical activity and find application when they are suited to our purposes and the enablements and constraints of biophysical and sociocultural reality.

In Martin's elaboration of Mead's theory, human psychological development issues from the simultaneous positioning of an individual within two or more perspectives and the growing capacity to discern, occupy, and coordinate multiple perspectives. Very early in development, infants are positioned by caregivers in simple sequences of interaction and prompted to simulate the roles and actions that comprise them—for example, offering and receiving food or other objects. With repetition, the infant begins primitively to register and anticipate the significance of social gestures and to distinguish among individuals and objects in its immediate surround. The infant operates prereflectively and preconceptually. However, as the child gradually becomes independently capable of performing and even initiating these basic sequences of activity, the caregiver moderates her assistance accordingly. Martin identifies this transition from assisted to prereflective/preconceptual participation as an important initial accomplishment in a developmental process during which perspective taking becomes an increasingly reflective and abstracted means of orienting toward possibilities for action.

As the child repeatedly assumes and practices social roles, she retains something of her experiences of them. These memories make it possible for the child to recall and anticipate being in one social position while occupying a related social position. For instance, in a game of hide-and-seek, as seeker, the child may remember a successful experience as a hider, and search in that same location for her hiding playmate. The child's repetitive participation in simply structured games with alternating roles and positions (e.g., hide-and-seek, tag, peekaboo) allows the child to occupy, remember, and anticipate the different positions and perspectives by which such routines are structured and coordinated. Gradually the child's range of experiences in the social world expand and, concomitantly, her repertoire of perspectives. This repertoire consists largely of perspectives held in common by members of her community, shared orientations Mead referred to as the "generalized other."

As orientations to action, perspectives are configured within specific sequences of interactivity. However, perspectives are not fixed temporally to the present. As Martin explains, perspectives can be occupied imaginatively as well as actually in ways that give rise to increasingly complex, differentiated, and abstracted forms of activity. The ability to employ and coordinate perspectives imaginatively, augmented by growing facility with language and other forms of symbolic representation, enables the developing child to participate in the multiplying variety of social situations encountered. Moreover, this capacity to occupy simultaneously actual and imagined perspectives is requisite for a kind of self-reactivity through which reflexive self-awareness is acquired.

For reflexive self-awareness to develop, not only must the child be able to take and occupy perspectives, but it is also necessary that she be able to react to the perspectives she holds in relation to herself as these are generated in interactions with others. In Mead's theory, reflexive self-awareness begins with an individual reacting to her own actions as others do. The reactions of others are a means by which the individual can make herself an object to which she then can react. The child remembers the ways others act toward her and reacts to these memories. By adopting the perspectives others hold toward her (i.e., acting toward herself as others do), she is able to interpret herself as both subject and object. This self-reactivity fuels the development of self-awareness and psychologically capable agency.

Mead distinguishes between the "I" and the "Me" to capture conceptually the rendering of subjectivity through self-reactivity. The agentive "I," present only in the immediate moment of action, reacts to a recollected "Me" brought forward as an object of reflection. The reaction of the "I" to the "Me" produces a reconstituted perspectival understanding of the "Me." This reconstituted self is subsequently made present as the next recollected "Me" to which an immediately future "I" responds. The "I" is experienced, but not knowable. Subjective knowledge consists of the "Me" manifest as memories of actions both remembered and imagined of an agentive "I." In this way, selfhood and psychological subjectivity result from a self-determining agency that generates its own psychological emergence by simultaneous occupation of perspectives of a reconstructed past and an anticipated future, joined in deliberative determination of action in the present.

In light of Mead's account, psychological development is the movement toward increasingly differentiated and abstracted capacities for perspective taking. As Martin describes, gradually the child comes to recognize and understand others as intentional agents who possess perspectives that differ from her own. With further immersion and participation in educational and other social contexts and a growing array of perspectives encountered, there is opportunity for more advanced forms of interpersonal differentiation and generalization that grant increasingly sophisticated reflective attitudes toward one's own and others' perspectives. As adolescents and young adults coordinate their actions and interactions within broader social practices and conventions, they are confronted by the inevitable limits and inadequacies of interpersonal interaction. Such experiences provoke more critical forms of self-other understanding, reflective deliberation, and interpretive perspective taking required for practices such as the giving and receiving of, for example, reasons, empathy, negotiation, and compromise.

Martin's (2007a) interpretation of Mead's work responds to criticisms by those such as Vessey (1998) and Frie (1997), who allege that Mead's theory of the emergence of subjectivity and deliberative agency necessarily assumes the a priori existence of what he is attempting to explain. The thrust of the criticism is that, for perspectives to be internalized, there already is implicit a relation between self and other, differentiation of that relation, and a reflexive orientation to oneself that allows for such differentiation. Internalizing a perspective appears to presuppose an internalizing subject who already has a sense of self and self-other awareness. Martin asserts, however, that for Mead, perspective taking does not begin as internalization. Rather, reflexive subjectivity and the reflective capacity it requires are preceded by prereflective forms of perspective taking that need involve only interactivity with others and the assistance they provide in instantiating and coordinating the positions comprising social activities.

What is key, Martin emphasizes, is that perspectives be comprehended as relational, not mental, entities. Perspectives are created, sustained, and transformed in coordinated action and interaction. Our ability to occupy and use perspectives requires direction and assistance from others in learning to participate in the social activities from which perspectives are derived. The possibility of reflexive self-awareness and psychologically capable agency is provided by a developmental context of coordinated interactivity in which the transformation of prereflective into reflective forms of perspective taking is supported by others. As Martin (2007a) expounds,

> Perspectives and our selves are differentiated and emerge within our ongoing activity with others in the biophysical and sociocultural world. There is no need to assume a pre-existing reflective "internalizer" because what occurs is not initially a matter of internalization. Instead, it is a process of participation in sociocultural practices through assisted interactivity with others. Our self-consciousness and deliberative agency follow upon our social positioning, assisted functioning, and prereflective perspective taking as these gradually allow us to differentiate and locate our selves as centers of acting, experiencing, and perspective taking within our lifeworld. (p. 452)

Martin finds in Mead's metaphysics and developmental theory elements for a conceptualization of agentive psychological development that delivers the possibility of a self-interpreting and self-determining psychological agency while refusing essentialist and foundationalist notions of an a priori subject. In Martin's interpretation, Mead's theory reveals a continuously emergent, psychologically capable human agency that is conceived in established practices of social interactivity, especially through the efforts of caregivers to support prereflective social positioning and exchange, a multiplicity of perspectives, a developing capacity to occupy simultaneously plural perspectives, and self-reactivity. These elements situate agentive development in pragmatic orientations to action that have evolved with the history of social practice while, at the same time, allowing for the transformation of extant practices and perspectives through agentive activity.

What these contemporary versions of CHAT and Mead's perspectival realism serve to highlight is the way our development as persons with social and psychological capabilities of self-consciousness, self-understanding, rational and moral agency, and social and psychological identity unfolds in the wake of coordinated activity and interactivity within the biophysical and sociocultural world. While there are important differences between these developmental theories, much is shared between them in the ways they conceive personhood and agentive psychological capacities as emergent within worldly activity with others. In both approaches, it is structured interactivity that steers a developmental trajectory in which biophysically evolved humans learn to orient to and coordinate with others not only to promote agentive personhood but also to sustain a sociocultural world of social objects, semiotically mediated meanings, material practices, institutions, conventions, roles, perspectives, and traditions. In light of Stetsenko's extension of CHAT and Martin's elaboration of Mead's perspectival realism, persons are both products and producers of the conditions required for their ontological emergence. It is within a developmental context of coordinated interactivity with others that we emerge as persons with selfhood, identity, and moral and rational agency.

As both these developmental approaches make plain, psychological existence never can shed its origins in collective experience. Our ontology is relational and emergent. Personal being is existential, not essential, a consequence of the conditions of possibility created within specific socio-culturally and historically situated developmental contexts of coordinated activity and interactivity. The implication is that the exact forms our self-hood, agency, and personhood take depends greatly on the particular societies, cultures, and historical periods in which we live and act.

EPISTEMOLOGICAL CONSIDERATIONS

Given an understanding of persons as self-interpreting beings whose ontological status is constituted developmentally and is emergent through coordinating their actions with objects and others, psychological investigation and description of persons insinuate a unique set of considerations. To identify and comprehend persons as unique entities, it is important to recognize that the constitution and development of persons is ongoing, emergent, and mutable. Our particular ontological constitution enables us to react to our encounters and experiences within unfamiliar or unique circumstances in ways that evoke new forms of coordinating, interacting, and being. In other words, new practices provide new possibilities and ways of being persons. Psychological description holds particular significance in this regard. Drawing on the work of Hacking (1995a, 1995b, 1998, 2002, 2006), Sugarman (2009) elaborates how, in describing and understanding themselves as psychological agents, persons are uniquely capable of reacting to their self-descriptions in ways that can constitute or reconstitute their perspectival relation with themselves. We come to define and act toward ourselves under psychological descriptions and, in the process, form and alter the kinds of persons we are.

Persons interact dynamically with the ways they are described and interpreted, a phenomenon Hacking (1995a) refers to as "the looping effect." As self-interpreting beings, humans can become aware of how they are described and classified within their groups, societies, and cultures; they can experience themselves in particular ways as a result of these descriptions and classifications; and they can act in ways that can alter their descriptions and classifications. For example, an individual told he is learning disabled may abandon aspirations of attending university in favor of more technical pursuits or may seek professional assistance in dealing with his disability. A drug user who is labeled an addict may persist in her current habit, commit crimes to support it, or decide to seek treatment. Such labels influence how human persons understand and interpret themselves—the perspectives they occupy in relation to themselves, their actions, and their interactions. Further, the reactions of persons to the ways they are described, classified and, consequently, treated often can result in those descriptions and classifications being transformed in dramatic ways. As Sugarman (2009) explains, persons may resist and rebel against the scientific, political, economic, medical, legal, educational, or religious institutions that describe, classify, administer, and govern them. Changes in human rights laws, policies, and practices, for example, have been realized as a direct consequence of the activities of multicultural and antiracism advocacy groups.

The looping effect connects the ontology of persons with our practices of psychological description. When the looping effect occurs and persons change the ways they interpret and describe themselves, they no longer can be considered quite the same kinds of persons they were before. Through a wide assortment of examples (e.g., adolescence, autism, child abuse, fugue, homosexuality, multiple personality disorder, suicide, teenage pregnancy, hip and square), Hacking illustrates how new descriptions and classifications of people, especially those invented and promoted by the human sciences, not only expand possibilities for action, interaction, and experience and create new kinds of personhood but also come in and out of existence.[*] In other words, the ontology of persons is unremittingly historical (Hacking, 2002; Sugarman, 2009).

When certain descriptions and categories prove useful in making our coordinated actions and interactions, experiences, and perspectives intelligible, in expressing common concerns, and in pursuing our various purposes, they can become "objectified" in the practices and conventions of cultures and societies. Such practices and conventions furnish normative criteria by which the actions of individuals and collectives are sanctioned and censured. Persons live within and through the descriptions, norms, and perspectives they provide and transmit them in developmental contexts of coordinated action and interaction from one generation to the next. As such, they become constitutive of the kinds of persons we are and the kinds of cultures and societies within which we live.

The ontological and epistemological significance of psychological description is that our experience and interpretation of ourselves as certain sorts of persons is the result of occupying and interpreting perspectives toward ourselves as focal objects of concern. Because we are self-interpreting and reactive within whatever practices we inhabit, our ongoing coordinations within such practices serve to transform both ourselves and the practices

---

[*] See Hacking, 1995a for adolescence, autism, child abuse, suicide, and teenage pregnancy; Hacking, 1995b for multiple personality disorder; Hacking, 1998 for fugue; Hacking, 2006 for homosexuality.

within which we are engaged. With new descriptions and perspectives, there is the possibility for new kinds of persons, new actions and interactions, and new experiences to emerge, while others disappear. Personhood is, in Ian Hacking's (2006) words, "a moving target."

A conception of persons as moving targets emphasizes their ontological mutability. A critical epistemological implication of this conception is that personhood is not pregiven or fixed, and there is no single absolute, universal, or ahistorical truth about persons that transcends the ontological features and conditions that derive from their worldly involvements. Persons are emergent within coordinated activity and interactivity that is situated within specific historically and socioculturally constituted practices. The kinds of persons we are, or can become, vary significantly across time and context. In other words, persons are defined by their embodied, embedded, and emergent capabilities to coordinate their worldly actions and interactions, not by any specific constellation or manifestation of these capabilities. The precise formulation of our experiences, actions, and interactions in situations will display considerable heterogeneity as we act and react within varied and evolving matrices of social practices. Such conditions of constant mutability preclude robust generalizations, let alone universal laws, about human behavior and experience. Notwithstanding, it is necessary for individuals and collectives to maintain some degree of stability in their coorientations, actions, and interactions. Without sufficient stability, the social practices within which individuals and collectivities are constituted and function would fail. However, it must be emphasized that such stability is the existential consequence of persons acting and interacting in worldly contexts, not a result of pregiven essential attributes that predate our worldly activity and interactivity.

CONCLUDING REMARKS

In conclusion, we wish to draw attention to what we believe sets our account of persons acting in worldly contexts apart from other psychological interpretations. We believe that our account and its emphases contribute a profoundly different starting point for considerations of human psychology. By granting primacy to action and interaction over reflection and coordination over imposition, we affirm coordinated activity and interactivity within the world to be conditions necessary for psychological existence, an existence that would be inconceivable in the absence of these conditions. In locating psychological existence at the dynamically evolving intersection of biophysical and sociocultural reality our interpretations of psychological being and knowing follow from the holistic coordinations and perspectival understandings that are forged within material and practical activity in worldly contexts. We suspect that the striking failure of psychology to ground its disciplinary investigations and theorizing on a conception of persons acting in worldly contexts (of the sort detailed herein) is a regrettable consequence of allegiance to a tradition of Western thought that has preserved, proclaimed, and promoted dualistic assumptions and reductionistic strategies.

In contrast to this tradition, we have conceptualized persons as contextually constituted, embodied, rational and moral agents with self-consciousness, self-understanding, and social, psychological identity. We have linked these conceptions to an ontological account of persons as unique entities constituted developmentally and emergent within contexts of coordinated activity and interactivity. Our particular constitution as persons: including our ontology as moving targets, demands of those who would investigate psychological existence, recognition of persons as unique ontological entities who cannot be reduced to their biophysical and sociocultural constituents. It is our hope that this chapter might inspire others to consider how the agenda for psychology might be refocused on understanding persons acting in worldly contexts.

REFERENCES

Frie, R. (1997). *Subjectivity and intersubjectivity*. Lanham, MD: Rowman and Littlefield.

Hacker, P. M. S. (2007). *Human nature: The categorical framework*. Oxford, UK: Blackwell.

Hacking, I. (1995a). The looping effect of human kinds. In D. Sperber, D. Premack, & A. J. Premack (Eds.), *Causal cognition: A multidisciplinary debate* (pp. 351–383). Oxford, UK: Clarendon.

Hacking, I. (1995b). *Rewriting the soul: Multiple personality and the sciences of memory*. Princeton, NJ: Princeton University Press.

Hacking I. (1998). *Mad travelers: Reflections on the reality of transient mental disease*. Charlottesville: University Press of Virginia.

Hacking, I. (2002). *Historical ontology*. Cambridge, MA: Harvard University Press.

Hacking, I. (2006, April 11). *Kinds of people: Moving targets*. The Tenth British Academy Lecture, London, UK.

Martin, J. (2005). Perspectival selves in interaction with others: Re-reading G. H. Mead's social psychology. *Journal for the Theory of Social Behaviour, 35*, 231–253.

Martin, J. (2006). Re-interpreting internalization and agency through G. H. Mead's perspectival realism. *Human Development, 49*, 65–86.

Martin, J. (2007a). Interpreting and extending G. H. Mead's "metaphysics" of selfhood and agency. *Philosophical Psychology, 20*, 441–456.

Martin, J. (2007b). Educating communal agents: Building on the perspectivism of G. H. Mead. *Educational Theory, 57*, 435–452.

Martin, J., Sugarman, J., & Hickinbottom, S. (2009). *Persons: Understanding psychological selfhood and agency*. New York: Springer.

Martin, J., Sugarman, J., & Thompson, J. (2003). *Psychology and the question of agency*. Albany: State University of New York Press.

Stetsenko, A. (2002). Vygotsky's cultural-historical activity theory: Collaborative practice and knowledge construction. In D. Robbins & A. Stetsenko (Eds.), *Vygotsky's psychology: Voices from the past and present* (pp. 174–179). Hauppauge, NY: Nova Science Press.

Stetsenko, A. (2005). Activity as object-related: Resolving the dichotomy of individual and collective planes of activity. *Mind, Culture, and Activity, 12*, 70–88.

Stetsenko, A. (2008). From relational ontology to transformative activist stance on development and learning: Expanding Vygotsky's (CHAT) project. *Cultural Studies of Science Education, 3*, 471–491.

Stetsenko, A., & Arievitch, I. (1997). Constructing and deconstructing the self: Comparing post-Vygoskian and discourse-based versions of social constructivism. *Mind, Culture, and Activity, 4*, 160–173.

Stetsenko, A., & Arievitch, I. (2004). The self in cultural-historical activity theory: Reclaiming the unity of social and individual dimensions of human development. *Theory & Psychology, 14*, 475–503.

Stetsenko, A., & Arievitch, I. (2010). Cultural-historical activity theory (CHAT): Foundational worldview, major principles and the relevance of sociocultural context. In S. Kirschner & J. Martin (Eds.), *The sociocultural turn in psychology: Contemporary perspectives on the contextual emergence of mind and self* (pp. 231–252). New York: Columbia University Press.

Sugarman, J. (2009). Historical ontology and psychological description. *Journal of Theoretical and Philosophical Psychology, 29*, 5–15.

Sugarman, J., & Martin, J. (2010). Agentive hermeneutics. In S. Kirschner & J. Martin (Eds.), *The sociocultural turn in psychology: Contemporary perspectives on the contextual emergence of mind and self* (pp. 159–179). New York: Columbia University Press.

Vessey, D. (1998, March). *On the incompleteness of George Herbert Mead's theory of the social self as an account of intersubjectivity: Re-reading Henrich after Habermas*. Paper presented at the annual meeting of the American Society for the Advancement of Philosophy, Milwaukee, WI.

Vianna, E., & Stetsenko, A. (2006). Embracing history through transforming it: Contrasting Piagetian versus Vygoskian (Activity) Theories of learning and development to expand constructivism within a dialectical view of history. *Theory and Psychology, 16*, 81–108.

Chapter 6

Development of individuality within a systems world

James L. Fosshage

The paradigm shift from intrapsychic to intersubjective or relational field theory and, more recently, to complexity or nonlinear dynamic systems theory has been nothing short of revolutionary in psychoanalysis. Its increased explanatory power of development and analytic interaction is contributing substantially to making psychoanalysis a growth-enhancing, effective treatment modality. Nonlinear dynamic systems theory is illuminating the intricate formative impact of experience that occurs within a context of multiple systems—individual, familial, ancestral, peer, community, cultural, national, and world systems (e.g., Coburn, 2002; Ghent, 2002; Lichtenberg, 2002; Shane, Shane, & Gales, 1998; Stolorow, 1997). Within this theoretical context of a systems world the issue of how we understand and account for the origins of individuality, the topic of this book, becomes especially salient.*

Each person develops within ongoing relational systems. With the current advances in cognitive science, neuroscience, infant, and dream research, our observations and understanding of developmental processes are achieving much greater specificity with regard to the interplay of constitutional and environmental elements. While it is commonly accepted that genetic and environmental factors participate in individual development, psychoanalytic relational field or systems-based models, in my view, tend not to recognize sufficiently constitutional factors (Fosshage, 2003). Our consideration of these factors and their impact—for example, self-regulatory capacities, temperamental dispositions, strength of motives, and physical and cognitive capacities—facilitates our recognition and appreciation of the uniqueness of the individual. Within the psychoanalytic arena, we, in turn, are better able to foster the development of the individual.

Because motivation (desires, urges, intentions, wishes) plays such a pivotal role in an individual's development and ongoing process throughout the life span, in this chapter I focus specifically on and redefine a psychoanalytic

---

* Joseph Lichtenberg conceived of this issue as the focus for the 2008 Self Psychology Conference, for which a group of these chapters was invited.

motivational concept I term *developmental motivation* and a closely related concept I term *developmental direction*. I have chosen to focus on these two related concepts for the following reasons: (1) motives and intentions are central in understanding thoughts, actions, and meanings; (2) these concepts have a meaningful history within psychoanalysis; (3) these concepts include biological givens that emerge from within the individual and can be distinguished from environmental influences at least in early infancy; (4) these concepts have considerable clinical utility; and (5) these concepts need to be updated and redefined to reflect the advances in neuroscience, cognitive science, infant research, dream research, and systems theory.

NATURE/NURTURE

Most would agree that the development of a person is a vastly complex, multivariable interactive process of genetic, neurobiological, and environmental elements (see Siegel, 1999 for a neuroscience perspective). Observations based on systems theory have revealed three general patterns involving these elements: (1) frequently the complexity of interaction prevents differentiation of constitutional and environmental elements; (2) many developmental features that were previously seen as driven by an inherent, genetically based design are unpredictable (nonlinear) developments emergent out of the interplay of genetic, neurobiological, and environmental factors; and (3) recognition of previously unseen primitive aspects of certain functions (biological givens) within the baby that later emerge nonlinearly into more mature functions.

It has been asserted by some that systems theory "transcends" the nature/nurture controversy, meaning that the complexity of interaction prevents differentiation of constitutional and environmental elements (Thelen & Smith, 1994). Transcendence, in this sense, does not negate the multiplicity of genetic and environmental factors that play a role in human development. While differentiation of these elements is often not possible, at times dynamic systems theory through its microscopic focus on process does differentiate and reveal biological givens and environmental factors. In the domain of cognitive/motor development, for example, Thelen and Smith note the presence of primitive aspects of certain functions (biological givens) within the baby that later emerge nonlinearly into fully developed functions (to be delineated). In other words, with its consistent focus on process dynamic, systems theory, in my view, contributes to the resolution of the nature/nurture controversy in three ways: (1) recognition that the interplay is too complex to delineate constitutional and environmental elements; (2) developmental features previously seen as driven by genetic design are, instead, viewed as new features spontaneously emergent within the system; and (3) recognition of previously unrecognized primitive aspects of certain functions (biological givens) within the baby that later emerge nonlinearly into fully developed functions.

Human beings, as with all living systems, have an inherent tendency to be self-organizing systems that receive, integrate, and organize vast amounts of internal and external stimulation—from genes, neurobiology, physical surroundings, and interpersonal interaction. Identification of any of these factors potentially contributes to our understanding of individual development as it occurs within a nonlinear dynamic systems world.

Take, for example, the contribution of genetic factors. Oliver Sacks (1993) in his summary of Gerald Edelman's work states, "Clearly there are some innate biases or dispositions at work; otherwise the infant would have no tendencies whatever, would not be moved to do anything, seek anything, to stay alive" (p. 44). Think of the impact of the variable genetic components of physical attributes and capacities, temperament (Kagan, 1971, 1984; Thomas & Chess, 1977, 1980), cognitive/emotional capacities (Bucci, 1985, 1997; Fosshage, 1983, 1997; Paivio, 1971, 1986, 2007; Siegel, 1999), language capacities (Chomsky, 1968, 1995; Pinker, 1994), self-regulatory (resilience) and interactive-regulatory capacities (Anthony, 1987; Beebe & Lachmann, 2002; DiAmbrosio, 2006, 2007; Fajardo, 1991; Lichtenberg, Lachmann, & Fosshage, 1992, 1996; Sander, 1977), and physical and psychological anomalies (e.g., cerebral palsy, cystic fibrosis, autism, schizophrenia). Addressing the findings of behavioral genetic research, Pinker (2002) concludes, "... Identical twins reared apart are highly similar; identical twins reared together are more similar than fraternal twins reared together; biological siblings are far more similar than adoptive siblings. All this translates into substantial heritability values, generally between .25 and .75" (p. 374).

In differentiating relational theory from the drive model, Mitchell (1988) notes, "In the drive model, 'anatomy is destiny' (Freud, 1924b, p. 178); social factors are shaped by inherent, underlying drive pressures. In the relational model biology and interpersonal processes constitute perpetual cycles of mutual influence" (p. 4). In our relational systems-based theoretical accounts of development, however, our enthusiasm over the extrication from the deterministic drive model, combined with the increased sense of agency, "soft assembly" (Harris, 2005) of personality features and explanatory power of relational systems has resulted in the neglect of constitutional factors. The postmodern impulse has been to eschew "human essences" (Teicholz, 1999) as the pendulum has moved, and many view biological givens warily as too limiting, too deterministic, and too diminishing of the observed power of relational systems.

There are, of course, notable exceptions to this neglect of constitutional factors. Bowlby (1969, 1973, 1988, 1989) identified five biologically rooted types of behavior: the attachment, exploratory, parenting, sexual and eating behavioral systems. Lichtenberg (1989), Lichtenberg, Lachmann, and Fosshage (1992, 1996, 2003), and Lichtenberg et al. (1992, 1996) posit that individuals are born originally with five, and now seven (Lichtenberg,

Lachmann, & Fosshage, 2010), innate needs and response patterns that emerge and develop through relational experience into functional or non-functional motivational systems: (1) the psychological need for physiological regulation; (2) attachment to individuals; (3) affiliation with groups; (4) caregiving; (5) sensuality/sexuality; (6) exploratory/assertive; and (7) aversive. These systems contribute to the development, maintenance, and restoration of self-cohesion or self-organization.

Based on Chomsky's (1968, 1995) work on a constitutionally based foundation for learning language, what he calls "linguistic deep structure," Ogden (1986) refers to "psychological deep structure," a genetically based foundation for psychological development. Slavin and Kriegman (1992), integrating evolutionary biology and psychoanalysis, posit an adaptive design or an evolving psychological deep structure of the human psyche, an innate complex architecture of the mind, that "guides the process of organizing experience, including such processes as the creation of a subjective sense of self." More recently, Gentile (1998, p. 69) formulates the idea of "a developmental trajectory, which reflects both the particularity of the intersubjective context and the universality of a deep structural foundation to developmental experience..." (p. 72).

Shane, Shane, and Gales (1998), in delineating two developmental pathways to the consolidation of self and self with other, refer to trauma due not only to "parental failures" but also to "constitutional difficulties in the child" (p. 1). Their conception of self, the system of mind/brain/body, includes biologically based motives and the neurophysiology of the development of brain function.

Infant researchers are delineating how infants have considerable wired-in capacities and motivational proclivities at birth. To mention a few, Stern (1983) asserts on the basis of infant research that infants are "predesigned to discriminate and to begin to form distinct schemas of self and of other from the earliest months of life" (p. 50). And Emde (1988) refers to four basic infant motivations: (1) activity; (2) self-regulation; (3) social fittedness; and (4) affective monitoring, that is, the propensity to monitor experience according to what is pleasurable and unpleasurable. Lastly, considerable research demonstrates how rapid eye movement (REM) stage sleep enhances learning and establishes neural patterns (maps). REM sleep begins in the fetus during the third trimester of pregnancy and is online at birth (Fosshage, 1997).

Bollas (1989) writes about one's "personal idiom" and a "destiny drive." Greenberg (1991) argues for a dual motivational model of safety and effectance. Ghent (2002), positing two types of needs—"homeostatic safety" and "expansion of function"—concludes, "Depending on circumstances in a person's life, basic needs will develop in unique ways, reflecting (1) the potential talents and skills, as well as handicaps, that were organized on the basis of genetic programming and prenatal experience and (2) the facilitative and thwarting environmental influences in personal life" (p. 789).

MOTIVATION

Motivation is central in our lives, for motives are primary in "directing" and giving meaning to our thoughts and actions. When listening to patients, psychoanalysts search for and assume, either implicitly or explicitly, motivations or intentions, for they are pivotal in understanding patients. Cognitive psychologists (Bruner, 1986, 1990, 2002) have suggested that motives are the "basic mental unit" for understanding human behavior. Correspondingly, the Boston Change Process Study Group (BCPSG, 2008) writes, "... Intention is the fundamental psychological meaning. Sequences of intentions give motivated human behavior its psychological existence, coherence, and finally its meaning. ... Intentions fit into larger movements of orientation and directionality given by motivational systems" (pp. 129–130). So important are intentions in understanding human behavior that "intention detection centers" in the brain have been identified that are activated when a person observes behaviors that lead him or her to infer an intention in another person (Rujby & Decety, 2001, referred to in BCPSG). And the mental process itself by which we parse "human behavior into intentions and motives is considered a mental primitive, in the sense that it appears to be an innate mental tendency necessary for adaptation in a social world of other motivated beings" (BCPSG, p. 129). It is not surprising, thus, that motivational models provide the fulcrum for every psychoanalytic theory.

Motives or intentions refer to an experiential sense of seeking (being pulled or pushed toward) goals and taking action to achieve those goals (Lichtenberg, 1989, 2002; BCPSG, 2008). The BCPSG states, "In other words, some fundamental (nonverbal) process-structure, like an intention that unfolds in real time, must exist" (p. 130). They describe the "intention unfolding process" as "a line of dramatic tension as the intention fulfills or fails to fulfill its destiny as it becomes revealed" (p. 131). With motivation so pivotal in "moving/directing" as well as understanding human beings, tracking, what the BCPSG calls the "intention unfolding process" becomes central in clinical work.

How do intentions or motives arise within us? What are the biological givens or preexperiential influences? Can we delineate biological givens and environmental factors that give rise to motives through microscopic study of process? I turn first to Edelman's work and then to systems theory (Ghent, 2002; Lichtenberg, 2002; Shane et al., 1998).

In his theory of neuronal group selection process, Edelman (1987, 1989, 1992) proposes that neural and psychic structure develop in each individual by two forms of natural selection in interactive neuronal patterns: developmental and experiential. In Edelman's theory developmental selection refers to the "processes of self organizing microanatomical selection that occur in embryological time and lead ultimately to the formation of the large-scale neuroanatomy characteristic of any given species" (Ghent, 2002, p. 776). In contrast, experiential selection addresses an individual's immediate processing and adaptive selection in the establishment of neuronal patterns. In his edifying summary of Edelman's work, Sacks (1993) writes:

> These basic biases Edelman calls "values" [not to be confused with the customary meaning of human values]. Such [biases or] values are essential for adaptation and survival; some have developed through eons of evolution, and some are acquired through exploration and experience. Thus if the infant instinctively values food, warmth and contact with other people (for example), this will direct its first movements and strivings. These "values"—drives, instincts, intentionalities—serve to differentially weight experience, to orient the organism toward survival and adaptation, to allow what Edelman calls "categorization on value," e.g., to form categories such as "edible" and "non-edible" as parts of the process of getting food. It needs to be stressed that "values" are experienced internally as feelings. ... At a more elementary physiological level there are various sensory and motor "givens," from the reflexes that automatically occur (e.g., in response to pain) to innate mechanisms in the brain, as, for example, the feature detectors in the visual cortex that, as soon as they are activated, detect such things as verticals, horizontals, and boundaries angles in the visual world. Thus, we have a certain amount of basic equipment, but in Edelman's view very little else is programmed or built in. It is up to the infant animal, given its elementary physiological capacities and given its inborn values, to create its own categories and to use them to make sense of, to construct a world—and it is not just a world that the infant constructs, but its own world, a world constituted from the first by personal meaning and reference.
>
> Daniel Stern (1985) in describing an "emergent self" notes [how infants] "have distinct biases or preferences with regard to the sensations they seek. ... These are innate. From birth on, there appears to be a central tendency to form and test hypotheses about what is occurring in the world ... [to] categorize into ... patterns, events, sets, and experiences" (p. 44).

Edelman (1992) adds, "Brains contain multiple maps interacting without any supervisors and yet bring unity and cohesiveness to perceptual scenes" (p. 69), and "...the ability to carry out categorization is embodied in the nervous system" (p. 87). In other words, genetically based features of the brain include the capability and powerful propensity to categorize information as well as to create unity and cohesiveness, qualities of a self-organizing system. Edelman's theory delimits from a neuroanatomical perspective biological givens in brain function that influence the formation of an individual within a relational systems world.

DEVELOPMENTAL MOTIVATION AND DEVELOPMENTAL DIRECTION

For the self-theorists Carl Jung, Donald Winnicott, and Heinz Kohut, a fundamental motivation to grow or develop, along with a developmental direction or trajectory, is inherent in every individual. More recently, a fundamental striving to develop is viewed as an overriding motivation by Lichtenberg (1989) and Lichtenberg et al. (1992, 1996, 2003) and corresponds with the notions of "destiny drive" (Bollas, 1989), effectance (Greenberg, 1991), and "expansion of function" (Ghent, 2002). Bollas's "personal idiom" is similar to the concept of developmental direction.

The concepts of developmental motivation and direction offer considerable clinical utility. Picking up on the "forward edge" of the patient's articulations (Miller, 1985; Tolpin, 2002; Lachmann, 2008), allying with the patient's strivings to grow has proven clinically to enhance a patient's sense of agency and efforts to grow. While self psychologists theoretically and clinically posit and use a developmental motivational model, expositions based in systems theory, however, rarely address it directly.

Emanating from recent contributions of neuroscience, infant research, cognitive science, and nonlinear dynamic systems theory, we are in a better position to note some of the biological givens that the baby brings into his or her systems world. On the basis of these contributions I update and redefine the concepts of developmental motivation and direction in an effort to delineate the interaction of biological givens and experience in development of an individual within a systems world.

On a micro level, Edelman's hard-wired "values" or "biases" differentially weight and categorize experience in keeping with adaptation and survival requirements. In addition to adaptation and survival requirements, it is likely that a host of endogenous and exogenous factors contribute to the shifting priority of these "values." These "values" refer to innate preferences, "tendencies to seek (act) and guides for such actions" (Lichtenberg, 2002). For example, Sander's (1977, 1980) observation that during an "open space" when physiological requirements are satisfied the infant will spontaneously explore the environment suggests an innate preference for exploration (the exploratory/assertive motivational system discussed in Lichtenberg, 1989). I suggest that *the shifting priorities and strengths of motivational values or preferences substantially contribute on a moment-*

to-moment basis to an individual's developmental direction. I propose the term *developmental* for each momentary actualization of intention or motivational preference contributes incrementally to a sense of agency, vitality, and increasingly complex levels of self-organization. Intentions involve a wide range of preferences, including exploration/assertion (curiosity/mastery), attachment intimacy, aggression to fortify protection, caregiving, sexual intimacy, and physiological regulation. *By developmental motivation I am referring to an inherent tendency in human beings to grow or develop, meaning to expand in function, to self-organize with increasing complexity in keeping with basic and evolving motivational values or preferences.* While exploratory activities can easily be viewed as expanding in function, similarly moments of withdrawal for self-regulatory purposes, sleep for physiological regulation, or aggressive bolstering of assertion, when successful, also enhance a sense of agency and vitality.

When motivational values are thwarted, a motivational thrust (also called resilience; see DiAmbrosio, 2006, 2007; Fajardo, 1991) to overcome or to expand kicks in. Borrowing from Waddington's (1947) study of biological systems, Lichtenberg et al. (1992, 1996, 2003) use the term *self-righting* to indicate an inherent tendency within living organisms to rebound and continue their direction when obstacles are removed or overcome. A good example is Stechler's (1987) description of a 14-month-old child, Jane, assertively moving a push toy along slowly and then more forcefully when seeing 8-month-old Laura in front of her as a potential obstacle. Appraising the situation, a caretaker creatively suggests to Jane to shift the push toy to the other hand to create open space on her right side to move around Laura. As Jane does so, she starts to push the toy with increasing vigor. "Her facial expression becomes more joyfully excited. Finally she stands up and walks the toy across the room, pleasantly vocalizing" (p. 348). Stechler views the child as initially asserting her preferences, feeling potentially thwarted, which activates aggression, and then joyfully returning to asserting her preferences as the obstacle was, in this instance, overcome by the caretaker.

An example of shifting motivational priorities during a 20-year lifespan, involves my patient, a woman of 47 years, who begins psychoanalytic treatment with a clear intention and intense desire to break out of a previously accepted, now constricting orthodox Jewish wife role and to develop more fully her talents and skills in a musical career. Previously her primary intention to marry and have children, corresponding with her husband's desires, took precedence and her motivational "value" for singing and her career in music receded in importance. Their orthodox Jewish culture and community (systems) strongly sanctioned the stay-at-home wife and mother role. Now with her children close to "leaving the nest," her desire for her musical career reascended in priority. My patient's desire to resume her career, however, would require far more time outside of the home, intensely conflicting with her husband's wishes and her current role. While she struggled with guilt, she also rebelled against her husband's "controlling" ways and was turned off by his emotional inaccessibility. With great effort she finally proved successful in getting him to marital therapy, only to have him leave after three sessions, denigrating therapy as "baby stuff." She, however, is learning to articulate and express herself more fully. While it is unclear as to how she will negotiate her marriage, she is already pursuing her musical career.

As we listen carefully for implicit and explicit intentions within complex relational scenarios, a guiding beacon, as it has been with this patient, is when an emotional moment is sufficiently in keeping with an one's motivational value and direction, and that moment is experienced at a feeling level as authentic, profoundly right, in keeping with one's integrity, one's core, one's self.

To discuss these concepts further, I first turn to psychoanalytic self-theorists to assess how original psychoanalytic conceptualizations of self contain notions of developmental motivation and direction and, then, track its more recent emendations. I then turn to nonlinear dynamic systems theory itself to delineate specifically the contributions of systems theory that, perhaps surprisingly, offer support for the concepts of developmental direction and motivation as I have defined them.

CONCEPT OF SELF AND DEVELOPMENTAL MOTIVATION

The self-theorists Jung, Winnicott, and Kohut all view the self as having an intrinsic design and posit a primary motivation to develop or realize that design. Jung (1953, 1959) conceptualizes the self as the "unconscious organizing principle of personality" and posits a fundamental striving "to fulfill one's innate potentials." Winnicott (1965) conceptualizes the "true self," referring to the "'inherited potential' of a child that comprises the core of his personality" (Twyman, 2006, p. 473).

Kohut (1984) places at the center of psychological development the self striving "to realize" "its intrinsic program of action" within a "self-selfobject" matrix (p. 42). The "intrinsic program of action" refers to hard-wired factors, some of which are universal (e.g., mirroring, idealizing, twinship selfobject needs) and some of which are unique (e.g., talents). Development of the self, for Kohut, as for Jung and Winnicott, referred not to development of any self but to development of the self, that is, in keeping with an individual's unique intrinsic design. For Kohut, striving "to realize" the self is primary, a developmental motivational model. Interestingly both Jung and later Kohut suggested that the self was far too new a concept to attempt to be more definitive.

Recognition and emphasis of the formative power of relational fields offered a fundamental counterpoint to Jung's, Winnicott's, and Kohut's intrinsic developmental direction and motivation inherent in the concept of self. Mitchell (1988) created the term *multiple selves* to accent how different we are in different relational fields. Simultaneously, a general phenomenological movement was underfoot to counter the abstract intrapsychic metapsychology that had been so much a part of classical psychoanalysis and ego psychology. In self psychology, we have replaced the more difficult-to-define concept of self with a more phenomenologically based "sense of self." While self psychologists have retained the motivational model of developmental strivings, our focus has changed from the development of Kohut's conception of self with its intrinsic program of action to the development and maintenance of a "positive cohesive sense of self." While the term *sense of self* is experientially accessible, it also bypasses the issue of hard-wired features.

CONTRIBUTIONS OF SYSTEMS THEORY

Within sciences at large and psychoanalysis specifically, nonlinear dynamic systems theory, through its empirical focus on process, explains the emergence of new organizations and new properties. A nonlinear dynamic system refers to independent and interdependent elements that over time mutually influence and transform each other in a relatively unpredictable fashion. An inherent property of any system—and this is what I wish to emphasize—is that it becomes self-organizing; that is, it establishes patterns that, in turn, become the more predictable features of the system. This property to self-organize is inherent within each individual and between them.

In their classic text, the developmental psychologists Thelen and Smith (1994) use dynamic systems theory to explain development of cognition and behavior. They found that the interactive processes of a system are typically too complex to differentiate constitutional and environmental constituents. Yet Thelen and Smith also reported that what previously may have appeared as an innate feature of cognitive development they, when looking more closely at the process, discovered previously unseen elements or precursors in the baby that are subsequently transformed into an emergent property of the system. For example, in contrast to Piaget's theoretical claims of (1) an impoverished beginning state, (2) global discontinuities in cognition across states, and (3) monolithic cognitive growth, with greater magnification the data show that the beginning state is not impoverished but that the human infant possesses highly structured perceptual and conceptual skills. Where Piaget indicates that representations are discontinuous across stages, there is evidence of precursors to mature thought that can be detected early in life. For example, "infants show elements of abstract numerical thought, a complex naïve physics, and 'theories' of causality. There is a common core, a continuity, in the thinking of babies and adults" (Thelen & Smith, 1994, p. 22). Thus, in contrast to a notion of phasic maturation of an organism, when looking microscopically at interactive processes, they observed previously unseen elements that show a continuity in thinking, precursors of cognitive development that interact in the system in a nonlinear, unpredictable fashion as development moves along.

Thelen and Smith (1994) describe what development looks like from two different perspectives: the "view from above" and the "view from below." First, the view from above:

> Over the broad sweep of time, the most global quality of developing organisms is that they go from being small and simple to being bigger and more complex. By complexity, we mean simply an increase in the number of different parts and activities, and relations among them. Development is linear and quantitative, as growth is always incremental. At the same time, development is also nonlinear and qualitative, since complexity invokes new forms and abilities. (p. xvi)

Note that the property of increasing complexity is inherent in all developing organisms. Thelen and Smith (1994) add:

> There is a remarkable orderliness to this process...We can describe quite precisely the behavioral and physiological repertoire of the human newborn and predict with great certainty that all intact humans will walk, speak the language of their culture, form social relationships, reach reproductive maturity, and engage in certain mental operations... The sweep of development is more than just orderly, it is progressive or directional. (p. xiv)

The view from above that development is inherently "progressive or directional" corresponds with observations within the psychoanalytic arena where development appears from "the view from above" to be inherently directional and motivated.

When viewing development from below (or at a local level), however, the description changes:

> The grand sweep of development seems neatly rule-driven. In detail, however, development is messy. ... What looks like a cohesive, orchestrated process from afar takes on the flavor of a more exploratory, opportunistic, syncretic and function-driven process in its instantiation. ... The paradox is that the organism moves along as an adapted, integrated whole as the component structures and processes change

in fits and starts....The boundaries of progressive stages are equally blurred by seeming regressions in performance and losses of well-established behaviors. (Thelen & Smith, 1994, pp. xvi–xvii)

This appears to be a strikingly apt description of psychoanalytic treatment from a process (view from below) perspective. The point I wish to emphasize is that from a longitudinal perspective (view from above) the overall progressive direction of development becomes apparent. Development can occur, however, only in a moment-to-moment process level that is fluid and messy with fits and starts and changing contexts and not in accordance with a grand plan. "The primary thrust of development" according to Thelen and Smith, "is the generation of novel structure and behavior" (p. xvii). I suggest that this "primary thrust of development" supports what we have come to recognize clinically as developmental motivation and direction.

GENETIC FEATURES

In explaining cognitive and behavioral development, Thelen and Smith (1994) suggest that systems theory transcends the nature/nurture controversy in that interactive processes of a system are too complex to differentiate constitutional and environmental constituents. Yet in their last chapter they, too, address genetic factors:

Infants come into the world with a rich set of adaptive biases, epigenetically acquired, but having strong selective value. These surely include the motivation to suck and seek nourishment, motivation for contact and warmth, preferences for certain moderate levels of sensory stimulation and preferred dynamics. ... The basic wiring of the brain, Edelman's primary repertoire, strongly implicates a value component in all processes of learning and memory. ... Tendencies to do one activity over another can be conceptualized as forces driving behavior toward attractors, the strength of the attractor indicating the strength of the particular motivational valence associated with the stimulus or task space. (p. 316)

Shane et al. (1998) describe a conversation with Edelman and Tononi that occurred in 1995:

It is not yet known how simple or complex these values are in the neonate or how predictably these values progress into motivational systems. It is known is that the values include a repertoire of 100 inborn reflexes, including such value-based behavior as rooting, sucking, startle, reaching, and grasping. [There may] be more complex values inherent in earliest life, including, for example, attachment per se, but that as of now, such inclusion of complexity in developmental theory is not possible. There is just not enough known about how values organize and reorganize neuronal nets and brain maps in the growing child. (p. 41)

These hard-wired motivational values are present at birth, and I suggest that their relative strengths contribute to the development of individuality. This is part of what a newborn, already an individual, if you will, brings into relational systems.

CONCLUSION

The development of an individual person is a vastly complex, multivariable interactive process of constitutional factors and environment. While systems theory has further clarified that the interaction of elements is often too complex to be able to differentiate constitutional and environmental factors, I have argued that systems theory does not negate the hard-wired factors that each individual brings into the systems world.

In this chapter I have focused on genetic components of individual development and, more specifically, on the genetic factors inherent in the concepts of developmental motivation and developmental direction, two concepts that have profound clinical implications. In their concept of self, Jung, Winnicott, and Kohut posit innate potentials unique to each individual and a striving to develop or actualize those potentials, what I have termed *developmental direction* and *motivation*. On a micro level I have set forth that the shifting priorities of motivational "values" or preferences substantially contribute on a moment-to-moment basis to an individual's developmental direction. The shifting priorities are occurring within and influenced by ongoing self and interpersonal systems. While it is often difficult clinically in the psychoanalytic arena to differentiate the various influences occurring within a patient, we attempt to do so. I have suggested that each momentary actualization of motivational preference contributes incrementally to sense of agency, vitality, and increasingly complex levels of self-organization. And, of course, there are often conflicts between motivational preferences. By developmental motivation I am referring to an inherent tendency in human beings to grow or develop, to expand in function, to self-organize with increasing complexity in keeping with motivational values or preferences.

I have argued that certain observations and generalizations emanating from systems theory as applied to cognitive and behavioral development support the psychoanalytic concepts of developmental motivation and direction: (1) an inherent property of every system is that it becomes self-organizing; (2) an inherent property of every system is that it becomes increasingly complex; (3) development viewed "from above" is "orderly" and "progressive or directional"; (4) development "viewed from below" is messy and nonlinear; and (5) the primary thrust of development is novel structure and behavior. In my view, these observations and generalizations support the same emanating from psychoanalytic work in which development appears to be inherently directional, motivated and messy.

Recognizing that developmental strivings carry the momentum of treatment enables us to foster a patient's creation of his or her unique developmental pathway (Fosshage, 2003) or, as Marian Tolpin (2002) aptly described it, to listen carefully for the "tendrils of forward edge strivings" (p. 169).

On a number of occasions I have found patients arrive at a psychological place that feels "right" and with a profound sense of conviction call it in their dreams or waking life their "destiny." I am reminded of a patient a number of years ago who had developed a successful medical career. She was a woman in her mid 50s, had a number of previous analyses, and came into treatment with me by phone since she lived in another country. She began treatment with a sense of being thwarted and "unfulfilled." Fairly soon, she began thinking of her aborted career as a ballet dancer. She had been a serious, very gifted dancer who was dancing in her national ballet. All of a sudden, at the age of 19, she precipitously stopped dancing, never to return. She later recognized that her mother's incessant pressure had "killed her desire for dancing." Now, in the afternoon of her life, she began thinking about dancing, imagining it more and more frequently. One day she announced to me that she was going to begin choreographing. She felt that it was her "destiny." She later established a ballet company, in addition to her medical career, and became "happier" and "more fulfilled than ever before."

My patient's rediscovery of a sequestered set of motivations were now no longer encumbered in a battle with her mother. She, in turn, was able creatively to actualize her intentions and aims, actualization that felt "right" in the core of her being and enhanced her sense of agency and vitality. These intentions provided a developmental direction and a developmental motivational thrust to achieve her aims. Listening carefully for implicit and explicit intentions within the psychoanalytic encounter serve as a guiding beacon for the developmental motivation and direction of our patients, enhancing our ability to foster the their unique individuality.

REFERENCES

Anthony, E. J. (1987). Risk, vulnerability and resilience: An overview. In J. Anthony & B. Kohler (Eds.), *The invulnerable child* (pp. 3–48). New York: Guilford.

Beebe, B., & Lachmann, F. (2002). *Infant research and adult treatment*. Hillsdale, NJ: Analytic Press.

Bollas, C. (1989). *Forces of destiny: Psychoanalysis and human idiom*. London: Free Association Books.

Boston Change Process Group. *Forms of relational meaning: Issues in the relations between the implicit and reflective–verbal domains, 18, 2*, 125–148.

Bowlby, J. (1969). *Attachment*. New York: Basic Books.

Bowlby, J. (1973). *Separation*. New York: Basic Books.

Bowlby, J. (1988). *A secure base*. New York: Basic Books.

Bowlby, J. (1989). *Loss*. New York: Basic Books.

Bruner, J. S. (1986). *Actual minds, possible worlds*. Cambridge, MA: Harvard University Press.

Bruner, J. S. (1990). *Acts of meaning*. New York: Basic Books.

Bruner, J. (2002). *Making stories: Law, literature, life*. New York: Farrar Strauss.

Bucci, W. (1985). Dual coding: A cognitive model for psychoanalytic research. *Journal of the American Psychoanalytic Association, 33,* 571–607.

Bucci, W. (1997). *Psychoanalysis and cognitive science: A multiple code theory*. New York: Guilford Press.

Chomsky, N. (1968). *Language and mind*. New York: Harcourt, Brace and World.

Chomsky, N. (1995). *The minimalist program*. Cambridge, MA: MIT Press.

Coburn, W. (2002). A world of systems: The role of systemic patterns of experience in the therapeutic process. *Psychoanalytic Inquiry, 22,* 655–677.

DiAmbrosio, P. (2006). Weeble wobbles: Resilience within the psychoanalytic situation. *International Journal of Psychoanalytic Self Psychology, 1,* 263–284.

DiAmbrosio, P. (2007). "Wobbly weebles" and resilience: Some additional thoughts, response to William J. Coburn. *International Journal of Psychoanalytic Self Psychology, 2*(4), 475–481.

Edelman, G. M. (1987). *Neural Darwinism*. New York: Basic Books.

Edelman, G. M. (1989). *The remembered present: A biological theory of consciousness*. New York: Basic Books.

Edelman, G. M. (1992). *Bright air, brilliant fire: On the matter of the mind*. New York: Basic Books.

Emde, R. N. (1988). Development terminable and interminable: 1. Innate and motivational factors from infancy. *International Journal of Psychoanalysis, 69,* 23–42.

Fajardo, B. (1991). Analyzability and resilience in development. In J. Winer (Ed.), *The annual of psychoanalysis, vol. 19* (pp. 107–126). Hillsdale, NJ: Analytic Press.

Fosshage, J. (1983). The psychological function of dreams: A revised psychoanalytic perspective. *Psychoanalysis and Contemporary Thought, 6*(4), 641–669.

Fosshage, J. (1997). The organizing functions of dreams. *Contemporary Psychoanalysis, 33*(3), 429–458.

Fosshage, J. (2003). Contextualizing self psychology and relational psychoanalysis: Bi-directional influence and proposed syntheses. *Contemporary Psychoanalysis, 39*(3), 411–448.

Freud, S. (1924). *The disollution of the Oedipus Complex. SE, 19,* 173–179.

Gentile, J. (1998). Listening for deep structure: Between a priori and the intersubjective. *Contemporary Psychoanalysis, 34*(1), 67–90.

Ghent, E. (2002). Wish, need, drive: Motive in the light of dynamic systems theory and Edelman's selectionist theory. *Psychoanalytic Dialogues, 12*(5), 763–808.

Greenberg, J. (1991). *Oedipus and beyond: A clinical theory.* Cambridge, MA: Harvard University Press.

Harris, A. (2005). *Gender as soft assembly.* Hillsdale, NJ: Analytic Press.

Jung, C. G. (1953). *Two essays on analytical psychology.* New York: Pantheon Books.

Jung, C.G. (1959). *The archetypes and the collective unconscious.* New York: Pantheon Books.

Kagan, J. (1971). *Change and continuity in infancy.* New York: Wiley.

Kagan, J. (1984). *The nature of the child.* New York: Basic Books.

Kohut, H. (1984). *How does analysis cure?* Chicago: University of Chicago Press.

Lachmann, F. (2008). *Transforming narcissism: Reflections on empathy, humor, and expectations.* New York: Analytic Press.

Lichtenberg, J. (1989). *Psychoanalysis and motivation.* Hillsdale, NJ: Analytic Press.

Lichtenberg, J. (2002). Values, consciousness and language. *Psychoanalytic Inquiry, 22*(5), 841–856.

Lichtenberg, J., Lachmann, F., & Fosshage J. (1992). *Self and motivational systems: Toward a theory of technique.* Hillsdale, NJ: Analytic Press.

Lichtenberg, J., Lachmann, F., & Fosshage, J. (1996). *The clinical exchange: Techniques derived from self and motivational systems.* Hillsdale, NJ: Analytic Press.

Lichtenberg, J., Lachmann, F., & Fosshage, J. (2003). *A spirit of inquiry: Communication in psychoanalysis.* Hillsdale, NJ: Analytic Press.

Lichtenberg, J., Lachmann, F., & Fosshage, J. (2010). *Psychoanalysis and motivation: A new look.* New York: Analytic Press.

Miller, J. (1985). How Kohut actually worked. In A. Goldberg (Ed.), *Progress in self psychology, vol. 1* (pp. 13–30). New York: Guilford Press.

Mitchell, S. (1988). *Relational concepts in psychoanalysis.* Cambridge, MA: Harvard University Press.

Ogden, T. (1986). *The matrix of the mind.* Northvale, NJ: Jason Aronson.

Paivio, A. (1971). *Imagery and verbal processes.* New York: Holt, Rinehart & Winston.

Paivio, A. (1986). *Mental representations: A dual coding approach.* New York: Oxford Universities Press.

Paivio, A. (2007). *Mind and its evolution: A dual coding theoretical approach.* Mahwah, NJ: Lawrence Erlbaum Associates.

Pinker, S. (1994). *The language instinct: How the mind creates language.* New York: William Morrow and Co.

Pinker, S. (2002). *The blank slate: The modern denial of human nature.* New York: Viking.

Sacks, O. (1993, 8 April). Making up the mind. *New York Review of Books, 40,* 42–52.

Sander, L. (1977). The regulation of exchange in the infant-caretaker system and some aspects of the context-content relationship. In M. Lewis & L. Rosenblum (Eds.), *Interaction, conversation, and the development of language* (pp. 315–327). New York: Basic Books.

Sander, L. (1980). Investigation of the infant and its caregiving environment as a biological system. In S. I. Greenspan & G. Pollack (Eds.), *Infancy and early childhood* (pp. 177–202). Washington, DC: Department of Health and Human Services.

Shane, M., Shane, E., & Gales, M. (1998). *Intimate attachments: Toward a new self psychology.* New York: Guilford Press.

Siegel, D. (1999). *The developing mind: Toward a neurobiology of interpersonal experience*. New York: Guilford Press.

Slavin, M., & Kriegman, D. (1992). *The adaptive design of the human psyche*. New York: Guilford Press.

Stechler, G. (1987). Clinical applications of a psychoanalytic systems model of assertion and aggression. *Psychoanalytic Inquiry, 7*, 348–363.

Stern, D. N. (1983). The early development of schemas of self, other, and "self with other." In J. Lichtenberg & S. Kaplan (Eds.), *Reflections on self psychology* (pp. 49–84). Hillsdale, NJ: Analytic Press.

Stern, D. N. (1985). *The interpersonal world of the infant*. New York: Basic Books.

Stern, D. N., Sander, L., Nahum, J., Harrison, A., Lyons-Ruth, K., Morgan, A., et al. (1998). Non-interpretive mechanisms in psychoanalytic therapy: The "something more" than interpretation. *International Journal of Psychoanalysis, 79*, 903–921.

Stolorow, R. (1997). Dynamic, dyadic, intersubjective systems: An evolving paradigm for psychoanalysis. *Psychoanalytic Psychology, 14*, 337–346.

Teicholz, J. (1999). *Kohut, Loewald, and the postmoderns*. Hillsdale, NJ: Analytic Press.

Thelen, E., & Smith, L. (1994). *A dynamic systems approach to the development of cognition and action*. Cambridge, MA: MIT Press.

Thomas, A., & Chess. S. (1977). *Temperament and development*. New York: Brunner/Mazel.

Thomas, A., & Chess, S. (1980). *The dynamics of psychological development*. New York: Brunner/Mazel.

Tolpin, M. (2002). Doing psychoanalysis of normal development: Forward edge transferences. In A. Goldberg (Ed.), *Progress in self psychology, vol. 18* (pp. 167–190). New York: Guilford Press.

Twyman, M. (2006). True self. In R. M. Skelton (Ed.), *The Edinburgh international encyclopedia of psychoanalysis* (p. 473). Edinburgh: Edinburgh University Press.

Waddington, C. (1947). *Organizers and genes*. Cambridge, UK: University Press.

Winnicott, D. W. (1965). *The maturational processes and the facilitating environment: Studies in the theory of emotional development*. New York: International Universities Press.

Chapter 7

Perspectives on individuality

From cells to selves

Frank M. Lachmann

INTRODUCTION

As psychoanalysis moved from a one-person drive model to a two-person interactive model, it increasingly emphasized connection with others, attachment, and, specifically in self psychology, the selfobject milieu. These shifts have been spearheaded by a multitude of clinicians (e.g., Beebe, Knoblauch, Rustin, & Sorter, 2005; Beebe & Lachmann, 2002; Greenberg & Mitchell, 1983; Stolorow, Brandchaft, & Atwood, 1987). Absent from these discussions have been a recognition and articulation of the patient's unique individuality—that is, what the patient brings to the encounter that is uniquely his or her own. As a result, the unique contributions of both the patient and the analyst have been subsumed within the interactive matrix. In addition, the patient's heredity, family, and culture are sometimes conflated with psychopathology rather than an articulation of individuality. This chapter will argue that we need to capture and address explicitly a person's uniqueness in addition to what has been interactively organized, or "cocreated." This is not an argument against the importance of "cocreation" but rather an attempt to redress an imbalance that has crept into our theorizing and clinical practice. We need to pay equal attention to what the patient brings as his or her own and not solely to what is cocreated in the analytic situation.

Recent psychoanalytic developmental theory has sought to bridge individuation and attachment and provides a model for thinking about individuality. When Karlen Lyons-Ruth (1991) reviewed Margaret Mahler's films of the separation-individuation developmental phase, she found evidence to rename that phase attachment-individuation. She thereby emphasized the qualities of attachment that visibly remain with the child and are essential to the individuation process. Fonagy, Gergely, Jurist, and Target (2002), in spelling out the benefits of mentalizing, emphasize how the child "... can fit his thinking to the world without feeling he has to change himself in order to change his mind [thereby] losing continuity with the self that thought before" (p. 264). Furthermore, Fonagy et al. argue that, as people's actions become predictable, moment-to-moment dependency on others is reduced. These are "important component(s) in the process of individuation" (p. 264).

When the contributions of Lyons-Ruth (1991) and Fonagy et al. (2002) are linked together, the process of individuation can be seen as a forerunner and contributor to the development of individuality. Lyons-Ruth recognizes that individuation remains embedded in an evolving attachment process. Fonagy et al. add that, in the process of recognizing one's mental life as one's own and of manipulating one's thoughts on one's own, the person relies less and less on concrete "lived" attachments in the moment. Individuation in the context of attachments, rather than separation, contributes to one's unique individuality. To redress the imbalance and to restore individuality as an equal partner with "cocreation" in clinical theory, I will focus on the shaping of our unique individuality in the development of the sense of self.

Humans live, and in fact can survive only in a world that contains caring and nurturing others and that fulfills the requirements essential for life, such as oxygen. However, the place occupied by these necessary life supports varies. It ranges from a silent background to an essential, noisy participation in our growth and survival. For example, for most of us the oxygen in the air is sufficient, and we breathe it silently. But for those with congestive heart failure or other diseases, dragging around a portable supply of oxygen is essential for breathing and staying alive. For Kohut (1981) the "empathic human milieu" is as essential for our survival in infancy as is the oxygen in our environment. For adults, this empathic milieu at times can be a critical foreground presence and at other times an unobtrusive background presence; both are necessary but not sufficient for our unique individuality to flourish.

I maintain that the development of individuality can be examined from four different perspectives: (1) the cellular; (2) the organismic; (3) the self psychological; and (4) the clinical. To explicate these perspectives, I now focus on those instances in which the presence of a caring human surround is a necessary but not sufficient dyadic background and in which individuality is essentially "self-created."

THE CELLULAR

Biologists use the term *developmental noise* to describe a "random atomic jostling inside cells" (Lehrer, 2007, p. 50) in living organisms. This phenomenon can account for the fingerprints of the left hand being different from those of the right. Neurobiologist Fred Gage (cited in Lehrer) refers to such developmental noise as "junk genes," and they are present in unusually high numbers in neurons. In fact he states that these "troublemaking scraps of DNA insert themselves into almost 80% of our brain cells, arbitrarily altering their genetic program" (p. 50). Gage puzzled over the finding that our brain would be engaged in arbitrary and conceivably self-destructive activity, such as altering our genetic program. These junk genes defy heredity. But then Gage proposed a rather cheerful solution: "All these genetic interruptions created a population of perfectly unique minds, since each brain reacted to these junk genes in its own way" (p. 50). Furthermore, he asserts that "chaos creates individuality" (p. 50) in that we each pick and respond to similar facets of the world in unique ways. No other person would organize their choices or biases—their experience—in exactly the same way. As an example, think of a salad bar; there are only a finite number of dishes on the counter from which to choose. But notice that as diners walk away from the salad bar after they have taken their share, each plate is unique. It is filled with different choices, or even similar choices, but in different proportions. And the salad on each plate is arranged differently. Based on the random jostling of junk genes and elaborated in myriad ways, no two plates are alike.

Context and what is contextualized are interchangeable; each can function as a context for the other. At the rudimentary level of junk genes and DNA, both coexist from the start. And so we begin life at our core as randomly, chaotically, and hence, uniquely created individuals. Of course our unique brains cannot survive in isolation. A dialectic is established between unique individuality and a survival that relies on giving care to others. This context of caregivers will be a background presence for individuality to emerge as well as an organizing presence in its own right. Here is where individuality and complexity theory join forces (see Coburn, 2007). Individuality prizes a degree of stability, and complexity theory prizes fluidity. This dialectic operates on several different levels within each person and in interactions with others. It not only applies to the relation between stability and fluidity but also opens up a range between these two. It thus affords possibilities for innovation, diversity, creativity, novelty, and change. Most important, however, is the recognition of the necessity for both stability or structure and continuity. Think again of the plate on which that salad is carried. Without it, we would be dripping salad dressing all over ourselves. We need the plate to sustain our unique choices. That is, our unique choices are derived from a finite number of opportunities and must be organized in a recognizable way and sustained over time. Continuity, self-sameness, and structure, defined by Rapaport (1960) as a slowly changing process, are a property of the empathic, human milieu, as well as of the individual.

THE ORGANISMIC

Moving from the cellular to the organismic level, I turn to the contributions of developmentalist and systems thinker Louis Sander (2002). He not only recognizes dyadic, interactive, or intersubjective systems but also holds that the self is a living system. Like any other system, the self is self-organizing, self-regulating, and self-correcting within its environment. These three "self" activities—organizing, regulating, and correcting—contribute to the unique agency of the individual. Furthermore, Sander argues that striving toward a coherent sense of self as agent draws on, and thereby integrates, the biological and developmental levels. Here the contributions of Gage at the cellular level join forces with Sander. Uniqueness and agency are undisputed properties of the individual, affected by context but possessing fluidity, continuity, and stability.

Self-stability is maintained, on a procedural level, through a system of dynamic equilibrium. In the principle of equilibrium, biological structures of the person balance opposing tensions. For example, opposing tensions might serve, on one side, to widen one's options in the service of opening the system and, on the other side, to narrow one's options in the service of sharpening the focus. Interplay of these counteracting forces is required to maintain coherence in one's sense of identity. This balance creates an equilibrium that maintains a coherent sense of the self as agent within the context of life support.

According to Sander (2002), self-assembly, a dimension of the self-organizing system that contributes to the uniqueness of the individual, is promoted by two principles. They are "matched specificity" and "rhythmicity." Matched specificity refers to the uncanny coordination between, for example, a baby and its caregivers, whereby the split-second nonconscious (procedural) actions of the caregiver dovetail exquisitely with movements and requirements of the infant. This nonconscious coordination of the two partners can lead the fussy infant to calm down and go to sleep. Fast forward now to adult psychotherapy, where therapist and patient can access and articulate to themselves and to each other, these nonconscious, implicit interactions. Ed Tronick (Tronick et al., 1998) refers to this process as the dyadic expansion of consciousness. In this process, each partner implicitly expands his or her own organization or self-awareness. For each partner, a sense of self-coherence increases, and each partner gets to know himself or herself better as well. That is, the dyadic, interactive, or intersubjective processes that further the self-organization of each partner increase self-coherence, and simultaneously the expanded self-organization expands the dyadic organization.

The second principle articulated by Sander (2002) is rhythmicity. Self-assembly, both stable and resilient, is also "held together" by the entrainment and synchrony of biological rhythms. Sander contrasts two feeding schedules in neonates and shows that they influence the infant's sleep–wake cycle. In one schedule, infants are fed on demand, whereby the caregiver responds to cues from the baby. In the other, infants are fed by the clock. On-demand feeding establishes the sleep–wake cycle more rapidly than by-the-clock feeding, illustrating the power of rhythmicity, specifically when the infant's innate rhythmic cycle is matched by the caregiver. Through rhythmicity, self-organizing components, distinct from each other, can reach a coherence or unity within the organism.

So far I have argued that given an adequate regulating surround, individuality begins at the cellular level and builds toward a unique self-organization. Using the contributions that Fonagy et al. (2002), Tronick et al. (1998), and Sander (2002) have drawn from studies of early development within a systems sensibility, I have described the acquisition of a self that is agentic. It is self-organizing, self-regulating, self-correcting, and mentalizing in the context of the interactive surround. A sense of self is the end product. My 3-year-old grandson's toilet activities illustrate this process. First he became aware of bodily sensations. These sensations were organized and connected to behavioral and verbal signals. Self-regulation then required a balancing act: recognition of his need to use the toilet, fascination with the game he had been playing, interruption of his fun to go to the toilet. At first he withheld to continue to play. His preference not to be bothered to use the toilet was balanced by his parents' admonitions and his awareness of his own and his parents' subsequent greater comfort when he used the toilet. Correcting for misjudgments in time and place, he eventually used the toilet. Once that had been achieved, there is a sense of success as agent when he proudly displays his accomplishment to his parents. These self-organizing, self-regulating, self-correcting, and mentalizing activities occurred in the context of the interactive surround, his parents. They also occurred on a procedural level, and implicitly an agentic sense of self develops.

Sander (2002) proposes that the brain's integrative capacity provides the bridge that connects biological, developmental, and psychological levels. Indeed, the integration among these levels takes place during the process of interaction and exchanges between the infant or child and its caregivers. At the same time, it occurs through self-organizing processes. The transition from the biological to the psychological level is promoted through the infant's acquisition of social expectancies. For example, infants learn this-is-how-things-go-when-I-am-put-to bed through the mutual, reciprocal adaptation of infant and caregiver. Again, rhythmicity or recurrence, for example, the cycle of the neonate going to sleep every few hours, plays a powerful role in shaping social expectancies. These expectancies, available in the first year of life, can be considered a "prelanguage" and evolve into "ways of being with the other" (Stern, 1985) and into implicit relational knowing (Lyons-Ruth, 1999).

Expectancies and adaptations are negotiated in interaction between infant and caregiver and play a crucial role in the self-organization of the infant and child (Beebe & Lachmann, 2002; Bretherton & Beeghly, 1982; Butterworth, 1990; Sander, 1995). A study by Singer and Fagan (1992) demonstrates the connection between expectations leading to the detection of contingencies and achieving a sense of agency. These researchers studied 2-month-old infants by tying a ribbon to their leg and tying the other end of the ribbon to a mobile. The infants learned that by kicking their leg they moved the mobile. In this phase of the study, infants were found to detect contingencies between what they did and what the environment did immediately following their actions. The infants thus discovered that they could cause the mobile to move. Moreover, the infants' repeated use of this contingency and the obvious pleasure they took in it show that it had an affective meaning for them. In the second phase of the study, the ribbon was disconnected, and the infants reacted with surprise and distress when their kicking failed to bring about the expected response from the mobile. The researchers concluded that detection of the contingency between kicking and the mobile moving facilitates the infants' development of a sense of agency or efficacy.

Expectancies develop through ongoing regulations between infant and caretaker "from birth and even before" (Beebe & Lachmann, 2002, p. 151). The development of expectancies exercises an enormous influence on organizing experience, including self-regulation. Finding the world to be contingent, that is, predictable and affectively responsive, accrues to initiative and self-assertion as well as to patterns of interactive regulation. Such patterns include the acquisition of language whereby the developing 2-year old can express perceptions of his or her state, intentions, and thought content. All of these shape individuality or, in Kohut's terms, the self as an active and unique organizer of experience (1971).

THE SELF PSYCHOLOGICAL

I now add a self psychological vantage point to the "organismic" level. In 1968, Heinz Kohut published a paper on the treatment of narcissistic disorders with the subtitle "An outline to a systematic approach." A wealth of literature was inspired by this outline. The next generation of self psychologists placed Kohut's "self" into a dyadic, intersubjective system. No self is an island, it was argued. But that's not entirely true. Living on, or being an island, can ensure one's self-delineation, offer a sanctuary from certain pressures of social living, and, most importantly, reinforce one's distinction from those who live on the "mainland." Coming from a slightly different perspective, Sander (1977) identified this necessary dimension of experience of "open spaces" in the infant's day. These are times when the infant has been nourished and lies on its back, happily and content, examining or playing with his fingers. Sander holds that these open spaces are the beginnings of creativity. Here we find an overlap between creativity and individuality, a topic to which I will soon return.

As I have been arguing, in the emphasis placed on our connection with others, on our attachments, and on the selfobject milieu, we have lost sight of the centrality of the *sense* of self. Goldberg (2008) refers to self psychology as a one-person psychology. He thereby reverts to Kohut's (1971) definition of the self as a "place," as an independent center of initiative and perception, regulating psychic equilibrium. From this perspective, through empathic immersion, the analyst's individuality is suspended, and a sharp focus is directed toward the patient's "self." Subsequently, over the years not only the patient's but also the analyst's individuality, and the bidirectional impact of patient and analyst, received increasing attention. In this shift, however, we have lost sight of the power of self-organizing processes beginning with the contribution of those junk genes and their noisy role in shaping our unique individuality.

Recognition and emphasis on intersubjectivity, connections, the dyad, or organizing systems was never intended to replace, ignore, or diminish the development of individuality. Somehow, however, the enthusiasm with which these perspectives have been taken up, and the widened horizons they afforded the self psychological clinician, may have dwarfed our appreciation of the individual, apart from the dyad. Attention was drawn away from the striving of a "self" toward integration, in favor of a striving for attachments and connections with others.

Kohut's contributions with respect to the "self" had enormous clinical implications. However, while expanding our horizons in one direction, they foreclosed on some flexibility in the other direction. In the heyday of the psychoanalytic adventuresomeness of the 1940s, '50s, and '60s, the goal of psychoanalytic treatment was to push analysands toward new frontiers of autonomy, individualism, even rugged individualism, and independence, as exemplified in the work of Edith Jacobson (1964). This spirit has been diluted. A spirit of relationality (Greenberg & Mitchell, 1983; Mitchell, 2000) replaced the sense of our standing alone by and as our selves. But in making this shift we may have neglected our potential for self-organization, self-transformation, and self-regulation of affect and arousal in maintaining self-cohesion, self-continuity, and positive self-regard (Stolorow & Lachmann, 1980). We can replace the lost individuality implicit in the individualism that we promoted in the analytic literature of the mid 20th century with a respect and recognition of our capacity to self-transform.

Previously I (Lachmann, 2008) described Igor Stravinsky, as he was observed sitting at his piano composing *The Rite of Spring*, to illustrate the process of self-transformation. Stravinsky was described by an observer as appearing enthralled by the sounds he produced as he composed this piece at the piano. In turn, the now enthralled, self-transformed Stravinsky composed music as neither he, nor anyone, ever had before. Responding affectively to his playing created a feedback loop that constituted a process of continuous self-transformation.

Self-transformation in the case of Stravinsky is not an isolated or even uncommon occurrence. It is not only found among artists creatively composing or painting or sculpting. It is also found among physicists creatively theorizing. There are anecdotal reports of physicists (Wallace-Well, 2008) who leave their tenured university appointments and isolate themselves from their academic families and the cultural conventions of their profession. They retreat to an isolated farmhouse or a snow-bound cabin in the mountains of Colorado or a beach shack in Maui. After some years, they emerge with new, revolutionary, groundbreaking ideas that clarify what had been murky to other scientists for many years. I cannot claim that they completely disregarded the conventions they had been taught, or that they had no human contact during that time. But in relative isolation, they all thrived and produced new work in profoundly creative ways.

Gleick (2003) described the isolated, creative scientist in his biography of Isaac Newton. Mathematics, Newton's field, was well suited for someone who chose to live in isolation. Gleick noted, "When Newton got answers, he could usually judge whether they were right or wrong, no public disputation necessary" (p. 36). Newton grew up impoverished and neglected by his parents, a condition that did not alter much throughout his life. At age 23, he was elected a fellow at Trinity College where "chastity was expected, marriage forbidden" (p. 67), and one either took holy orders upon the completion of one's studies or resigned. Eventually Newton did resign, not because of these restrictions but because he disagreed with certain theological issues. Clearly, human contact, other than with the authorities in his fields of study, seemed to have been of little interest to Newton. He harbored an intense hatred for both of his parents who treated him shabbily. "Sometimes he wished his step-father dead, and his mother, too: in a rage he threatened to burn their house down over them. Sometimes he wished himself dead and knew the wish for sin" (p. 11). Certainly Newton was not a man devoid of passion, but what sustained him? At a young age he began to fill a thousand-page notebook with notes he took while reading whatever he could lay his hands on in the fields of mathematics and science. His notes "... mutated seamlessly into original research. He set himself problems, considered these obsessively; calculated answers, and asked new questions. He pushed past the frontiers of knowledge (though he did not know this). The plague year was his transformation. Solitary and almost incommunicado, he became the world's paramount mathematician" (p. 34).

In effect, Newton and other scientists probably carried away a few sustaining selfobjects from that salad bar. If nothing else, music for Stravinsky or mathematics for Newton may well have fulfilled selfobject functions, particularly in the area of affect regulation. At the very least, both music and mathematics are reliable, contingent "mirroring" responses. The inventiveness of these artists and scientists emerged after extraordinary intellectual and emotional efforts that were a product of their unique self-organization. Arguably such retreats are possible because a firmly internalized selfobject milieu had been previously established. At the same time, some of these extraordinary people were delusional, grandiose, and unable to tolerate other people. A firm self–selfobject matrix cannot account for their creativity and ingenuity. It seems more likely that their individuality required some degree of isolation from others to flourish. And what of the case of Isaac Newton? It appears to me that he was sustained by his driven obsessional curiosity and his passion to learn everything that could be learned, to search where others had not had the curiosity to search. Perhaps remaining unaware of the severe deprivations he tolerated throughout his life was self-sustaining. Other than his passion for his work, Newton did not need or desire more than a few professional contacts.

In discussing Stravinsky, Newton, and the physicists, it is important to acknowledge the distinction between individuality and creativity; in this chapter, I straddle the border between the two. Previously I (Lachmann, 2008) used an operational definition of creativity: creativity as the product (e.g., music, painting, laws of physics) that recognized, professionally acclaimed, creative artists produce. Individuality, on the other hand, is understood as the uniqueness of an individual's organization that enables the emergence of creative product in the first place. In turn, such product then loops back upon the individual and informs the further elaboration and expression of that person's individuality, that person's sense of self. In systems theory, this is referred to as *recurrency*. For many of these innovative individuals, their uniqueness was most apparent in their creative output.

THE CLINICAL

Participation in the psychoanalytic process shares similarities with creative, self-transformative processes. Analytic self psychologists attend faithfully to how they impact the patient and how the patient impacts on them. But we have neglected the process by which we impact ourselves and thereby self-transform. As a result of the attention paid to the transference of the patient and the countertransference of the analyst, we have become biased in the direction of emphasizing interactional influence. At best we may recognize how the patient or analyst behaved in a particular way that reflects a process of self-regulation. For example, we may know how the patient or analyst redress states of despair, emptiness, or anxiety by engaging in some self-enlivening behavior, such as speaking more or less, faster or slower. But the "leading edge" (Lachmann, 2008) here, as

Clement (2004) proposes, is the "patient's persistent search for the self-initiating agentic experience that exists within, or in dialectical relationship to, the development of the self within the dyad" (p. 65). Along similar lines, Beatrice Beebe and I (Beebe & Lachmann, 2002) have argued that "internalization" entails a reordering of one's inner or subjective world in tandem with transactions with one's environment.

There is a self-organization that is not only impacted but may accommodate, resist, or imaginatively elaborate the environment on which it has an impact. This unique self, with its multifaceted individuality, resides in a culture, a family, and in a dyad. When Kohut spoke of the self as a center of initiative and perception, he acknowledged a dimension of subjective experience that deserves equal analytic attention, alongside the dyadic, interactive, or intersubjective context in which the self resides (1971).

CONCLUSION

Creativity and individuality, in my view, share a common developmental trajectory. In the open space, the infant's needs for nurturance and caretaking are quiet, and the infant explores, for example, his or her hands, making shapes with them and moving them about. It is done for its own sake, and no two infants will do this in identical ways. The beginnings of creativity and an emergent individuality can both be located here. As development proceeds, creativity will bear the stamp of its creator. Further developments are promoted or inhibited within this biological, psychological, familial, and cultural context. To the extent that creativity is nurtured, rather than impeded by the context, it will flourish. At best it emerges as a unique product, a personal work of art, or an exquisite mathematical formula or law of physics. Similarly, as development proceeds, cellular, organismic, psychological, familial, and cultural processes will further or impede the organization of a unique individuality.

I have outlined the emergence of individuality from four different perspectives: (1) the cellular; (2) the organismic; (3) the self psychological; and (4) the clinical. Our basic structure at the cellular level already contains our uniqueness. And our individuality emerges from the human milieu in which we live. But although this milieu actively cocreates our individuality, it also provides a background, like the oxygen in the air. The picture of individuality and the individual, as posited here, simultaneously expands and delimits our continually burgeoning, contextualist, and systems perspectives. Whereas we may conceptualize the individual as relentlessly embedded in a larger relational, self–selfobject matrix, this embeddedness does not obviate that we are, in many respects, self-sustaining islands to which we retreat for longer or shorter stretches, to engage in self-transformation, invention, and creativity. And what we ourselves create thereby we may share with others—or perhaps not.

REFERENCES

Beebe, B., & Lachmann, F. M. (1994). Representations and internalizations in infancy: Three principles of salience. *Psychoanalytic Psychology, 11*, 127–165.

Beebe, B., & Lachmann, F. M. (2002). *Infant research and adult treatment: Coconstructing interactions.* Hillsdale, NJ: The Analytic Press.

Beebe, B., Knoblauch, S., Rustin, J., & Sorter, D. (2005). *Forms of intersubjectivity in infant research and adult treatment.* New York: Other Press

Bretherton, I., & Beeghly, M. (1982). Talking about internal states: The acquisition of an explicit theory of mind. *Developmental Psychology, 18*, 906–921

Butterworth, C. (1990). Self-perception in infancy. In D. Cicchette & M. Beeghly (Eds.), *The self in transition: From infancy to childhood* (pp. 119–137). Chicago: University of Chicago Press.

Clement, C. (2004). Self communication in the intersubjective field. *Psychoanalytic Dialogues, 14*, 65–72.

Coburn, W. (2007). Psychoanalytic complexity: Pouring new wine directly into one's mouth. In P. Buirski & A. Kottler (Eds.), *New developments in self psychology practice* (pp. 3–22). New York: Jason Aronson.

Fonagy, P., Gergely, G., Jurist, E., & Target, M. (2002). *Affect regulation, mentalization, and the development of the self.* New York: Other Press.

Gleick, J. (2003). *Isaac Newton.* New York: Vintage Books.

Goldberg, A. (2008). Boundary exegesis: Response to commentaries on "Some limits of the boundary concept." *Psychoanalytic Quarterly, 77*, 915–919.

Greenberg, J., & Mitchell, S. (1983). *Object relations in psychoanalytic theory.* Cambridge, MA: Harvard University Press.

Jacobson, E. (1964). *The self and the object world.* New York: International Universities Press.

Kohut, H. (1968). The psychoanalytic treatment of narcissistic personality disorders: Outline of a systematic approach. In P. Ornstein (Ed.), *The search for the self, vol. 1* (pp. 477–510). Madison, CT: International Universities Press.

Kohut, H. (1971). *The analysis of the self.* New York: International Universities Press.

Kohut, H. (1981). On empathy. In P. Ornstein (Ed.), *The search for the self, vol. 4* (pp. 525–536). Madison, CT: International Universities Press.

Lehrer, J. (2007). *Proust was a neuroscientist.* Boston: Houghton Mifflin Co.

Lachmann, F. M. (2008). *Transforming narcissism: Reflections on empathy, humor, and expectations.* New York: Analytic Press.

Lyons-Ruth, K. (1991). Rapprochement or approchement: Mahler's theory reconsidered from the vantage point of recent research on early attachment relationships. *Psychoanalytic Psychology, 8*, 1–21.

Lyons-Ruth, K. (1999). The two-person unconscious, intersubjective dialogue, enactive relational representations, and the emergence of new forms of relational organizations. *Psychoanalytic Inquiry, 19*, 576–617.

Mitchell, S. (1988). *Relational concepts in psychoanalysis*. Cambridge, MA: Harvard University Press.

Mitchell, S. (2002). *Relationality*. Hillsdale, NJ: The Analytic Press.

Rapaport, D. (1960). *The structure of psychoanalytic theory: A systematizing attempt*. Madison, CT: International Universities Press.

Sander, L. (1977). The regulation of exchange in the infant-caretaker system and some aspects of the context-content relationship. In M. Lewis & L. Rosenblum (Eds.), *Interaction, conversation, and the development of language* (pp. 133–156). New York: Wiley.

Sander, L. (1995). Identity and the experience of specificity in a process of recognition. *Psychoanalytic Dialogues, 5*, 579–594.

Sander, L. (2002). Thinking differently: Principles of process in living systems and the specificity of being known. *Psychoanalytic Dialogues, 12*, 11–42.

Singer, J., & Fagan, J. (1992). Negative affect, emotional expression, and forgetting in young infants. *Developmental Psychology, 28*, 48–57.

Stern, D. (1985). *The interpersonal world of the infant*. New York: Basic Books.

Stolorow, R., Brandchaft, B., & Atwood, G. (1987). *Psychoanalytic treatment: An intersubjective approach*. Hillsdale, NJ: Analytic Press

Stolorow, R., & Lachmann, F. (1980). *Psychoanalysis of developmental arrests*. New York: International Universities Press.

Tronick, E. Z., Bruschweiler-Stern, N., Harrison, A., Lyons-Ruth, K., Morgan, A. C., Nahum, J. P., et al. (1998). Dyadically expanded states of consciousness and the process of therapeutic change. *International Journal of Mental Health, 19*, 290–299.

Wallace-Wells, B. (2008, 21 July). Surfing the universe. *New Yorker*, pp. 32–38.

Part 4

Reflections on the challenges of individuality

Chapter 8

Recontextualizing individuality and therapeutic action in psychoanalysis and psychotherapy*

William J. Coburn

Theories of individualism and their attendant attitudes have increasingly given way to a variety of contextualist and systems sensibilities in psychology, psychoanalysis, and psychotherapy.[†] These attitudes invariably have shaped our ideas about what it means to be individual. As reflected in the introduction of this book, many questions and corresponding challenges for theorists and clinicians have emerged—above all, how to understand the role of the individual and of individuality given our increasing contemporary appreciation of the contextualized nature of emotional experience and the meaning-making process. The contributors to this book have each addressed potential solutions to these questions and challenges and, while doing so, imply, if not explicitly state, their respective views on therapeutic action in the treatment setting. Theoretical and clinical attitudes about individuality, about what it means to be human, and about the notions of dysfunction and psychopathology are inherently based on ideas about what heals and what constitutes therapeutic action in psychoanalysis and psychotherapy. This chapter thus investigates the salient contentions of each chapter and explores the corresponding implications for meaning making,

---

* I am deeply indebted to Roger Frie for his editorial insight, recommendations, and unwavering support in the revision of this chapter (and throughout the entire preparation of this book) and to Kristen Leishman for her editorial assistance throughout this project.

[†] For examples from complexity theory, see Bacal and Herzog (2003), Beebe and Lachmann (2001), Bonn (2006), Charles (2002), Coburn (2002), Dubois (2005), Galatzer-Levy (1978), Ghent (2002), Harris (2005), Lichtenberg, Lachmann, and Fosshage (1992), Magid (2002), Miller (1999), Moran (1991), Orange (2006), Palombo (1999), Pickles (2006), Piers (2005), Sander (2002), Sashin and Callahan (1990), Scharff (2000), Seligman (2005), Shane and Coburn (2002), Shane, Shane, and Gales (1997), Sperry (in press), Spruiell (1993), Steinberg (2006), Stolorow (1997), Sucharov (2002), Thelen (2005), Thelen and Smith (1994), Trop, Burke, and Trop (2002), VanDerHeide (2009), Varela, Thompson, and Rosch (1991), and Wiesel-Barth (2006).

therapeutic action, and, ultimately, a more contemporary, contextualist approach to clinical practice.

Understanding the contributors' cogent responses to the challenge of individuality hinges on an appreciation of the distinction between thinking and speaking *phenomenologically* (addressing the realm of lived experience) and thinking and speaking *explanatorily* (addressing the realm of theory and explanations presumed to account for emergent experience). Acknowledging and delineating each of these dimensions of discourse position us to appreciate more effectively our assumptions and attitudes about the ontology of the individual, the contextualization of the *experience* of individuality, and the consequent epistemological values that permeate the therapeutic milieu. Indeed, the contributors either allude to or address directly this distinction in elaborating their views on individuality, agency, relationship, development, and the meaning-making process.

Whereas the contributors all reject subjectivist conceptions of isolated individuality, they define and organize individuality and the idea of the individual rather differently. An array of useful, innovative perspectives on therapeutic action emerge throughout the course of the chapters, powerfully expanding our thinking on what is useful and transformative in the treatment setting. Thus, the contributors provide essential tools and perspectives with which to better grasp and appreciate how truly contextualized human beings are. In the process, they also leave us with more questions and more challenges.

I begin by briefly addressing the distinction between phenomenological and explanatory dimensions of discourse and then delineate the salient themes of each of the book's chapters. I highlight each contributor's approach to subverting and reorganizing traditional subjectivist conceptions of individuality. I then consider and elaborate the therapeutic implications of each author's perspective. My conclusion argues for the additional benefits of psychoanalytic complexity theory to alter radically any remaining worldviews that are grounded in the traditional precepts of individualism and to substantially advance current ideas on therapeutic action.

DIMENSIONS OF DISCOURSE

Many of the hypotheses or seemingly self-evident truths philosophers, theorists, and clinicians have constructed, or "discovered," over time are the result of distilling, reducing, and reifying personal lived experience and then elevating it to the status of "truth and reality." René Descartes' conclusions about mind–body dualism, the separation of reason and passion, and the "radically disengaged" nature of human thought doubtless emanated from his first-hand experience of feeling separated and estranged from his world context (see Stolorow, 1992). In other words, if I *experience* myself to be a "punctual self" (Taylor, 1989), then I must *be* one. This reifying activity relies on the conflation of two dimensions of discourse: the phenomenological and the explanatory. Elsewhere I (Coburn, 2002, 2007, 2009) underscored and elaborated the necessity of acknowledging this distinction, in contexts of theorizing, conversing, teaching, and engaging in psychoanalytic practice, lest we confuse whether we speak of personal lived experience or the contexts presumed to give rise to such experience.

In the absence of this distinction, it is unclear whether we are investigating and attempting to describe (not explain) emergent emotional experience and meaning or whether we are examining the sociocultural-relational-historical contexts in which we are fundamentally and relentlessly embedded. A striking example of this potential for confusion can be drawn from Heinz Kohut's use of the term *self* (1977). Depending on the dimension of discourse in which one is thinking and speaking about the self, it could be understood as a dimension of experience, an ontological entity (agent), or an intrapsychic structure. Muddling or ignoring differences between the phenomenological and explanatory dimensions has far-reaching, negative implications not only for the outcome of professional dialogue but also for the relationship and truth-finding trajectory of clinical engagements.

Each contributor, implicitly or explicitly, relies upon this distinction in accounting for the impact of the historically influential paradigm of individualism. And each has his or her own ideas about what had been diminished of the person in constructing the decontextualized individual born of individualism. For Frie (Chapter 1), the decontextualized individual has been stripped of its embeddedness in socio-cultural contexts, whereas for Cushman (Chapter 2), the prehermeneutic self has been denuded of the explicitness of its origins in moral dialogue in favor of masking it under the guise of the "approved [and verifying] practices" of objective science. Frie's "Marlboro Man," acting independently and courageously, provides his own explanation for his independence and fortitude (his dependency on nicotine notwithstanding). Ironically, the very symbol of his rugged masculinity and independence may have proved to be the instrument of his demise. For Sugarman and Martin (Chapter 5), the decontextualized person, relieved of history, society and culture, acts in a worldly vacuum, not a worldly context; this person is consequently reducible to "physical, biological, or sociocultural properties." For Orange (Chapter 3), as for Stolorow (Chapter 4), the decontextualized individual rests on the premise of "isolated mind" thinking and must be recast in irreducible, intersubjective contexts that can account for I-You relating, for understanding through conversation, for the face of the other, and for the contextualized nature of human development and creativity. For Fosshage (Chapter 6), the postmodern systems approach obscures developmental motivation and developmental direction, especially the dynamism and uniqueness of genetic predispositions. Similarly, for Lachmann (Chapter 7), the traditional self psychology conception of the individual is rendered inept and vapid in the absence of a selfobject milieu, lacking creativity and potential for self-transformation.

For all the contributors, the precontextualized, solitary, rational individual, the so-called punctual self of Descartes and Locke, exists only in a solipsistic, imaginary world. By considering context and the emergent quality of the products and properties of larger systems, the contributors posit and clarify that the surface of personal, emotional *experience* does not always reflect all the multiple contexts responsible for the emergence of such experience. Furthermore, as Stolorow underscores, "individualized selfhood is grasped always and only as a dimension of personal experiencing," not as the various possible explanations presumed to account for it. Indeed, drawing from Husserl (1900/1913), Stolorow suggests that "careful phenomenological description of structures of experience is a precondition for adequate theoretical explanations of them." Thus, for theorists historically to have defined the individual by means of positing idiosyncratic, explanatory assumptions about what the individual is effectively decontextualized the person. By rejecting this decontextualizing process, each author seeks to redefine the notion of individuality.

SUBVERTING INDIVIDUALISM AND REDEFINING THE INDIVIDUAL

Social, cultural, and political contexts

In the first chapter, Frie argues from a sociocultural-historical perspective that individualism simply cannot capture who and what we are as human beings. An individualist perspective that is grounded in individualism effectively denudes the person of its radical and seamless embeddedness in sociocultural-historical contexts. These larger contexts define and inform the person as an individual, just as the person transforms her life contexts through activity. A theoretical and practical preoccupation with the "inner self" and with "individual self-fulfillment" exacerbates what is already disengagement, if not estrangement, from our socio-cultural milieu. Drawing from a hermeneutic perspective that is grounded in the works of Martin Heidegger, Hans-Georg Gadamer, and Ludwig Binswanger, Frie successfully challenges the "artificial distinction between self and world" by arguing for the irreducibility of contexts of (hermeneutic) understanding that forms the basis for human development, experience, and meaning making.

For Frie, individuality is redefined as "situated personal experience," which definition repositions our vantage point in both phenomenological and explanatory terms. He emphasizes that personal, lived experience and its concomitant emotional meanings do not reside only in our minds or in "separate registers and dimensions" but are informed by and distributed throughout a world of "shared understandings" that form the fabric of our lives. Whereas Frie's model focuses on understanding personal *experience* through dialogue and appreciation for context, his phrase "situated personal experience" does not conflate but artfully combines both dimensions of discourse, the phenomenological and the explanatory. His individual, thus redefined, enjoys the capacity for agency, for uniqueness, and for having a say in one's world surround. Embeddedness in a world context, for Frie, does not relegate the individual to a life of fatedness (Strenger, 1998), of being at the mercy of one's context. Indeed, drawing from Martin, Sugarman, and Thompson (2003), Frie underscores that the individual is as influenced by his sociocultural milieu and by his interpretations of the milieu, as his milieu is influenced by the individual. Frie does not deny the existence of the individual but reorients and grounds him in a contextualized life of personal experience that is unequivocally and relentlessly "situated." This presumption of situatedness has profound implications for reconfiguring our ideas about therapeutic action.

In Chapter 2, Cushman defines politics as "exercise of power" and underscores what it is we want power over: What it means to be human. Social practices, or "everyday living," configure the individual and, once formulated through moral dialogue, what it means to be an individual becomes institutionalized and subsequently structures the bases for political struggle. The individual unwittingly has been informed and shaped repetitively by the very instruments purporting to investigate it dispassionately, rigorously, and objectively. Cushman's pointed subversion of individualism emerges as a challenge to mainstream, "scientific" social psychology and its presumptions about what of the self must be "universal, natural, and the most proper an infant can develop." Alternatively, for Cushman, sociocultural context and political struggle constitute the individual. Invoking a philosophical hermeneutic, interpretive perspective, Cushman's individual coheres instead through sociocultural-political practices and is as context sensitive as social psychology research is predictably verifying of the principles of Western individualism. He states, "[b]y unknowingly propping up the hegemony of individualism through laboratory findings, psychology is preventing individuals from having the ability to see into how political structures impact the individual and how much these structures are responsible for the suffering of the victims and the crimes of the perpetrators." He avers that "two-person psychologies," such as object relations and self psychology, are a "kind of intellectual tokenism," not radical and substantial enough to subvert the deleterious effects of individualism that perpetuate the pathologizing of the person, or the dyad, instead of examining and questioning the larger political systems of which they are but a constituent. For Cushman, the dark side of the presumption of the personal freedom of individualism is the denial of "social influence and political allegiances." Arguing to reinstate a spirit of moral responsibility and communal commitment radically contextualizes the person and also, notably, harmonizes well with Orange's plea for committing ourselves to privileging and caring for the face (and the needs and the suffering) of the other.

Philosophical contexts

In light of the radical challenges to individuality posed by intersubjective systems theory (Stolorow & Atwood, 1992; Stolorow, Atwood, & Orange, 2002), Orange, in Chapter 3, begins by questioning whether the concept of individuality is even worth rescuing. Placing aside "chaos, systems, and complexity theories," she turns instead to the works of Martin Buber, Hans-Georg Gadamer, and Emmanuel Lévinas to reconfigure what individuality might be. Orange's individual thus becomes quintessentially relational, coming to life through how he or she might stand in relation to the other: "Meeting the other as a Du changes us both by the word that is spoken." For Buber, and for Orange—to paraphrase them both—a word from an other that "happens to me" demands an answer. A word from an other, then, may be seen as an invitation to respond to the other in a way that transforms each person into an individual who is other than an outside observer or investigator. This potential transformation—or perhaps *opportunity for relating* might be a better description—involves experiences (or perhaps ways of being) of *confirmation* (for who one is) and *inclusion* (of who one is). For Orange, these dimensions of relating imply (1) a "self-building quality of Kohutian mirroring" and the experience of "having a presence in the being of the other" (Buber, 1988) (confirmation), and (2) "both belonging to the human community together and a warmth of embrace within this commonality" (inclusion). In this light, any sense of individuality, or of being individual, is derivative of relation.

Similarly, Orange's Gadamer subverts the notion of the Cartesian, isolated person through an emphasis on "genuine dialogue" centered on advancing (or negotiating) one's perspective with the other while, importantly, always doing so with the "expectation that the other can teach us something." Understanding thus emerges not through persuasion or coercion but rather through a "play of conversation." In a different context, this is reminiscent of the oft-referenced contention in complexity theory that the rules of the game change as a result of the play, that a sense of personal individuality emerges as a result of the cooperative interaction of individual persons. For Orange, privileging the "self" over the shared endeavor for meaning making and understanding reflects a "reversion to the romantic hermeneutics and to the Cartesian view of the self-enclosed mind." Thus, in this context, the individual emerges as cooperative, dialogic, but not self-abnegating.

Radically transformed, the individual in Orange's Lévinasian perspective is profoundly relational, if with potentially challenging moral and ethical overtones. One is confronted not only with the truly individual face of the other—*truly individual* in the sense that the other is something or someone other than the presumed idea of the other I hold in my mind—but also with an obligation to respond to her "infinite demand for protection and care." The face of the other is irreducible and not to be treated as "something to be studied or understood." Thus, I, as a person, am "unutterable" and "radically responsible for the other," even prior to meeting (Lévinas, 1987). For Lévinas, and for Orange, I become *individualized* in my relation to the other. Drawing from these three philosophers, Orange's striking redefinition and subversion of individuality poses compelling if at times anxiety-provoking implications for conceptualizing therapeutic action.

Stolorow's approach to individuality in Chapter 4 focuses on the nature of individualized selfhood and the preconditions necessary for its development, as distinct from traditional notions of "self" as structure or as autonomous agent. For Stolorow, individualized selfhood, including personal identity, distinctiveness, and agency, constitutes neither reified, objectified, isolated things in the world nor fantasies, illusions, or theoretical constructs devised for purposes of intellectual play. Instead, it is understood as comprising very real dimensions of experience that take form within the nexus of intersubjective systems and are thus highly context sensitive and context-dependent. He underscores that understanding an individual's experiential world as an emergent property of a larger intersubjective system does not render it an illusion, does not nullify it. As he says, "Contexualizing is not nullifying." Drawing on concepts from philosophical phenomenology, Stolorow argues that one salient feature of individuality—or more precisely, the *experience* of individualized selfhood—is the sense of personal ownership, or "mineness," of one's experiential life. Here we witness Stolorow's insistence on distinguishing between the phenomenological and explanatory dimensions of discourse.

Stolorow further argues that an "attuned relationality"—emanating from an other's "attunement to and understanding of one's distinctive affectivity"—is an essential ingredient in any relational system in which one's sense of *mineness* may be facilitated and sustained. This reflects an enormous leap in our understanding of empathy, affect regulation, affect tolerance, and generally the process of coming to know oneself through one's relationships. It also elegantly contextualizes the process by which we become more acquainted with our *throwness* (Heidegger, 1927), our unremitting embeddedness in a larger world context, our potential for freedom in such contexts, and our sense of personal ownership of our emotional life. However, perhaps even more central to his chapter and to his efforts at relationalizing individuality is his argument that (1) "authentically taking ownership of our finitude" is the very action that individualizes us (Heidegger), and that (2) one must integrate not solely one's experience of finitude into one's sense of ownership but also the "finitude of all those to whom one is deeply connected." This substantially "relationalizes" and extends the work of Heidegger in important ways. In this view, the individual, thus radically contextualized and redefined, remains ever vulnerable to one's finitude and to the ever-present, potential, and inevitable loss of one's connections with others. Indeed, it is from within this particular life-situatedness that individuality, or individual selfhood, emerges.

Developmental contexts

Turning next to the work of Sugarman and Martin in Chapter 5, the authors approach the challenge of individuality from a perspective of "persons acting in worldly contexts." They consider their "psychology of personhood" through developmental, ontological, and epistemological perspectives, effectively replacing traditional individualism with a sensibility that radically redefines the individual, or person, without eliminating him or allowing him to be consumed by privileging context over personal, emotional life and meaning. Building upon the work of Vygotsky, Leontiev (Cultural-Historical Activity Theory), and Stetsenko and her colleagues, Sugarman and Martin, argue for a developmental ontology that recasts the individual as an emergent property of "developmental contexts of coordinated activity and interactivity." Through this process, persons achieve the status of ontological entities, as agents in their own right, though ever irreducible, perpetually emergent, and continually transformed within a "dialectic relation of acting and being acted upon."

Additionally, extending the perspectival realism of G. H. Mead (Martin, 2007a, 2007b), Sugarman and Martin underscore the role of perspective taking in the development of the person. "Perspectives have ontological force. ... [They] are real." Perspective taking orients individuals toward "possibilities for action" and, over time, reach higher and higher levels of sophistication in the person. This development does not unfold as a function of an isolated psyche, predesigned and preprogrammed. Instead, in this view, the individual gains reflexive self-awareness by taking and occupying perspectives and also by being able to "react to the perspectives she holds in relation to herself as these are generated in interactions with others." Thus, not unlike the other authors under consideration here, Sugarman and Martin posit a quintessentially intersubjective, relational model of individuality in which (1) personal lived experience and growth are understood as emergent properties of an intersubjective system (Stolorow, Atwood, & Orange, 2002) (explanatory), and (2) coming to know one's own perspective—to know one's "self"—emerges and evolves in the context of other individuals' perspectives and past perspective taking contexts (phenomenological).

In Fosshage's Chapter 6, we find a remarkably thorough exploration of individuality and the development of the individual in the context of larger complex systems. Fosshage argues that "relational systems-based theoretical accounts of development tend to neglect constitutional factors," and thus his focus is on reconsidering the realm of genetic predispositions, or "hard-wired motivational valences." Here his interest resides in the genetic and bio-neuro-physiological makeup that the newborn brings to the otherwise emergent, relational contexts of human life. Like Sugarman and Martin, Fosshage eschews biological-genetic reductionism. He argues instead for revisiting the vital role that genetics play in human development as well as the context-dependent nature of the formation and activation of those genes responsible for human uniqueness. He organizes his treatment of individuality around the key concepts of *developmental motivation* and *developmental direction*, providing the fulcrum for gaining insight into the nature of the individual, contextualized self. Ideally, developmental motivation and direction "contribute incrementally to vitality, self-esteem, and increasingly complex levels of self-organization." Innate potentials in the person, in concert with a striving to actualize those potentials, are, for Fosshage, what is indeed unique about the person. Appreciating this view of the individual, as we shall see, has enormous therapeutic implications.

Responding to the "postmodern impulse ... to eschew 'human essences'" (Teicholz, 1999), Fosshage clearly supports the presumption of an "inherent tendency in human beings to grow or develop, to expand in function, to self-organize with increasing complexity in keeping with basic motivational values or preferences." This reflects another instance in which distinguishing between phenomenology and explanation is critical. Whereas it is the individual person who exhibits theses developmental tendencies, the individual per se is not responsible alone for this life-infused propensity. Of course, the very genetics or "hard-wired motivational valences" that are present at birth and may be experienced directly do not emerge on their own. Rather, they are themselves the product and property of larger, historical, complex, relational systems that precede the emergence of individual life.

In Chapter 7, Lachmann emphasizes "those instances where the presence of a caring human surround is a necessary *but not sufficient*" precondition for the development of individuality and self-creation. Lachmann privileges self-transformation, understood as individual activity, in defining and investigating the nature of individuality. Drawing from the work of Louis Sander, the Boston Change Process Study Group, and his own work with Beatrice Beebe, Lachmann joins the concept of individuality and the theory of complexity and investigates the development of individuality through four different perspectives, successively expanding or reframing outward from the cellular/genetic to the organismic to the self psychological to the clinical levels of discourse. This approach effectively traverses incrementally from the realm of the explanatory (including ideas about self-organization, self-assembly, specificity, rhythmicity, nonconscious implicit interactions, intersubjectivity, and the development of expectancies) to that of the phenomenological (the *experience* of being an independent center of initiative and perception, the *experience* of attachments and relationality, and the *experience* of self-transformation and creativity). For Lachmann, much of individuality rests on the complexity theory concept of *recurrency*—in other words, the personal affective responses to experiencing one's own creations that in turn create a "feedback loop ... [constituting] a process of continuous self-transformation." However, Lachmann's argument, based in self-transforming experiences, does not obviate the continual and central role of the contextual bath in which we relentlessly swim and that perpetually informs even our self-transformative experiences. There is no escape from what Taylor (1989) refers to as our embeddedness in "webs of interlocution" or "webs of music." These contextual webs, as Lachmann suggests, may not determine who we are and what we can create: They contextualize; they provide the medium in which we might create and self-transform. Though emphasizing the concept of self-transformation, he posits that the "dyadic, interactive, or intersubjective processes [are responsible for] further[ing] the self-organization of each partner," thereby laying essential groundwork for the opportunity for individualized, self-transformative experiences.

In some ways resonant with Fosshage's arguments, Lachmann's contentions challenge the more extreme versions of postmodernism in which context is thought to determine and define the individual, thus rendering the person practically illusory. Thus, to recapture a viable and lively sense of personal individuality, Lachmann reinstates and privileges the concept of self-transformation that may emerge apart and separate from everyday relational experience. If Orange argues for the emergence of individuality as a function of encountering the face of the other, Lachmann refocuses our attention toward what is to be gained from encountering our own face through physical sequestration and the creative process.

THERAPEUTIC ACTION AND THE INDIVIDUAL

Therapists' attitudes about what is true and real and about what is valued and desired inform much of how they think and how they work. These attitudes affect what is considered relevant and what is foreclosed upon, thereby substantially informing the trajectory of the therapeutic relationship. Clinicians are always doing *something*, are always looking for something, though admittedly they are often not clear about what that is until they have found it. In accounting for therapeutic action and therapeutic change, it is therefore essential to examine the role of therapists' attitudes, which often remain implicit or are not explicitly articulated. In considering each of the authors' chapters, along with many other theorists of therapeutic action, it is increasingly evident that the attitudes that accompany a therapist's interventions and ways of being serve a central and pivotal role in the patient's personal development and the likelihood for meaningful change. This was clearly announced—though only briefly—by Glover (1937) when he stated that "... a prerequisite of the efficiency of interpretation is the attitude, the true unconscious attitude of the analyst to his patients" (p. 131). More recently a number of theorists, including Daniel Stern, Karlon Lyons-Ruth, and Wilma Bucci, argue for the role of the implicit/procedural processing and "experiencing" as the essential conduit for therapeutic action (Bucci, 2001; Lyons-Ruth, 1999; Stern et al., 1998). Doubtless much change happens implicitly, just as the personal, subjective attitudes responsible for such change are often (though not always) conveyed on the implicit level. Personal attitudes—the notion of how one feels and thinks about things—can also run the gamut from obviously explicit and outspoken to completely nonconscious and unformulated (Stern, 1997; Sullivan, 1953).

In arguing for the utility and conceptual elegance of a psychoanalytic complexity perspective, I have explored and elaborated (Coburn, 2007, 2009) the essential role of the analyst's attitudes in understanding therapeutic action and resulting change. Regardless of theoretical background and clinical proclivities, one's theoretical perspective is necessarily accompanied by specific attitudes that reflect that viewpoint as well as one's history, one's current state of mind, and one's environment (Coburn, 2007). Shane (2009) supports this view when she comments that "it is the attitude of the analyst toward the patient and toward the process that is most potent in whatever that change process may be" (p. 236). Similarly, Orange (2009) contends that attitude—"a complex, amalgam of outlook, emotional perspective, and disposition taken up"—remains a central constituent in the process of therapeutic action and human relating. She reminds us of what Friedman (1982) once averred: "[A]ttitudes are undeliberate interpretations." The therapeutic advantages of a psychoanalytic complexity perspective do not reside in technical prescriptions or developmental expectations but rather through the medium of the therapist's attitudes and presuppositions about the patient, the relationship, the nature of systems, how we are always contextually situated, and how we arrive at our conceptions of truth and meaning (Coburn, 2009).

All of the chapter authors, in addition to many authors not considered herein, provide fertile ground from which more contextualist-informed attitudes emerge. How might they inform and expand our contemporary understanding of therapeutic action? I begin with our social, cultural, and political contexts in considering this question.

From a sociocultural-historical and hermeneutic perspective, Frie argues for a vision of individuality that encompasses both the phenomenological and explanatory dimensions of discourse: Redefined, individuality becomes "situated personal experience." And of course this applies to the analyst as well as the patient. Thus, adopting an attitude of personal situatedness—that each of us is irrevocably situated and relentlessly influenced by our "time and place," our cultures, and our relationship to one another—will necessarily permeate our thinking process, our choices, and phrasings of our interpretative activity. This includes how we comport ourselves to our patients (e.g., as contextually embedded individuals in a specific culture and in a quest for understandings that are not entirely of our own making). Conveying to our patients that our understandings are necessarily delimited and subject to contextual forces may potentially liberate certain patients from the constraints of complete personal responsibility for one's emotional life and from the burden of having to achieve an illusory objective perspective on self and other. When oriented in this view, a clinician may not be covertly demanding of the patient to assume responsibility for where and how she finds herself. Instead, the therapist may convey a sense of compassion for one's personal situatedness and for the current constraints on understanding one's life predicaments. Herein lies an attitude about therapeutic change—that change does not occur inside a "patient's interior life or structures of mind" but in one's relationship to one's self and to others in the world. This implies the process of perspective taking (see Aron, 2006) and foreshadows some of the implications of the work of Sugarman and Martin. Understanding clinically that the therapist's as well as the patient's horizons of understanding are simultaneously freeing and delimiting implies a degree of fatedness as well as potential freedom (Heidegger, 1927). This may help patients who otherwise tend to position themselves at either of the extreme ends of the fatedness/authorship spectrum (Strenger, 1998). For Frie, aspects of the therapeutic dialogue might even include examining how "such concepts as the individual and individuality are used in our culture because they carry hidden and not so hidden values and assumptions, which have very real political and ethical implications." This articulates well with Cushman's perspective, which, if more openly political, has equally powerful implications for therapeutic action.

Cushman, also drawing from a hermeneutic and interpretive perspective, is outspoken in his views on how the decontextualized individual was constructed. Through his (along with Altman, 1995) "three-person psychology," he provides a useful and potentially subversive framework for helping patients reconsider what society and "science" have made of them. In the absence of Cushman's hermeneutic and radical contextualist attitude, therapists may be inclined to support implicitly the hegemony of the traditional political structures and the mainstream scientism that perpetuates them. Alternatively, however, Cushman's therapeutic attitude enjoins therapists not to take for granted a patient's insistence on the static and resolute experiences of separateness, autonomy, and definitiveness that heretofore may have defined the patient. Patients no longer need be told, or at least accommodate to what they have been told, about the desirable, sought-after values of Western individualism to which they may have adhered. Through these potential clinical attitudes—again, most likely implicitly conveyed—the therapist invites the patient to reconsider and perhaps redefine his sense of what it means to be free. Personal freedom need not be defined as the "*absence* of social influence and political allegiances." At the least, Cushman alerts clinicians to beware of theories that "glorify individuation" and that "proclaim separation as the ultimate goal of child development." In this way, therapeutic action may emerge from a challenge to "maintaining compliance with a particular cultural terrain" and from a radical rejection of what remains in our personal attitudes of mainstream developmental and psychoanalytic psychologies (see Mahler, Pine, & Bergman, 1975, for a striking example).

For Cushman, a hermeneutic and interpretive attitude invites both therapist and patient to consider the "ongoing psychological processes that we unknowingly use" to perpetuate a nonconscious accommodation with a particular cultural landscape—one which should not be taken for granted. In this light, the individual and her personal psychology is as "soft assembled" (Harris, 2005) as are the cultural landscapes that have dictated the illusions of inherent objectivity, autonomy, and independence. Similar to those of Frie, these attitudes may usefully subvert those forces that have conspired to define a patient's personhood and articulate well with the systems of pathological accommodation theory of Brandchaft (2007). In her never-ending decision making about what to attend to and what to think and speak about in the clinical setting, the clinician, given these attitudes, may be more alert to the presence of "health and maturity moralit[ies]" (Kohut, 1979) that otherwise seamlessly and silently pervade the fabric of our clinical conversations.

Turning to philosophical contexts, Orange's emphasis on the emergence of human individuality and personhood in contexts of human relating and concern for the other opposes the traditional precepts of technical prescription, objective observation, and implicit health-and-maturity judgments. Orange's combined interpretations of Buber, Gadamer, and Lévinas provide powerful attitudes about what it means to be human and about how humans should be with one another. Doubtless these attitudes, including the experiences of compassion, witnessing, "undergoing the situation" (Orange, 1995), and suffering with, have profound implications particularly for patients whose histories have centered on the dehumanizing reverberations of trauma, abuse, and humiliation. Indeed, to be treated as a whole person, and not as an object and function intended for one's personal narcissistic use, conveys a "radical hope" (Lear, 2006) for a life in which one might have possibilities other than subservience, accommodation, neglect, or exploitation.

If Cushman's is political, Orange's attitude is intensely moral and ethical, particularly as evidenced in her interpretation of Lévinas. Whereas being with the other through confirmation and inclusion (Buber, 1988), in concert with the expectation of and openness to learning something *from* the other (Gadamer, 1975/1991), repositions the clinician as a caring and receptive participant (instead of an observing and educating authority), the implications of turning toward the (face of the) other (Lévinas, 1987) radicalizes and challenges the simple notion of a benevolent presence in therapy. Some clinicians may find confusing the idea that it is my "answerability to the other that makes me an individual," if, conversely, as a patient, I am working with a clinician who is endeavoring to be answerable to me. Alternatively stated, how might the patient realize personhood when her potential efforts at "abdicating [her] position of centrality" are thwarted by the clinician who is attempting to privilege the needs and experiences of the patient? Additionally, for certain clinicians, the idea, perhaps a misinterpretation of Orange's perspective, that one "deposes," "dethrones," or "abdicates" oneself in the service of the patient might be construed as needing to attempt to collapse one's subjectivity in the face of the other, which presumably one cannot ultimately do, given our understanding of interpersonal actions, interactions, and information sharing that exist within the realm of the implicit. Certain clinicians may construe this perspective as a moral, therapeutic directive that painfully confirms and substantiates preexisting invariant organizing principles (Stolorow, Atwood, & Orange, 2002) that center on pathological accommodation (Brandchaft, 2007) and the presumption of personal subjugation to the "dictates of authority" (Brandchaft, 2007). Additionally, some theorists (e.g., Hoffman, 1994) have argued for the therapeutic action derived from the patient witnessing the *analyst* change, indeed struggle, in the process of psychoanalysis. Clinicians should keep in mind that Orange's sensibility, as reflected here, may not preclude an openness to this way of relating and self-disclosing in the treatment setting. Hence the oft-quoted phrase in psychoanalysis, "context is everything," should always be considered in one's decision making.

This particular set of clinical attitudes may need to be approached cautiously by the less experienced clinician. More experienced clinicians, however, may discover far-reaching and powerful advantages by reentering their clinical settings with such an intense willingness (and capability) to "undergo the situation" with patients and relentlessly to keep in mind that one can never really presume to know the other fully. Particularly helpful is Orange's continual questioning about what theorists and clinicians may learn from these philosophers—what they may learn given that our Western individualism and its concomitant concepts of individuality "have served us badly." Clearly, for Orange, a truly therapeutic attitude emerges in contexts in which "generosity, care, and protection of the other become our central values." Alternatively stated, the spirit of Orange's contentions resides in the necessity for the therapist to be present, to really show up, in relation to the patient, in good faith. Doubtless this entails caring for the other while also being oneself.

Turning to the next chapter, Stolorow draws from Zahavi's three delineations of notions of the self, namely, the Kantian self, the narrative self, and experiential selfhood, the latter of which pertains to the first-person sense that my experiences are indeed mine. It is this latter definition of self—that of originary selfhood—that Stolorow underscores and that, in concert with his relationalization of finitude, informs what emerge as therapeutic attitudes. He also places strong emphasis on the role of the other's attunement and understanding of one's "distinctive affectivity" in the coalescence and sustenance of the experience of ownership of one's emotional life. Perhaps more than any of the other authors, Stolorow explicitly acknowledges and delineates the two dimensions of discourse that I have referenced throughout this chapter.

Historically, Stolorow has eschewed any tendency toward universalizing psychoanalytic concepts, and certainly so when it comes to talking about dimensions of experience (Stolorow & Atwood, 1992). One reason for this, presumably, is that clinicians tend to find in others what clinicians, a priori, assume is universally there to be found. Therapists who have presumed innate aggression (Freud, 1915; Klein, 1957) most certainly have found it (or have engendered it) or have declared something wrong if it remained "hidden." In his current chapter, however, Stolorow advances an exception to his otherwise antiuniversalizing posture by arguing for an inherent, prereflective, implicit sense of mineness in all personal self-experience. In a manner akin to the work of early German romantic and phenomenological philosophers (Bowie, 1990), Stolorow suggests that individuality and individual experience is defined by an implicit and unthematized quality that is presumed to be present in all individuals—that of *mineness*. Stolorow makes clear that this sense of mineness, of personal ownership of one's experience, is present or emerges in a wide range of varying degrees across many varied and unique contexts.

A vital therapeutic attitude derived here lies in the developmental implications of the presumption of mineness: The reflective *experience* of mineness is not something we are born with but instead coheres via the "other's ongoing validating attunement to and understanding of one's distinctive affectivity," or, conversely, it can be thwarted and truncated when to have and to own one's own affectivity threatens a needed tie with a malattuned or affect-intolerant other (Brandchaft, 2007). Thus, a clinician with this sensibility may be inclined to assess, prereflectively or otherwise, the patient on the basis of his relative sense of *experienced* ownership of his emotional life. Such a sensibility, or attitude, inevitably would infiltrate the clinical surround and perhaps privilege keeping an eye on the patient's experience of mineness and on how the therapeutic relationship advances or thwarts such an experience of ownership. This would be particularly vital for patients whose emotional and relational histories have centered on pathological accommodation or on deficits in their "sense of the real" (Coburn, 2001).

Stolorow also argues for the Heideggerian idea that authentic existence is one in which the finitude of one's individual life is avowed and death is apprehended and lived with as one's ever-present, "ownmost" possibility that is inevitable though temporally indeterminate. He further states that "Heidegger's characterization of existential anxiety [not to be confused with death anxiety] bears a remarkable resemblance to the phenomenology of traumatized states." In addition, and perhaps most central to his thesis, Stolorow relationalizes our finitude by underscoring that to be finite beings also is to confront that we will inevitably lose our connections with others, either through our own demise or through the demise of a cherished other. His references to Jacques Derrida bring this actuality into bold relief. From his thesis and attendant arguments, clinicians may derive intensely determining therapeutic attitudes that certainly would inform the trajectory of the therapeutic relationship. In this light, it is presumed that a sense of individualized selfhood emerges via experiencing a relational home for one's own unique affectivity, including one's emotional experiences of finitude and its relationality.

Following Stolorow's paradigm, what might an analyst do and what might she look for? On the one hand, clearly the therapist would analyze, work within a spirit of inquiry, be concerned with affect, with investigating organizing themes, and with the contexts that give rise to them. But this attitude suggests that he would also be attempting to expand, strengthen, and thematize a felt sense of mineness in the affectivity of his patients and would be looking for and attempting to be attuned to existential anxiety as well. This indeed poses a challenge for clinicians, as it does for all finite beings, namely, to remain open to themes of death anxiety, existential anxiety, and particularly anxiety and dread about the potential loss of cherished others. Many clinicians' proclivity may be to minimize the inevitability of our demise or the demise of our loved ones and may remain squeamish at empathizing with and validating the truth of our inexorable losses, past, present, or future. In fact, time does *not* heal all wounds, and many wounds are yet to come. A therapeutic attitude that embraces an awareness of such inevitable losses affords the potential for a more expanded affective life and concomitant emotional meanings. This attitude also prepares the clinician for transference experiences in which a sense of finitude emerges in the therapeutic relationship. Just as Winnicott (1949) speaks of the therapist's hate for the patient as perhaps concretized in his ending of a session, similarly a palpable sense of the analytic dyad's sense of finitude may be encapsulated and reflected upon in the meanings associated with the ending of a session or with a hiatus in the treatment. A rendition of this attitude, invaluable to both the analyst and the analysand, is found in Lear's (2003) comment that the "analyst lives with a lively sense of death...that the end was always in sight" (pp. 54–57). Indeed, if we can reflect upon them, our ends—the terminations of all our relational connections—are potentially always in sight. Openness to this fact, to speaking of it, is in this view an essential attribute of a truly therapeutic system.

Turning now to developmental contexts, Sugarman and Martin eschew perspectives that perpetuate understanding human subjective experience through an "interior mentalistic focus or environmental restriction and simplification." As they state, "Brains [alone] cannot decide, learn, be creative, or commit crimes. Only persons [acting in worldly contexts] can be said to do and be these things." In their stead, they propose a vision of personhood that is developmentally emergent in contexts of activity and interactivity. What is emergent become "uniquely constituted ontological entities." From this sensibility and the therapeutic attitudes that it implies, clinicians may help patients grasp more effectively a deeper sense of what constitutes their unique selfhood—its origins and its present-day and imagined-future contributors—and the potential ontological solidity that accrues over time. To contextualize an individual's emotional life is not to reduce and simplify it. Instead it affords the therapist and patient a deeper appreciation for the complexity of human experience and its attendant meanings.

In some ways similar to Stolorow's contention about a person's inherent (albeit initially prereflective) sense of mineness or ownership of her selfhood, Sugarman and Martin's thesis suggests that therapeutic change in part involves a relatively gradual process of delineating and elaborating the patient's status as an ontological entity in her own right. The therapeutic value of illuminating the patient's status, as such, obtains as the patient and therapist explore the continuing role of her (the patient's) "coordinated action and interaction" in her sociocultural contexts. To be contextualized also means to be individual. This provides a substantial and useful corrective to the assumption that we are either, on one hand, predominantly self-determining, separate individuals, left to our own devices in a fragmented and separate world or, on the other hand, are constructed by the indeterminate whims and currents of our sociocultural environment. To accept either position alone serves only to decontextualize the person in ways they may have already been, and in ways that may have necessitated seeking a therapeutic relationship in the first place.

For Sugarman and Martin, persons are both products and producers of the preconditions for their emergence: "[A] developmental context of coordinated interactivity with others" provides the matrix for persons emerging with a sense of selfhood, identity, and agency. In their developmental schema, it is not only vital for the child to "take and occupy" perspectives but similarly essential to be able to respond to the perspectives he holds in relation to himself. For these authors, the development of self-awareness and personal agency derives from this form of self-reactivity—a kind of recurrency in which experiences of self and other, in concert with others' experience of our self and others, congeal and take on personal meaning. This developmental schema implies attitudes that may usefully inform clinicians' therapeutic choices. In this light, a clinical dialogue may be encouraged in which perspective taking—for example, self as experienced self, self as experienced other (by the other)—lays vital groundwork for the emergence of self-reflexive capacities. It implies the use of verbal exploration of the patient's experience of her selfhood and of her experience of the therapist's experience of the patient. This ongoing perspective taking provides the scaffolding for future, increasingly complex experiences of "I" and "Me." Fundamentally, this attitude privileges, and consequently invites patients into, reflective processes that ultimately transform how "they interpret and describe themselves," transform the persons they once were. The potential therapeutic change here rests in a "movement toward increasingly differentiated and abstracted capacities for perspective taking." This articulates well with the perspective taking sensibility reflected in the work of Aron (2006), in which he summons the notion of the third in encouraging alternate points of view of self, other, and the world (instead of remaining locked into either/or dimensions of experience). Furthermore, this process, engendered by an attitude of underscoring perspective taking, also conveys an implicit attitude of "ontological mutability" in which personhood is not conceptualized as predesigned and static. Instead, it is pictured as dynamic and subject to transformation, which, in turn, conveys an implicit sense of hope and possibility for personal authorship and ownership of one's life.

Turning to the next chapter, Fosshage underscores the persuasive inclusion in psychology and psychoanalysis of a variety of intersubjective, relational, and complexity perspectives. In addition, he emphasizes the renewed importance of a multidisciplinary approach that includes ideas from cognitive science, neuroscience, infant research, and dream research. Employing and integrating these perspectives, Fosshage argues that many relational field or systems based models tend to underemphasize constitutional factors in conceptualizing the individual. For Fosshage, understanding the uniqueness of the person rests not solely in appreciating the ongoing contextualization of emotional experience but largely in acknowledging the constitutionally informed arena of developmental motivation and developmental direction, as outlined earlier. Although innate dispositions doubtless coalesce originally from within historical complex systems of their own, their presence at birth provides an essential developmental landscape from which our "desires, urges, intentions, [and] wishes" take form and subsequently may or may not emerge in increasing degrees of sophistication in the person, depending on the surroundings.

Attitudinally, Fosshage's emphasis in treatment inclines the therapist to convey a deep respect for the uniqueness of the patient and for the necessity of the therapeutic dyad to attend to what is uniquely emergent—what is alive, vital, and creative—in the patient's experiential world. By positioning personal motivational values and motivational directions at the heart of what is individual about the person, Fosshage opens up substantial and fruitful avenues of investigation and growth for patients. He contends that an "emotional moment that is sufficiently in keeping with an individual's motivational value and direction is experienced at a feeling level ... as authentic; profoundly right; in keeping with one's integrity, one's core, one's self." Armed with this clinical sensibility, clinicians would be more inclined to remain alert to examining the specificity of a given patient's unique motivational values and directions, to learn how to identify them, and, especially, to underscore and articulate to the patient those "emotional moment[s]" that reflect these values and directions. Remaining thus alert, patients may then be more inclined to likewise adopt an attitude of attention to what Fosshage references as "forward edge" (Lachmann, 2008; Miller, 1985; Tolpin, 2002), developmental strivings in themselves. This attitude—of the presumption of the inherent, human propensity to grow and expand in accord with one's unique motivational values or preferences"—cannot be considered a given in many individuals' emotional worlds. Indeed, many may feel that what appears to be the specificity of human emotional development is predesigned, teleological, isomorphic, and inexorable in all persons. Many individuals' sense of developmental stagnation and fatedness (Strenger, 1998) lies at the heart of their problems and discord, and Fosshage's developmental attitude enjoins the clinician to remain alert to this sense in their patients and similarly to acknowledge and elaborate the emotional moments of vitality, passion, and emotional meaning—that which we perpetually seek in psychoanalysis and psychotherapy but cannot force or create on our own.

In some ways similar to Fosshage's emphasis on individual uniqueness and personal striving for expansion and growth, Lachmann's complex considerations of the human propensity for self-transformation and creativity provide a substantial framework from which instrumental therapeutic attitudes emerge. Addressing four levels of discourse—the cellular, the organismic, the self psychological, and the clinical—this framework, whereas quintessentially contextualist in many ways, foregrounds what has been deemphasized in all our contextualizing, situating, and interpreting: Our inherent human propensity for self-transformation and the resulting potential for creativity. A contextualism that is denuded of the phenomenology of personal experiencing virtually disregards what can be transformative in oneself, by oneself. Thus, for the therapist, holding a contextualist sensibility should not obviate or obstruct the patient's personal experiences of self-transformation and creativity by immediately relegating them to the larger sociocultural surround. Lachmann avers that whereas intersubjectivity, contextualism, and ideas about organizing systems were never meant to "replace, ignore, or diminish the development of individuality," enthusiasm for these perspectives "may have dwarfed appreciation of the individual, apart from the dyad."

In this view, perhaps a central goal of clinical work might be to investigate, elaborate, and encourage those life circumstances that are likely to increase an individual's propensity toward self-transformative experiences, self-expression, and creativity. Similarly, a related goal might include clinicians striving to identify and acknowledge when indeed they are witnessing self-transformational experiences in their patients. This attitude potentially deepens therapists' appreciation not only for how self-organizing processes are partly informed by the surround but also how these processes may at times resist—perhaps must resist—or imaginatively elaborate the environment on which they have an impact.

CONCLUDING REMARKS

At the risk of deindividualizing this book's contributors and their unique perspectives, what might the implications of their collective work be? Developmentally, a sense of individuality, as experienced by the individual person, clearly is essential in emotional growth. It is clear by now that this is not to be confused with what traditionally has fallen under the rubric of achieving independence, autonomy, separation, individuation, and detachment. Each of these authors supports an unremitting spirit of contextualism in concert with valuing a sense of mineness, unique developmental aspirations, relationality, personal self-expression, and creativity. Notice that each author privileges and encourages self-expansion and an existence—as anxiety-filled as it may be—characterized by multiple perspective taking and an ongoing, development momentum. We witness how inextricably intertwined ideas about development are with conceptualizations of individuality. As elegantly reflected in these chapters, doubtless each of us is highly individualized, though such characteristics can obtain only via the medium of the greater relational and systemic contexts of which each of us is a part and in which each of us develops. And therapeutically speaking, clinicians look for, and attempt to encourage, a sense of individuality, uniqueness, vitality, energy, self-ownership, self-expression, and self-transformation in their patients as well as in themselves. This can be accomplished through a lens or attitude of our being relentlessly situated and embedded in a larger context; of hermeneutics, political subversion, interpretation, and challenge to traditional, sociopolitical hegemony; of respecting the face of the other and of privileging dialogic understanding over self-aggrandizement; of acknowledging the emotional ownership, personal finitude, and inescapable relational loss inherent in what it means to be human and conscious; of perspective taking and the reflexive process; of appreciating developmental motivation and direction and remaining astute to emergent aliveness, spontaneity, and meaning; and of the primacy of self-transformative growth and creativity. To the extent we may capture a sense of ownership of our emotional lives, contact and embrace our developmental motivations and directions, embody our potential for self-transformation, or be moved by the word of the other, we are faced with a vital question: What will we do with how and where we find ourselves, as situated individuals, in our own particular life context?

This book's introduction asked whether there is a place for the individual in a contextualist approach to theory and practice. Can an ineradicable contextualist and systems sensibility mesh with an acknowledgment of and appreciation for the uniqueness of the individual and his sense of individuality? The answers to these questions are unequivocally affirmative and have emerged through an evocative array of contemporary ideas. One essential and unifying conduit through which this has been accomplished lies in the unremitting attention to delineating and distinguishing between phenomenological discourse and explanatory discourse. Failing to recognize this distinction thrusts us back into reifying complex emotional experience and distilling it into one-person model accounts of the person. Despite the powerful influence of the contextualist, interpretative turn of the last 50 years, clinicians working with the highly specific dimensions of emotional life can still easily lapse into reductionism by hunting for and assigning responsibility for the origins of specific subjective experiences. Certain remnants of traditional psychoanalysis, such as the continued use of the term *transference*, or even the concept of "*self*-regulation," can steer the therapeutic dialogue into realms that tend to assign certain emotional experiences to very specific origins: For example, this is from the patient's history, this is from the therapist's countertransference, this is from the patient's neurobiological (mal)functioning, this is from the patient's difficulty in self-regulating or in mentalizing (Bouchard et al., 2008). Indeed it is challenging to maintain a spirit of contextualism in everyday practice when our natural human propensity is to want to locate with clarity and specificity the origins of painful affectivity and the organizing principles associated with it.

The phenomenological/explanatory distinction is, in itself, a useful attitude that is implicated in therapeutic action. Through this attitude, clinicians may convey to their patients that whereas we may speak in the language of phenomenology—indeed assigning origins and causes from one day to the next to aspects of the patient's emotional life—we also may perceive and organize our understandings through a lens of complex systems. With such systems in mind, neither the clinician nor the patient can ever demarcate accurately and precisely the lines dividing one's history, one's current state, and one's environment, or one's past, one's present, and one's imagined future. This entails learning to live with the indeterminacy of contextualized, emotional life and meaning.

Broadly speaking, might these perspectives, once absorbed into the attitudinal framework of the clinician, become yet another ideology purporting to know the mind of the patient and presuming to know what the patient needs? If accepted as the next dogma, especially by less experienced practitioners, perhaps yes. If pondered and played with in the spirit of understanding persons as uniquely contextualized and contextualizing beings, then perhaps not. The attitudes derived from these theoretical sensibilities contain important implications for the clinician interested in revisiting and subverting the traditional assumptions about individuality and its developmental dimensions.

REFERENCES

Altman, N. (1995). *The analyst in the inner city: Race, class, and culture through a psychoanalytic lens.* Hillsdale, NJ: Analytic Press.

Aron, L. (2006). Analytic impasse and the third: Clinical implications of intersubjective theory. *International Journal of Psychoanalysis, 87,* 349–368.

Bacal, H., & Herzog, B. (2003). Specificity theory and optimal responsiveness: An outline. *Psychoanalytic Psychology, 20,* 635–648.

Beebe, B., & Lachmann, F. M. (2001). *Infant research and adult treatment: A dyadic systems approach.* Hillsdale, NJ: Analytic Press.

Bonn, E. (2005). Turbulent contextualism: bearing complexity toward change. *International Journal of Psychoanalytic Self Psychology, 5*(1), 1–18.

Bouchard, M.-A., Target, M., Lecours, S., Fonagy, P., Tremblay, M., Schachter, A., et al. (2008). Mentalization in adult attachment narratives: Reflective functioning, mental states, and affect elaboration compared. *Psychoanalytic Psychology, 25,* 47–66.

Bowie, A. (1990). *Aesthetics and subjectivity from Kant to Nietzsche.* Manchester: Manchester University Press.

Brandchaft, B. (2007). Systems of pathological accommodation and change in analysis. *Psychoanalytic Psychology, 24,* 667–687.

Buber, M. (1988). *The knowledge of man: Selected essays.* Atlantic Highlands, NJ: Humanities Press International.

Bucci, W. (2001). Pathways of emotional communication. *Psychoanalytic Inquiry, 21,* 40–70.

Charles, M. (2002). *Patterns: Building blocks of experience.* Hillsdale, NJ: Analytic Press.

Coburn, W. J. (2001). Subjectivity, emotional resonance and the sense of the real. *Psychoanalytic Psychology, 18,* 303–319.

Coburn, W. J. (2002). A world of systems: The role of systemic patterns of experience in the therapeutic process. *Psychoanalytic Inquiry, 22*(5), 655–677.

Coburn, W. J. (2007). Psychoanalytic complexity: Pouring new wine directly into one's mouth. In P. Burisi & A. Kottler (Eds.), *Contemporary trends in self psychology practice*. Northvale, NJ: Jason Aronson, 3–22.

Coburn, W. J. (2009). Attitudes in psychoanalytic complexity: An alternative to postmodernism in psychoanalysis. In R. Frie & D. Orange (Eds.), *Beyond postmodernism: New dimensions in clinical theory and practice*. London: Routledge, 183–200.

DuBois, P. (2003). Perturbing a dynamic order: Dynamic systems theory and clinical application, prepublished paper.

Freud, S. (1915). Instincts and their vicissitudes. In J. Strachey (Ed. & Trans.), *The standard edition of the complete psychological works of Sigmund Freud* (Vol. 14, pp. 159–215). London: Hogarth Press.

Friedman, L. (1982). The humanistic trend in recent psychoanalytic theory. *Psychoanalytic Quarterly, 51*, 353–371.

Gadamer. H. G. (1975/1991). *Truth and method*. New York: Crossroads.

Galatzer-Levy, R. (1978). Qualitative change from quantitative change: mathematical catastrophe theory in relation to psychoanalysis. *J Am Psychoanal Assoc, 26*, 921–935.

Ghent, E. (2002). Wish, need, drive. *Psychoanalytic Dialogues, 12*, 763–808.

Glover, E. (1937). Symposium on the theory of the therapeutic results of psychoanalysis. *International Journal of Psychoanalysis, 18*, 125–189.

Harris, A. (2005). *Gender as soft assembly*. Hillsdale, NJ: Analytic Press.

Heidegger, M. (1927). *Being and time* (J. Macquarrie & E. Robinson, Trans.). New York: Harper & Row, 1962.

Hoffman, I. Z. (1994). Dialectical thinking and therapeutic action in the psychoanalytic process. *Psychoanalytic Quarterly, 63*, 187–218.

Hoffman, I.Z. (2000). At death's door: Therapists and patients as agents. *Psychoanalytic Dialogues, 10*, 823–846.

Husserl, E. (1900/1913). *The shorter logical investigations* (J. Findlay, Trans. & D. Moran, Ed.). New York: Routledge, 2001.

Klein, M. (1957). Envy and gratitude. In *Envy and gratitude and other works, 1946–1963*. New York: Delacorte Press/Seymour Laurence.

Kohut, H. (1977). *The restoration of the self*. Madison, CT: International Universities Press.

Kohut, H. (1979). The two analyses of Mr. Z. *International Journal of Psychoanalysis, 60*, 3–27.

Lachmann, F. M. (2008). *Transforming narcissism: Reflections on empathy, humor, and expectations*. New York: The Analytic Press.

Lear, J. (2003). *Therapeutic action: An earnest plea for irony*. New York: Other Press.

Lear, J. (2006). *Radical hope: Ethics in the face of cultural devastation*. Cambridge, MA: Harvard University Press.

Lévinas, E. (1987). *Collected philosophical papers* (A. Lingis, Trans.). Boston: Nijhoff.

Lichtenberg, J., Lachmann, F., & Fosshage, J. (1992). *Self and motivational systems: Toward a theory of psychoanalytic technique*. Hillsdale, NJ: Analytic Press.

Lyons-Ruth, K. (1992). The two-person unconscious, intersubjective dialogue, enactive relational representations, and the emergence of new forms of relational organizations. *Psychoanalytic Inquiry, 19*, 576–617.

Magid, B. (2002). *Ordinary mind: Exploring the common ground of Zen and psychotherapy*. Boston: Wisdom.

Mahler, M., Pine, R., & Bergman, A. (1975). *The psychological birth of the human infant: Symbiosis and individuation*. New York: Basic Books.

Martin, J. (2007a). Interpreting and extending G. H. Mead's "metaphysics" of selfhood and agency. *Philosophical Psychology, 20,* 441–456.

Martin, J. (2007b). Educating communal agents: Building on the perspectivism of G. H. Mead. *Educational Theory, 57,* 435–452.

Martin, J., Sugarman, J., & Thompson, J. (2003). *Psychology and the question of agency*. Albany: State University of New York Press.

Miller, J. P. (1985). How Kohut actually worked. *Progress in Self Psychology, 1,* 13–30.

Miller, M. L. (1999). Chaos, complexity, and psychoanalysis. *Psychoanalytic Psychology 16,* 355–379.

Moran, M. G. (1991). Chaos theory and psychoanalysis—The fluidic nature of the mind. *Int Review of Psycho-Analysis, 18,* 211–221.

Orange, D. (1995). *Emotional understanding: Studies in psychoanalytic epistemology*. New York: Guilford.

Orange, D. M. (2006). For whom the bell tolls: Context, complexity, and compassion in psychoanalysis. *International Journal of Psychoanalytic Self Psychology, 1*(1), 5–22.

Orange, D. (2009). Kohut Memorial Lecture: Attitudes, values and intersubjective vulnerability. *International Journal of Psychoanalytic Self Psychology, 4*(2), 235–253.

Palombo, S. R. (1999). *The emergent ego : Complexity and coevolution in the psychoanalytic process*. Madison, Conn.: International Universities Press.

Pickles, J. (2006). A systems sensibility: Commentary on Judith Teicholz's "Qualities of Engagement and the Analyst's Theory." *International Journal of Psychoanalytic Self Psychology, 1*(3), 301–316.

Piers, C. (2005). The mind's multiplicity and continuity. *Psychoanalytic Dialogues, 15*(2), 229–254.

Sander, L. W. (2002). Thinking differently. *Psychoanalytic Dialogues, 12,* 11–42.

Sashin, J. I. & Callahan, J. (1990). A model of affect using dynamical systems. *Annual of Psychoanalysis, 18,* 213–231.

Scharff, D. E. (2000). Fairbairn and the self as an organized system. *Canadian Journal of Psychoanalysis, 8,* 181–195.

Seligman, S. (2005). Dynamic systems theories as a metaframework for psychoanalysis. *Psychoanalytic Dialogues, 15*(2), 285–319.

Shane, E. (2009). My life with self psychology. In N. Vanderheide & W. J. Coburn (Eds.), *Self and systems: Explorations in contemporary self psychology*. Boston, MA: Blackwell Publishing. 229–236.

Shane, E. & Coburn, W. J. (2002). Prologue. *Psychoanalytic Inquiry, 22,* 653–654.

Shane, M., Shane, E., & Gales, M. (1997). *Intimate attachments: Toward a new self psychology*. New York, Guilford Press.

Sperry, M. (in press). This better be good: Complex systems and the dread of influence. *International Journal of Psychoanalytic Self Psychology*.

Spruiell, V. (1993). Deterministic chaos and the sciences of complexity: psychoanalysis in the midst of a general scientific revolution. *J Am Psychoanal Assoc, 41*, 3–44.

Steinberg, M. C. (2006). Language, the medium of change: The implicit in the talking cure. Prepublished paper.

Stern, D., Sander, L., Nahum, J., Harrison, A., Lyons-Ruth, K., Morgan, A., et al. (1998). Non-interpretive mechanisms in psychoanalytic therapy: The "something more" than interpretation. *International Journal of Psychoanalysis, 79*, 903–921.

Stern, D. B. (1997). *Unformulated experience: From dissociation to imagination in psychoanalysis.* Hillsdale, NJ: Analytic Press.

Stolorow, R. D. (1997). Dynamic, dyadic, intersubjective systems: An evolving paradigm for psychoanalysis. *Psychoanalytic Psychology, 14*(3), 337–364.

Stolorow, R. D., & Atwood, G.E. (1992). *Contexts of being: The intersubjective foundations of psychological life.* Hillsdale, NJ: Analytic Press.

Stolorow, R. D., Atwood, G. E., & Orange, D. M. (2002). *Worlds of experience: Interweaving philosophical and clinical dimensions in psychoanalysis.* New York: Basic Books.

Strenger, C. (1998). The desire for self-creation. *Psychoanalytic Dialogues, 8*, 625–655.

Sucharov, M. (2002). Representation and the intrapsychic: Cartesian barriers to empathic contact. *Psychoanalytic Inquiry, 22*(5), 686–707.

Sullivan, H. S. (1953). *The interpersonal theory of psychiatry.* New York: Norton: MIT Press.

Taylor, C. (1989). *Sources of the self: The making of the modern identity.* Cambridge, MA: Harvard University Press.

Teicholz, J. (1999). *Kohut, Loewald, and the postmoderns.* Hillsdale, NJ: Analytic Press.

Thelen, E. (2005). Dynamic systems theory and the complexity of change. *Psychoanalytic Dialogues, 15*(2), 255–283.

Thelen, E. & Smith, L. B. (1994). *A dynamic systems approach to the development of cognition and action.* Cambridge, Mass

Tolpin, M. (2008). Doing psychoanalysis of normal development: Forward edge transferences. In A. Goldberg (Ed.), *Postmodern self psychology: Progress in self psychology, vol. 18* (pp. 167–191). Hillsdale, NJ: Analytic Press.

Tolpin, M. (2002). Doing psychoanalysis of normal development: Forward edge transferences. Chapter 11 in *Progress in Self Psychology, 18*, 167–190.

Trop, G. S., Burke, M. L., & Trop, J. L. (2002). "Thinking dynamically in psychoanalytic theory and practice." *Progress in Self Psychology.* (A. Goldberg, Ed.) NJ: The Analytic Press. 18, 129–147.

VanDerHeide, N. (2009). A dynamic systems view of the transformational process of mirroring. *International Journal of Psychoanalytic Self Psychology, 4*(4), 432–444.

Varela, F. J., Thompson, E. & Rosch, E. (1991). *The embodied mind: Cognitive science and human experience.* Cambridge, Mass.: MIT Press.

Weisel-Barth, J. (2006). Thinking and writing about complexity theory in the clinical setting. *International Journal of Psychoanalytic Self Psychology* 1(4), 365–388.

Winnicott, D. W. (1949). Hate in the counter-transference. *International Journal of Psychoanalysis, 30,* 69–74.

Index